CW00550132

Advance Praise for *Analysis of Genuine Karate*

We welcome this fascinating exploration of the many modern misconceptions about genuine Okinawan karate. The book explains that Okinawan Te was originally developed for the purpose of self-protection but that over the last several decades other purposes were added, namely physical education, recreation, meditation, and sports. It acknowledges that there were good reasons for these additions but strongly suggests that we not confuse them with the genuine intention of the art—as that art is taught at our and other traditional dojos.

> —Sensei Noel Smith, Kyoshi, 8th Dan
> Shorin Ryu, Shorinkan, head coach for
> the US karate team 1973 to 1978, USA
> Karate Hall of Fame inductee

Dr. Bayer has written an extraordinarily insightful book that will assist its readers in their personal growth and understanding of Okinawa's martial culture. His passion, curiosity, and finely honed research and analytical skills have resulted in a rare work of substance, enlightenment, and truth.

> —William (Bill) Hayes, Hanshi, 9th Dan
> Shorin Ryu, Shobayashi-Kan, inducted
> into the Karate Masters' Hall of Fame
> and into the American-Okinawan
> Karate Association Hall of Fame,
> major in the United States
> Marine Corps (retired)

Hermann Bayer's *Analysis of Genuine Karate* is extraordinarily interesting and informative. He brings clarity to many of the greatest misconceptions about karate, from cultural traditions and the mind-set of the founding fathers of traditional Okinawan karate to the modern worldwide promulgation of karate for fame and money. He leaves no stone unturned, addressing differences in training methods and goals that could mean the difference between life and death. In this book, Hermann Bayer has his finger on the pulse of authentic and traditional Okinawa karate-do and culture.

—Nestor Tadeusz Folta, 8th Dan Uechi-Ryu, Soke Shubukan, master instructor in the Uechi-Ryu Karate-Do Association, inductee to the World Martial Arts Hall of Fame 1996

Given the ever-widening gap between the karate practiced in Okinawa and the karate practiced elsewhere around the world, it was perhaps inevitable that a book such as this would be written. More than one man's opinion, *Analysis of Genuine Karate* is the result of the author's methodical academic research. Hermann has consulted widely and sought expert opinion. The result of his research awaits the reader. I have no doubt this book will spark a great many conversations about what is and what isn't "Genuine Karate."

—Michael Clarke, author, Kyoshi, 8th Dan Okinawan Goju-Ryu, author of *The Art of Hojo Undo, Shin Gi Tai,* and *Redemption*

Engaging, enlightening, and informative, this book reflects a love, devotion, dedication, and level of knowledge that is comparable to if not exceeds anything that has been published on the topic by anyone.

—Bernard N. Curry, PhD, LCSW, CSOTP, CCTP; university professor

Doctor Bayer's book will be an excellent addition to the library of anyone interested in the study of karate. He has made good use of his considerable experience training in traditional Okinawan karate and Japanese karate in his examination of their fundamental differences. His research gives the reader a good look at the historical, social, philosophical, and physical dynamics of the development of karate as it evolved from its origins in Okinawa to its adoption by the culture of mainland Japan.

—Raymond (Gene) Adkins, Renshi, 6th Dan Shorin Ryu, Shorinkan

Dr. Hermann Bayer's book on the cultural heritage and influences of Okinawan karate versus sport karate is well researched, well organized and well presented. Hermann's intelligent, sincere, and thoughtful approach helps both the novice and the experienced karateka "see" the brilliance behind kata and the deep well of potential preserved in the cultural art of Okinawan karate.

—Ted Jacobson, 5th Dan Shorin Ryu, Shorinkan

Analysis of Genuine Karate

Analysis of

GENUINE KARATE

*Misconceptions, Origins,
Development, and True Purpose*

Hermann Bayer, Ph.D.

YMAA Publication Center
Wolfeboro, NH USA

YMAA Publication Center, Inc.
PO Box 480
Wolfeboro, NH 03894
800 669-8892 • www.ymaa.com • info@ymaa.com

ISBN: 9781594398438 (print) • ISBN: 9781594398445 (ebook)

This book set in Adobe Garamond and Frutiger.

All rights reserved including the right of reproduction in whole or in part in any form.
Copyright © 2021 by Hermann Bayer
Edited by Doran Hunter
Cover design by Axie Breen
Photos by author unless otherwise noted
Charts and graphs by author unless otherwise noted

20211001

Publisher's Cataloging in Publication
Names: Bayer, Hermann, author. | McCarthy, Pat (Patrick), writer of foreword.
Title: Analysis of genuine karate : misconceptions, origins, development, and true purpose /
    Hermann Bayer ; foreword by Patrick McCarthy.
Description: Wolfeboro, NH USA : YMAA Publication Center, [2021] | Includes bibliographical
    references and index.
Identifiers: ISBN: 97815943988438 (print) | 9781594398445 (ebook) | LCCN: 2021943063
Subjects: LCSH: Karate—Japan—Okinawa Island. | Karate—Foreign influences. |
    Karate—Physiological aspects. | Karate—History—Errors, inventions, etc. | Karate—
    History—Sociological aspects. | Martial arts—History. | BISAC: SPORTS &
    RECREATION / History. | SPORTS & RECREATION / Martial Arts / General. |
    SPORTS & RECREATION / Martial Arts / Karate.
Classification: LCC: GV1114.3 .B39 2021 | DDC: 796.815/3—dc23

The authors and publisher of the material are NOT RESPONSIBLE in any manner whatsoever
for any injury which may occur through reading or following the instructions in this manual.

The activities physical or other wise, described in this manual may be too strenuous or dangerous
for some people, and the reader(s) should consult a physician before engaging in them.

Neither the authors nor the publisher assumes any responsibility for the use or misuse of
information contained in this book.

Nothing in this document constitutes a legal opinion nor should any of its contents be treated
as such. While the authors believe that everything herein is accurate, any questions regarding
specific self- defense situations, l egal liability, and/or interpretation of federal, state, or local
laws should always be addressed by an attorney at law.

When it comes to martial arts, self-defense, and related topics, no text, no matter how well
written, can substitute for professional, hands-on instruction. These materials should be used
for **academic study only**.

Printed in USA.

CONTENTS

Foreword by Patrick McCarthy, Hanshi, 9ᵗʰ Dan   vii
Preface by the Author   ix

**Chapter 1: Okinawan Karate's "Japanization," "Americanization,"
and "Commercialization"**   1

Okinawa Is the Birthplace of Karate   1
   Excursion: Empty-Hand Te Uses Weapons As "Extensions of the Body"   9
The "Disarmament" of Okinawan Karate in Japanese Karatedo   14
"Takeover Attempts" to Integrate Okinawan Karate into Japanese Karatedo   21
Worldwide Non-Okinawan-Karatedo "Inflation" after 1945   28
"Americanization" and Transformation of Karatedo into "Karate Commerce"   33

Chapter 2: Arguments to Maintain Okinawan Karate in Its Originality   45

Traditional Karate Is Okinawan Cultural Heritage   45
   Okinawa Maintains Its Subcultural Identity within Japan's Culture   46
   Okinawa Officially Promotes Karate as Its Cultural Heritage   50
Core Reasons to Maintain Okinawan Karate in Its Original Form   60
   Peaceful Minds through the Study of Lethal Okinawan Karate?   61
   #1: The Reason Not to Change Effective Techniques and Kata   65
   #2: The Reason Not to Obscure an Intangible Culture Heritage   78
   #3: The Reason Not to Call Sports Karate Derivations a Martial Art   84

**Chapter 3: Empirical Evidence and the Laws of Physics to Support the
Sociocultural and Historic Arguments**   91

First Practical Example:
   How Major Training Differences between Genuine Okinawan
     Karate and "Disarmed" Traditional Japanese Karatedo Lead to
     Contrasting Fighting Skills   92
   First Major Training Difference: The "Correct Way and
     Nothing Else" vs. "Individual Approach"   98
   Second Major Training Difference: "Closed System/Curriculum of
     Katas" vs. "Open System of Katas"   105
   Third Major Training Difference: Rank Requirements and Belt
     Testing vs. Holistic Rank Allocation   109
   Fourth Major Training Difference: Bunkai, Formalized Kumite,
     Sparring, and Combat Kumite Versus Sporadic Partner Exercises 111
   Conclusion: The Two Ways Lead to Opposing Combat Skills   122
Second Practical Example:
   Modern Nekoachi-dachi Modifications Prove the Superiority of the
     "Never Changing Kata Principle"   124
   How Changing the Traditional Low Nekoachi-dachi in Modern
     Kata Interpretations Weakens Block-Counters   125

The Difference between a Low and a Deep Stance/Position 128
Insights from the Laws of Physics into Higher Versus Lower
Stances/Positions 131
Examples and Proof: The Lower You Are, the Stronger You Are 133
Conclusion and Solution: Sitting Low in a Natural Stance/Position 135
Third Practical Example:
Modern Naihanchi-dachi Modifications Prove the Superiority of the
"Never Changing Kata Principle" 138
How Changing the Traditional Naihanchi-dachi in Modern Kata
Interpretations Increases a Karateka's Vulnerability 139
Confirming Traditional Naihanchi-dachi in Okinawa 2019 140
Modern Naihanchi- (Kiba-) dachi Variations 144
Block/Counter Delay When Using Modern Kiba-dachi Variations
Instead of Traditional Naihanchi-dachi 146
Knee Joint Damage When Using Modern Kiba-dachi Variations
Instead of Traditional Naihanchi-dachi 151
Consolidated Deduction from Empirical Evidence and
Final Thoughts 158

List of Abbreviations 161
Explanations of Asian Terms 163
List of Photos, Tables, and Graphs 173
References 175
Index 185

FOREWORD BY PATRICK MCCARTHY HANSHI 9TH DAN

Accurately understanding *why* is too crucial an element to dismiss when we seek to advance our skills and become successful in doing so. This couldn't be truer for an art developed for the purpose of self-defense.

In recent years there has been significant interest in finding a way back to the old-ways, to the original and more pragmatic approach to the art of karate. In spite of its current popularity as a cultural recreation and rule-bound competitive sport, much of today's karate has become wholly dysfunctional as a form of self-protection. Researchers involved with such a study have collectively revealed that changes made to original Okinawan karate, after it arrived on Japan's mainland in the 1920s, had transformed it to the point where it no longer reflected its original functionality.

Where does this leave us? When we embark on a search for accurate knowledge, we discover it can be a quite a challenge.

Too often, when seeking a better understanding of historical, technical, and tactical ambiguities of their original art, I've noticed that many enthusiasts tend to overlook factual knowledge of the cultural landscape and the social mind-set prevalent during the period in which their art evolved.

This oversight, unintentional as it may be, has great consequences for truly understanding how and why our karate "evolved" as it did. We are after all in search of karate success.

We are fortunate that Hermann Bayer's work penetrates deeply into the ambiguity which shrouds our understanding of the most important parts of this art; and he even reveals an almost forgotten path.

Supported by historical and socio-cultural facts, scientific analysis, and public records, Bayer examines how Japan reinterpreted Okinawan karate to best serve its own nationalistic agenda. Moreover, how and why both Japanese and American influences have resulted in creating something quite different from what the original pioneers intended. This fact becomes quite apparent within these pages. Through his collective analyses Bayer quantifies karate as an industry, and he reveals both a complex and a convoluted evolution, at times aptly illuminating the motivations behind various stake-holders.

As a longtime disciple of the art, and an astute researcher, Hermann Bayer's important contributions and inspirational leadership have not gone unnoticed. Delving into classical tradition, with contemporary insight, he has succeeded in portraying an untold journey that many of us have wondered about for so long.

I am confident that *Analysis of Genuine Karate: Misconceptions, Origins, Development, and True Purpose* will be highly regarded and go on to become mandatory reading for all serious enthusiasts looking to better understand their true history, evolution, and practical application of original karate. It's a fascinating exploration and makes a compelling case for better understanding genuine Okinawan karate.

I am pleased to lend my name to this work and highly recommend it.

Patrick McCarthy, Hanshi 9th Dan
Director, International Ryukyu Karate-jutsu Research Society
Naha, Okinawa

PREFACE

First and foremost I am profoundly thankful to all *sensei, senpai,* and fellow students I had the privilege to encounter during many years of studying martial arts. Every one of them made essential contributions to my personal development. In particular, I am deeply honored by the once-in-a-lifetime opportunity to have trained with a generation of *hanshi* and *kyoshi* who were directly taught by the senior authorities of the two approaches to karate I have trained in, *Okinawan Kobayashi Shorin Ryu* and *Japanese Shudokan-Doshinkan.*

This training experience is connecting me (better: directly linking me) to a tradition of more than five hundred years of Okinawan *Te*—a fascinating, almost overwhelming, and deeply humbling thought.

Both karate styles share common ancestries since both of their most senior representatives, Chibana Chosin Sensei and Tomaya Kanken Sensei, were practicing *Shuri-Te* under Itosu ("Anko") Yasutsune Sensei, before *Shudokan-Doshinkan Karatedo* in the years before, during, and after WWII transformed into the non-Okinawan *budo* philosophy of mainland Japan and consequently moved away from the Okinawan *self-protection* philosophy towards *self-perfection* and meditative athletics.

Compared to over five hundred years of *Te* and three hundred years of *Shorin Ryu* in Okinawa, mainland Japanese karatedo, with its more than ninety years of existence, is a relative new development with a different form, purpose, and philosophical superstructure, and it altered traditional Okinawan karate so significantly that it formed a new alternative system and a new approach of its own.

However, (mainland) Japan, the "karate-*reproducing*" country is—and used to be—the superior political power governing the "karate-*inventing*" region of Okinawa. Mainland Japan with its own, many centuries-old, martial arts, *samurai,* and *bushido* traditions did not hesitate to claim karate as a *Japanese* martial art, which is of course correct in terms of the governmental sphere, but which is incorrect in terms of subcultural heritage, and thus is not appropriately crediting the "karate-inventing" region of Okinawa.

Studying traditional, non-sports, (mainland) Japanese karatedo for many years as well as classical Okinawan karate, including its historic and sociologic evolution (in my seventies still being a hard training *deshi*), helped me to understand better. Nevertheless, my insight is limited, and I am in no position to claim that my opinions are as relevant as the ones contributed by any *hanshi, kyoshi,* and *renshi* who studied the art for several decades. All my thoughts and conclusions are based on my personal level of knowledge and insight. However, there is a chance that my academic socio-cultural research background and my analytic skills as a scientist—in combination with this current level of understanding—allow a fruitful perspective.

Though preferring the self-protection focus of *dentou* Okinawan karate, I think that there is an opportunity for both karatedo paths to complement each other. Since all karate combines physical, spiritual, and mental development, the initial contradiction may evolve into a new overarching unity—like night and day, *yin* and *yang*—not being mutually exclusive, but defining each other by contrast in order to come together into a new holistic entity. This only happens, however, when both approaches maintain karate's initial purpose of combat and lethality. Unfortunately this is not always the case; different paths underpin a contrast of "disarmed" Japanese karate-derivatives versus genuine Okinawan karate. Hence, such a synthesis is far from being achieved today and leaves Okinawan karate and Japanese karatedo as two relatively separated entities—unbridged for (sports-) political reasons and hubris rather than for logical or historical ones—which is an unfortunate situation without an easy resolution in sight. To this day the Okinawan karate groups, united in their own *Traditional Okinawan Karate Association*, do not belong to the *Japan Karate Federation*, nor do they intend to join.

Looking at other cultures bears the risk of misconception, especially when considering Asian cultures through a lens forged by Western socialization, Western norms, and Western values. The exploration of socio-cultural phenomena does require more than intellectual understanding; it needs open-minded holistic-hermeneutic avenues with broad perception, empathy, and emotional intelligence, which are all prone to individual limitations. Therefore, though having developed these social skills as a professional coach, and though going to great lengths to be objective in my arguments and conclusions, I cannot completely exclude bias, and I do apologize in advance for any misunderstanding or misinterpretation.

In this publication I follow the Japanese tradition of writing the first name after a last name for all Japanese individuals referred to. Honorary titles are not used; contrary to Western practice this is not appropriate in Japanese tradition. "In Japan this is considered to be in particularly poor taste as titles such as hanshi, kyoshi, and so forth are only usually listed with the first appearance of a name in, for example, a faculty list."[1]

---

1. The author is deeply grateful to David Chambers, author and publisher of *Classical Fighting Arts* magazine and *OPG Okinawa Goodwill Ambassador,* for this and other valuable advice; to Miguel Da Luz, who is in charge of Public Relations at the Okinawa Karate Information Center (OKIC), for his support; to Noel Smith, Sensei, 8th Dan *Shorin Ryu, Shorinkan,* a senior US-*Shorinkan* authority in direct lineage to Nakazato Shugoro Sensei, for training and sharing wisdom, experience and insight; to David Colaizzi, Sensei, 7th Dan *Shorin Ryu, Shorinkan,* for relentlessly forging my performance every week in conjunction with Sensei Smith, and to Michael Clarke, Sensei, 8th Dan *Goju Ryu, Jundokan,* Australian karateka and author, for his encouragement to continue my research and to publish my findings.

Chapter 1

Okinawan Karate's "Japanization," "Americanization," and "Commercialization"

Okinawa Is the Birthplace of Karate

Many martial arts historians agree that karate is an indigenous Okinawan martial art form, though written records about its origin do not exist due to centuries-long secrecy and destruction, specifically that caused by the Battle of Okinawa in 1945.

Consequently, the majority of historic karate arguments is based on secondary sources and on what historians call "oral history," that is, on interviews or conversations with karate authorities and other contemporary witnesses. Hence, all published historical claims should be carefully double-checked and should generally be taken with a pinch of salt.

On the other hand, the selection of reliable references for historical and socio-cultural arguments is of utmost importance, because—plausible from a cultural point of view, but unfortunate from the standpoint of precision—all martial arts history is prone to legends and myths, to misinterpretations, to wishful thinking, and even to personal and political agendas.

* * *

A prominent example is *taekwondo,* which, after 1945, positioned itself as an ancient native Korean art, though academic research makes a strong case that it developed out of Japanese karate during the decades of Japan colonializing Southeast Asia in the 20th century.[1] Korea, of course, like every other Asian country, has its ancient martial arts roots. *Taekwondo* itself, though, was most certainly molded by Choi Hong Hi Sensei, who studied *Shotokan* karate in Japan. After enforced enlistment in the Japanese army, he became involved in the Korean independence movement, which led to his imprisonment. Until his liberation at the end of WWII, he practiced and developed his martial art, and later led the effort to forge Korean martial arts into its "official" form for the instruction of the Korean military and civilians (Thomas/Hornsey 2008).

But surprisingly, "the tales of taekwondo's 'ancient' roots have been repeated so many times and for so many years that these accounts have actually become 'history' for a large number of worldwide taekwondo practitioners and followers. Under scrutiny, however, taekwondo history and tradition, as presented by the taekwondo establishment, comes perilously close to being little more than fiction" (Moenig/Minho 2016, p. 158).

This background, of course, detracts neither from *taekwondo's* specific role as a martial art, nor from its undoubted strengths as a fighting approach, nor from its importance as an Olympic sport. It simply serves as an example of unnecessarily emphasizing a myth over historic facts.

∗   ∗   ∗

When historic facts and documents are not available, which is the case with *Te* and karate, scientific research of secondary sources, oral history, and indirect witnesses' interpretations, for a start, yield a source-criticized collection of historic possibilities. To overcome the eclecticism of the notion that "everything may be possible and everything is equally

---

1. ". . . Taekwondo's historical claims have been universally questioned, but still, the tales of taekwondo's indigenous origins from Korea persist. The narratives have been propagated by the taekwondo establishment and popular culture as taekwondo's tradition for such a long time that it is difficult to correct the storyline. Moreover, Korea's sensitive political relationship with Japan, which is tied to historical and territorial disputes, nationalistic sentiments, and national pride, makes it almost impossible for the Korean taekwondo community to change the narrative and finally acknowledge taekwondo's roots in Japanese karate." (Moenig/Minho 2016, p. 157f).

important," and to move towards historical reasoning, the findings need to not just be stated, but to be *understood* through a "hermeneutic" lens. In other words, to make sense, the findings need to be interpreted within the context of the socio-economic conditions at that time. This is the approach we use here; "hermeneutic" in historic research has the same effect as "empathy" in psychology: it allows us to better understand.

In terms of Okinawan karate, "the earliest known records were from the 18th-century, and they tended to be vague and prone to misinterpretation. Therefore, the generally accepted theory was that there had long been an indigenous fighting method in Okinawa called *Ti* (hand)" (Chambers et. al. 2020, p. xiii), *"peculiar to Okinawa in its origins"* (Funakoshi 1973, p. 3).

"Te," or *"Ti"* (手 pronounced "tee"), meaning "hand," apparently developed more than five hundred years ago, some say more than 1000 years ago (ibid., p. 3), and it is supposed that it was initially cultivated, practiced, and promoted by the islands' royal government organization *hiki* under *King Sho Shin* (Quast 2015a, p. 1), before Japan's *Satsuma* nobility invaded and occupied the Ryukyu Islands' kingdoms.

The century that followed this invasion by the Japanese *Satsuma daimyo* (feudal vassals of Japan's *shogun*, or the military commander) in 1609 fertilized the soil for the blossoming of Okinawan martial arts within the Ryukyus' gentry and honed *Te* further as a unique and genuine Okinawan way of fighting, and as a predecessor of karate (Funakoshi 1973, p. 7f; Hokama 2000, p. 15; Nagamine 1976, p. 21; OKIC, n.d., n.p.), whereas some Western sensei and authors claim that karate was initially developed out of Chinese *ch'üan fa*; such as Mark Bishop in the USA (Bishop 1991), or Werner Lind in Germany (Lind 1991), and, more recently, in Europe/Sweden, Jesse Encamp (https://www.youtube.com /playlist?list=PLnepTzrhzuB-6k93Klo0L5GDwiMym3Y9a).

Though Chinese martial arts were undoubtedly included in *Te*,[2] *validated historic sources about its first seminal impact are missing*. It is rather believed that Okinawan martial arts experts versed in Chinese boxing "altered the existing martial art, called Okinawan-Te, weeding out its bad points and adding good points to it, thus working it into an elegant art" (Funakoshi 1973, p. 3).

---

2. Perhaps after the famous "thirty-six Chinese families" took up residence in Okinawa in the late 14th century to spread administrative skills, crafts, and arts (Quast 2016); perhaps because Okinawan nobility as well as Okinawan karate masters used to study in China too; or perhaps because Chinese sailors, guards, or military envoys taught the art to Okinawans.

Accordingly, our core argument is that *an existing Okinawan martial art, with its clear intention and purpose of self-protection and preservation of one's life, integrated foreign knowledge and skills as an improvement into its existing system and intellectual framework.* Our thought seems plausible, as *every Asian country or kingdom has its genuine ancient martial art.* This was a simple necessity to survive, because as long as tradition goes, records, memories, myths, and legends describe fights, battles, wars, violent crime, and combat as a constant throughout history. As one of these genuine ancient martial arts forms we find *Te* on the Ryukyu Islands, genuine as it can be. Chinese martial arts were later integrated into *Te* as improvements without sacrificing Okinawan karate's essence, i.e., its true purpose and intention of self-protection.

Te/Ti, as a native Okinawan martial art, flourished for several hundred years, with *Naihanchi kata* [3] as one of its original Okinawan forms. Before Itosu Yasutsune Sensei created the *Pinan* [平安] kata series in the early 20th century, *Naihanchi* was the first form taught to karateka, characterized by Okinawan karate's anchored stances and positions, controlled minimal hip torque, and hard-style short movements. The lethal concepts in this ancient form allow, in Chibana Chosin Sensei's words, "one technique, total destruction" (Chibana 2006, p. 20).

The purpose of this Okinawan fighting art, developed and practiced in complete privacy, some say secretly, was a simple one; after swords were confiscated and, during the Ryukyu Islands' centuries-long occupation by Japan, when carrying/owning weapons was forbidden,[4] the purpose became to *defend yourself and create the most possible damage to an opponent in the most effective way.* Hence, Okinawan kara-*Te* (term explanation below) was intended to be a weaponless lethal fighting art (however, see excursion below for "weapons in empty-hand *Te* as extensions of the body"), protecting Okinawa's inhabitants in potentially life-threatening situations, because "in an individual confrontation,

---

3. Since it is not a Japanese word, there are no *kanji* for *Naihanchi*; it usually is written in *katakana* as ナイハンチ. More remarks on this kata, considered to be "the heart and soul of *Shorin Ryu* karate," in Chapter III.

4. "Contrary to popular belief, Karate was never 'banned' in the 19th and 20th century by the Okinawan authorities, as has been reported. Instead it was practiced in private so as not to reveal too much of the art to outsiders. The concept of Karate being an illegal practice came from the mistranslation of a written character in Gichin Funakoshi's book, *Karate-Do: My Way of Life*" (CFA, Issue# 58, p. 11). It is claimed that until the official recognition of Okinawa as part of Japan in 1875, karate was practiced not just privately, but "in the strictest secrecy" (Nagamine 1976, p. 24).

armed with the element of surprise, a skilled martial artist might have a fighting chance" against a trained soldier, even if the latter is carrying steel-bladed weapons (Hokama 2000, p. 24).

Though validated historic sources about the first impact of Chinese martial arts on Okinawan *Te* are missing (assumptions are listed in Patrick McCarthy's publication of the *Bubishi*, pp. 14ff), legend has it that these arts were introduced in the late 17th and in the early 18th century into Okinawan *Te* by sailors and pirates like Chinto and by military envoys like Wanshu and Kushanku (which is actually a title rather than a name), all remembered from the kata named after them. Only the two military envoys' visits to Okinawa are documented by Japanese historical records (Clarke C. 2012b, p. 118), and whether Wanshu indeed was the name of an envoy or whether this term was used as a general term for a royalty is unclear (Quast 2015b, n.p.). Overall, the impact of Chinese martial arts during that period seems to be recognized by martial arts historians.

Te evolved into *Tode* [唐手; i.e., "China Hand"] and larger circular Chinese *ch'üan fa* movements and concepts are now found in advanced Okinawan kata.[5]

---

5. (Footnote continued on next page) The historic timeline and argument for its accuracy are supported by the following sources:
   A. The Okinawa Prefecture Board of Education's findings, which in 1994 organized the published results of the various research efforts into the question of origins, with the result that (Okinawa Karate Information Center, n.d., n.p., and Okinawa Prefectural Government, 2003, n.p.):
      (a) "Karate originates from 'Ti,' the original Okinawan martial art, which later was influenced by martial arts from China and other nations.
      (b) The origin of Karate traces back to the time of King Shō Shin (1477–1526), when Aji local rulers were gathered to reside in the surrounding of Shuri Castle and a sword hunt occurred [author's remark: supposedly a "sword confiscation" is meant here]. It was also influenced by the weapon prohibition enforced following the invasion of Ryūkyū by Satsuma in 1609.
      (c) At the time of Satto, trade with China started in 1372. Later, Chinese martial arts were introduced and formalized to match the natural features of Okinawa. Thus karate was born."

   B. Patrick McCarthy, translator of *Bubishi*, with his commentary, summarizes the three historically verified theories referring to the development of karate (McCarthy 2016, p. 138), which match and support the above quote:
      • one claims that it was primarily impacted by Chinese martial arts;
      • another claims wealthy landowners' needs for effective defense after king *Sho Shin's* weapon ban;
      • the third one says that Okinawan law enforcement and security personnel developed the art in response to the forbidding of weapons after *Satsuma's* invasion of Okinawa.

Around 1900, *Te/Tode* was practiced mainly in the Okinawan towns of Shuri, later called *Shuri-Te* [首里手], in Naha, later called *Naha-Te* [那覇手], in its port village Tomari, later called *Tomari-Te* [泊手], and in Itoman.

The term "kara-te" [空 手] was introduced to replace the initial term Te ("hand") shortly thereafter—initially as "China hand," to be renamed later, in the mid-1930s, into the more neutral term "open-hand," when Japan was engaged in its historic conflict with China and references to Chinese martial arts were not welcome in imperial Japan's militaristic world view.

> During this entire time, for more than 500 years, even for 1,000 years, karate was exclusively practiced in Okinawa and was essentially unknown in mainland Japan.

Though Okinawa's legendary karate authorities did not promote a distinction of the art into different "styles" and rather promoted its overarching purpose of forging individuals into entities of defense and offense, karate "styles" were introduced for a variety of reasons in the decades preceding WWII; a request for "styles" by mainland Japan's martial arts officials and the reason to not offend them politically being one of those. Hence, carefully avoiding any possible reference to Chinese influences on Okinawan *Te*, Okinawan karate masters explained some kata, when demonstrated to visiting Japanese royalties, martial arts officials or political dignitaries, as being representations of the above mentioned three town-specific *Te*-"styles." Later, the town-specific karate approaches were named as *Shorin Ryu*, *Goju Ryu* and *Uechi Ryu*, which became the only three officially recognized umbrella karate styles in Okinawa.

"Shuri-Te was considered to be the most indigenous style of Te, less . . . influenced by Chinese martial arts" (Clarke, C. 2012a, p. 27). It is based on Matsumura Soken Sensei's and his teacher Sakugawa Sensei's teachings

---

C. A high-quality historical analysis fresh off the printing press in May 2020 confirms the timeline as follows: "The earliest known records were from the 18th-century, and they tended to be vague and prone to misinterpretation. Therefore the generally accepted theory was that there had long been an indigenous fighting method in Okinawa called *Ti* (hand) and that this eventually became Okinawan karate when it was merged with selected self-defense concepts from China, and elsewhere" (Chambers et. al. 2020, p. xiii).

in the 1800s. Out of *Shuri-Te, Shorin Ryu* [少林流] originated as probably the oldest Okinawan karate style, named *"Shorin Ryu"* instead of *"Shuri-Te"* by Chibana Chosin Sensei in 1933. *Shorin Ryu* is also the common ground of its sub-styles *Matsubayashi Ryu, Kobayashi Ryu, Shobayashi Ryu, Matsumura Orthodox Ryu, Isshin Ryu* (a style overlapping *Goju Ryu* as well), *Seibukan,* and a few others.

Naha-Te and *Tomari-Te* based karate, combined with both *ch'üan fa* and Okinawan and Chinese *kenpo* [拳法; pronounced "kempo" and meaning "fist method"] evolved into *Goju Ryu* and *Uechi Ryu,* the other two indigenous Okinawan styles.

Though karate legend Miyagi Chojun Sensei gave the name "hard-soft" to the style in the mid-1930s, *Goju Ryu* [剛柔流] is based on Higaonna Kanryo Sensei's teachings more than half a century before that. In the late 1930s Miyagi Chojun Sensei appointed Yamaguchi Gogen Sensei to promote *Goju Ryu* on mainland Japan, which lead to the rapid growth and popularity of a *Goju Ryu* derivative on the mainland, including the style's official recognition as one of the "ancient martial arts"—a position that strangely enough was not awarded to any other Okinawan karate style and representing a decision that can only be understood completely within the big picture of governmental cultural integration efforts at that time (see next chapter).

Uechi Ryu [上地流], initially named *Pangainun Ryu,* was introduced to Okinawa and Japan in the early 1920s by its initiator, Uechi Kanbun Sensei, who like *Goju Ryu* predecessor Higaonna Kanryo Sensei, studied Chinese martial arts in Fuchou, China, in addition to studying Okinawan *Te.* In the 1940s, during the Chinese-Japanese war, either he himself renamed this style *"Uechi Ryu"* because, as stated earlier, Chinese references, terms, or connotations were not welcome in Japanese martial arts, or his students renamed it in honor of its creator after his death (Clarke, C. 2012b, p. 277). Over the following decades, his son, Uechi Kanei Sensei, created and promoted a systematic *Uechi Ryu* curriculum and initiated the worldwide spread of this style (Dollar 2017).

Today, as was the case for centuries, *dentou* Okinawan karate is preserved, practiced, and passed on to the generations in privately owned *machi* [町] dojo [道場] and it "will only survive if it is supported by vibrant *machi* dojo producing excellent instructors. That is, individuals who are willing to train for decades to achieve a standard that equals that of the past and by which others will be judged in the future" (CFA, Issue #58, p. 11).

Every Okinawan karate style has its *honbu* [本部 pronounced "hombu"] dojo; its administrative headquarters and central training hall, led by its presiding 10th dan sensei; as well as other associated, but independent machi dojo, sometimes led by 10th dan sensei as well—today totaling around four hundred all over the Okinawan islands. Such

Image 1: Shorin Ryu Shorinkan Honbu Dojo 1967 and 2019

Photographs by Noel Smith

Street Entrance 1967.   Street Entrance 2019.

Adobe with Imprinted Images of Shuri Castle
2019.

is Kuramoto Masaku Sensei's educated estimation (in his CFA interview 2020, p. 19).[6]

Since the author is most familiar with *Kobayashi Shorin Ryu* in the version promoted by *Shorin Ryu Shorinkan* [小林流小林館], this style is used in Chapter III as an empirical example to compare training variations between *dentou*/classical Okinawan karate and traditional (non-sports) Japanese karatedo.

* * *

Excursion: Empty-Hand Te Uses Weapons as "Extensions of the Body"

The notion that karate is a "weaponless fighting art" has to be modified in the sense that classical karate always used everyday tools and trade equipment as extensions of the body, tools which were sometimes slightly modified for easier handling or to do more damage. Without going into the specific history of the development of these weapons,[7] here are the best-known examples:[8]

---

6. "The book *Okinawa Karatedō Kobudō Dōiō List* was issued by the Okinawa Prefectural Board of Education in 2009" (http://okic.okinawa/en/archives/news/p2704). Based on this survey, Sensei Andreas Quast counted 420 Okinawan dojos in 2005 (http://ryukyu-bugei .com/?p=3048). "After that, the Okinawa Prefectural Karate Promotion Division conducted a 'Survey on Okinawa Traditional Karate and Kobudō' during the fiscal year 2016. According to this survey, as of the end of 2016 there were 386 dojos in the prefecture" (OKIC ibid.). The author's count in October 2020 of dojos listed at the OKIC website (http://okic.okinawa/en/dojo) was 364 dojos, which seems to be an updated figure. However, there may be not all active dojos listed, because "only the ones that approved the disclosure are being introduced" (ibid.), so that, in summary, Kuramoto Sensei's above quoted estimation of ca. 400 dojos seems pretty accurate.

7. Author and self-acclaimed "karate-nerd" Sensei Jesse Enkamp asserts that some of the listed weapons were not Okinawan farming tools, but equipment used by soldiers and law enforcement officers in China before their use in Okinawa (https://www.facebook.com /karatebyjesse/). Even if that is the case, it does not explain the origin of these weapons. Or is the proposition that they were explicitly developed for military use? In other words, that soldiers were using flails and forks instead of swords, spears, and halberds? The author dares to strongly doubt this. Sensei Enkamp's related statement that, contrary to the popular myth, farming-tool weapons were not introduced into Okinawan martial arts by "poor farmers fighting samurais" but by evicted *Ryukyu* nobility, is shared by the author—as it is by other martial arts historians as well.

8. *Everything* can be, was, and should be used as an extension of the body to succeed in a fight; this fierce and vigorous dedication to commission everything in a fighter's environment represents a significant part of the true karate fighting spirit.

- Staffs and sticks (*bo, jo, tanbo . . .*)
- Farming equipment, like flails and, perhaps, some parts of horse gear/ bridle[9] (*nunchaku*); parts of large sickles, or complete small ones (*kama*); handles to crank water from wells or turn millstones when grinding grains (*tonfa*); upper parts of forks (*sai*)
- Fishing equipment, like net-hauling tools that prevent coral cuts on fishermen's hands (*tekko*), gaffs/hitchers used to harpoon and to haul nets (*nunte bo*), oars (*eku*), and other utensils.

The art of using these weapons in traditional karate was and is called *kobudo* [古武道], which, in conjunction with weaponless karate, constitutes a mutually inclusive unity to be taught and practiced in unison at many Okinawan dojos.

Some Okinawan masters became famous for their unique way to master *kobudo* with either all or some specific weapon of their choice, which resulted in kata named after them; e.g., *Yamaine No Bo Shushi No Kun; Yamane No Bo Sakugawa No Kun; Nakaime No Bo Kubo No Kun; Tonaki No Nunchaku;* and so forth. This sometimes led to the misconception that *kobudo* is a martial art of its own. It never was, though in recent years *"Ryukyu kobudo"* or *kobujutsu* is to be found as a separate category for Okinawan Intangible Cultural Asset Holders and is offered as a "fourth style" in addition to the tree of official Okinawan karate styles for karate tourists who want to visit Okinawan dojos (more details on this matter later in the following chapters).

So, again, *karate and kobudo are the upside and downside of the same coin.* They are taught in unison at the author's US-based dojo as well as at the Shorin Ryu Shorinkan Honbu Dojo in Okinawa, represented by its own association, the *Okinawan Kobudo Kokusairengokai*. The unity may be illustrated by the name of a bo kata created by the legendary *Shorin Ryu* karate master Nakazato Shugoro Sensei, who included moves

---

9. The "bridle"-explanation was provided by Nagamine Shoshin Sensei, but challenged by Sensei Mark Bishop, who claims that "a nunchaku is a flail and has no connection with a horse bridle whatsoever . . . So where did this horse-bridle false history stem from? Well, my research showed that much of the historic misinformation about *kobudo* stemmed from, or was made up by, Shinken Taira (1897–1970); probably to be politically correct in the post-War era, when bushido was rather unpopular and Okinawans needed to put themselves over as humble farmers to their new American overlords" (https://www.facebook .com/mark.bishop.71271). Unfortunately this statement does not falsify the "bridle" reference, since both gadgets, flails as well as bridles, are farming tools. However, as a *deshi* the author does not have the authority or skill level to question either view.

from Sakugawa Sensei's above-mentioned kata into a form he created and named *Shugoro No Bo Sakugawa No Kun.*

The similarity of moves between *kobudo* and weaponless karate is fascinating. The author found the transfer from *kobudo* hand-positions, when working with the *bo, sai,* and *nunchaku,* into hand-coordination when practicing weaponless techniques (and vice versa), as explained in the following paragraphs, especially helpful and clarifying. Two illustrating examples for *bo* in this sense, which everyone may re-evaluate, are included here:

- the hand/fist positions when holding a *bo* correctly for a forward strike and
- the hand/fist positions when holding a *bo* correctly for an outside block.

In our first example, a *bo* forward strike, the correct grip needs the front hand to be turned "inward" in the way that the palm points down toward the weapon and toward the ground, and the knuckles point upward.

This correct hand position (left photo) prevents the weapon from slipping out of the hand at the moment of its forceful connection with its target. It completely transfers the kinetic energy of the strike into its target, and it prevents an opponent from hitting the *bo* out of the forward fist. The weapon is locked in the front hand.

In contrast, when the front fist knuckles are pointing to the side—or even if they are pointing down to the ground—the weapon is not locked in the forward hand (right photo). In this case, the *bo* may slip out of the front hand when it forcefully connects with its target, or opponents may knock the *bo* out of the front fist by pushing it upwards and sideways.

The correct hand position in this forward strike is similar to the one for a forward punch without a weapon (*chudan-, judan-,* or *gedan-tsuki* depending on the level; compare the first and the third photograph in Image 2 below), thus constituting one example of the stunning similarity of techniques and concepts in empty-hand karate and *kobudo,* the two pillars (or the two sides of the same coin) that conjointly constitute the art.

Our second example for this argument of the similarity of *kobudo* moves and weaponless karate is a *bo* outside block. The correct grip here needs the front hand to be turned "inward" so that its knuckles are pointing at least forward, and even a bit to the blocked side.

Image 2: Correct (and Incorrect) Fist Position for Bo Forward Strike Compared
to Empty Hand Forward Punch

Correct Fist Position.   Incorrect Fist Position.

Empty Hand Forward Punch.

Comparable to the first example of a forward strike, this hand position prevents the weapon from slipping out of—or being knocked out
of—the front hand, when it meets the opponent's weapon or body with
full force (left photo); the *bo* is locked in the forward hand.

The other advantage, and in this case of utmost importance, is that
this fist position prevents the front wrist from hurtful spraining, even
braking, at the moment of impact, because the wrist is in line with the
forearm.

This specific wrist vulnerability is given whenever karateka apply an
incorrect grip (right photo) for a blocking move with the *bo*. The

Image 3: Correct (and Incorrect) Fist Position for Bo Outside Block Compared
to Empty Hand Outside Block

Correct Fist Position.   Incorrect Fist Position.

Empty Hand Outside Block.

incorrect hand/fist position allows kinetic energy to "vector away" from the target, to "escape" at the counterproductively backward bent wrist. Unfortunately, this practice can be observed at many *kobudo* competition demonstrations all over the USA.

The incorrect grip for a *bo* outside block has the forward hand knuckles pointing down or even to the non-blocked side (right photo), which does not lock the weapon into the forward hand. So, again, an opponent may knock the *bo* out of the front fist by pushing it upwards/sideways—and, as mentioned, this fist/wrist position is extremely vulnerable because an opponent can force the already backward-bent front wrist to bend further backward. Thus the wrist is prone to sprain or even to fracture when the *bo* forcefully connects with its target.

The correct hand position in this second example is similar to the one for an outside block (*soto-uke*) in empty-hand karate without a weapon (compare the first and the third photograph in image 3 above) and thus provides another example for the stunning similarity of techniques and concepts between weaponless karate and *kobudo*, the two martial art systems which constitute the two sides of the same coin.

* * *

The "Disarmament" of Okinawan Karate in Mainland Japan

The specific role and purpose of a comparable lethal martial art in mainland Japan during the same time period was not represented by karate; it was *bujutsu*, better known as *jujutsu*, that served as a part of a warrior's education. *Karate was essentially unknown in mainland Japan until the early 1920s*, though some Chinese military *ch'üan fa* representatives may have visited before that and some Okinawan karate instructors may have travelled there sporadically.

Okinawan karate "officially" entered Japan with Funakoshi Gichin Sensei in 1922, when he demonstrated the art before a large gathering of interested Japanese spectators (Funakoshi 1983, p. 85). However, it took almost another decade, after much struggle, for Funakoshi Sensei to promote and shape his karate approach, later named Shotokan [松濤館] by his students, to gain broader public interest (ibid., pp. 85ff). Other Okinawan karate instructors followed and taught on mainland Japan, including karate legends Tomaya Kanken, Motobu Choki, Shinken Taira, and others.

They all deserve credit for helping win respect for the "new" art among Japanese government institutions and leading *budo* associations—however not without significant modifications to assimilate the path of other traditional Japanese martial arts forms and their sports-alterations (judo, aikido, kendo, etc.). This assimilation represents the "Japanization" of Okinawan karate, a process which seems to be motivated by a combination of reasons, such as:

- *governmental cultural integration efforts* to create some homogeneity within the cultural sphere of the nation (Johnson 2012)
- *sport-political considerations* to create an Olympic discipline as well as business opportunities (Kotek 2016; *Chambers* in CFA and email to the author)
- strategies to establish a Japanese "punch and kick alternative" to the then-popular sport of boxing (Enkamp, n.d., https://www.youtube .com/watch?v=jSLAcC5X8iE).[10]

In the mid-1930s, karate was officially accepted as a Japanese martial arts discipline on the mainland, after meeting the requirements of Dai Nippon Butokukai,[11] the governing and accreditation body of Japanese *budo* arts. As one result of the required adaptions, the initial Okinawan concept of self-protection underwent two revisions that distinguish Japanese karatedo considerably from its Okinawan origin:

- the *change of purpose* from self-*protection* to self-*perfection* in terms of recreation, spiritualism, health, and character development
- the *change of techniques* from "creating the most possible damage in the most effective way" to speedy, fencing sport moves with tagging contact.

---

10. The last aspect was enforced when fifty-year-old Motobu Choki Sensei defeated a big non-Japanese heavy-weight boxer/wrestler with an open-hand punch (Chambers et. al. 2020, p. 106f.)—a spectacular victory that was then incorrectly attributed to Funakoshi Gichin Sensei in the press (ibid., p. 107), supposedly to support the latter's role of spreading his specifically Japanized version of Shotokan karate on the mainland.

11. "The Dai Nippon Butoku Kai was originally established 1895 in Kyoto, Japan, under the authority of the Japanese government and the endorsement of His Majesty, Meiji Emperor, to solidify, promote, and standardize martial disciplines and systems throughout Japan. It aimed for the preservation of traditional budo and the nobility associated with Samurai culture. It was the first official and premier martial arts institution sanctioned by the government of Japan" (https://www.dnbk.org/index.php, n. d., n. p.). The organization was dissolved after WWII and other associations took over its function.

First, referring to the change of purpose: it is claimed that the leading Okinawan karate masters, for instance Funakoshi Sensei's famous and influential sensei, Itosu ("Anko") Yasutsune, permitted some of their students to teach the secret art in mainland Japan but advised them to change Okinawan karate in order to "disarm" it and keep specific techniques hidden.

In this view, "Funakoshi . . . represented, and even amplified, the Itosu-derived trend of removing or hiding the most effective and brutal aspects of Okinawa Te" (Clarke, C. 2012a, p. 157)—even moving further to alter, to "Japanize," the entire self-defense purpose to suit the spiritual way, the *"Do"* [道], of Japanese *budo* arts. In short, Funakoshi Sensei turned Okinawan karate "into karate-do, transforming it from a tough and effective art of self-defense into a means of spiritual perfection" (ibid.).[12]

As a result of these efforts, many classical lethal Okinawan karate's techniques were eliminated in Japanized karate, especially throws and sweeps, ground work, nerve suppression, joint locks, and limb, head, and neck manipulations.

It seems safe to assume that Funakoshi Sensei actually transferred some modified Itosu-based Okinawan *Shuri-Te*, later called *Shorin Ryu*, to mainland Japan. In his detailed analysis of "Gichin Funakoshi's Exquisite Art" (the title of the article series), Graham Noble gives several examples of how today's "deep" and "wide" *Shotokan* stances and postures were initially closer to the "low" and "natural" postures of Okinawan karate, how today's chest- and head-high *Shotokan* kicks were initially restricted to mid-level, and how hand movements were short and direct rather than extended (Noble 2020, p. 51).

American sensei, Bruce D. Clayton, 8th Dan *Shotokan*, ISKA, tries to reconnect *Shotokan* to ancient *bunkai* roots and calls it *Shotokan's Secret: The Hidden Truth Behind Karate's Fighting Origins* (Clayton 2010). To be precise, the material presented in that publication is not actually *Shotokan's* secret but the secret of Okinawan *Te*, primarily *Shuri-Te/Shorin Ryu*. In the author's humble opinion, there is no need to vindicate *Shotokan*, i.e., *Shorin Ryu's* "softened" and Japanized derivative, as an art specific to Okinawa when the original lethal and *dentou* form

---

12. As a *deshi* the author does not have the competency to verify or reject these claims. Interestingly, *Kobayashi Shorin Ryu* authorities in Okinawa shared this view with the author when discussing the matter in fall Nov 2019.

still exists in parallel. This rather looks a bit like an attempt to claim that a Japanese derivative is *dentou* Okinawan.

In summation, many techniques seem to have been radically changed through "Japanization"—either per request of the leading Japanese *budo* associations, or by Funakoshi Sensei himself, or by following sensei generations—and much of the original, Itosu-based style was lost in its transition from Okinawa to mainland Japan.

Initially, "karate was little understood and probably little regarded, coming as it did from Okinawa, the most distant and poorest prefecture of Japan" (Noble 2020, p. 44), and thus in mainland Japan *budo*-specific philosophical, Zen- and health-related superstructures for karate became more important than the original purpose of *dentou Shorin Ryu,* which was self-protection.

"This radical period of transition represented the termination of a secret self-defense art that embraced spiritualism and the birth of a unique recreational phenomenon" (McCarthy 2016, p. 147).

> "Karatedo" as a Japanese athletic-meditative path differs significantly from the classical Okinawan self-protection concept.

Second, with respect to the change from lethal techniques to speedy, fencing sport moves with tagging contact, establishing karate as "sport" was initiated and heavily pursued by the official Japanese *budo* and karate associations as part of their political efforts to establish martial arts as an Olympic discipline (see next chapter for more details). These efforts led to the fact that "these days there are two types of karate, traditional karate . . . and sport or competition karate" (Yagi interview 2018, p. 23).

Kiyuna Choko Sensei, former Director General of Okinawa Karatedo Shinkokai, regrets that in the late 1960s *this split the world of Okinawan karate into two groups; those who wanted to go with . . .* sport karate and the others who embraced Okinawan *dentou* karate" (Kiyuna interview, 2018, p. 11).

> Japanese "sports" karatedo, with it speedy fencing moves and tagging contact, differs significantly from the original Okinawan self-protection concept.

"In the case of sport karate, they are only interested in speed to score points. They also have 'safety zones' where attacks are not permitted and where penalties are given even for accidental contact. Therefore they are . . . not martial art in any way" (Yagi Interview 2018, p. 23).

In contrast to "sportsmanship," true combat does not have rules, and terms like "fairness" or "equitableness" do not apply when it comes to surviving a life-threatening situation—which contradicts these pointless stand-off scenes propagated in action movies, where a "noble hero" doesn't act on an advantage while combatting a villain but even drops a weapon to level the fight. As soon as any kind of rules are implemented, combat changes into some kind of game. Life-protecting fighting is no game. Life-protecting fighting is not pretty. Life-protecting fighting is pure violence and pitiless full-power action.

That does not mean, however, that "honor" is excluded in combat. Honor remains a core value of an individual code of ethics for every karateka. Acting honorably in combat is a matter of individual choice with all its consequences, as the Japanese *bushido* philosophy as well as the moral guidelines introduced by Okinawan karate legends aptly explain.

"Un-softened" Okinawan "karate has the unconditional philosophy of killing with one strike (*ichigeki hissatsu*) and complete self-protection. Therefore, when learning the techniques, it is necessary to assume a situation that corresponds to actual combat and to prepare for inevitable death" (Takamiyagi 2008, p. 1).[13]

Though this "one-punch kill" approach shouldn't always been taken literally—it is almost impossible to achieve in every strike—it is the required proper mind-set for full-power training and determined application of techniques. In real combat, an adversary is to be mentally and physically controlled and "set up" by a series of techniques during the chess-like flow of combat for the final application of an *ichigeki hissatsu* technique that ends the fight.

In line with Okinawan karate's disarmament, Funakoshi Gichin Sensei promoted karate as a peaceful way of meditative athletics, concentrated in the—sometimes misunderstood and sometimes called "sacred"—principle of "there is no first attack in karate."

---

13. On a side-note, this is a core reason why some karateka oppose teaching traditional martial arts to children. In the words of Raymond ("Gene") Adkins, 6th Dan *Shorin Ryu*, *Shorinkan*, "I am not a big proponent of children participating in martial arts. The developmental physical fights of children (generally wrestling types of things) don't need traditional adult fighting methods" (email to the author, 01/06/2020).

This principle needs to be rephrased as "karateka aim at not attacking first," but they will of course defend themselves by all means necessary if attacked, including pre-emptive strikes (which are blocks at the same time; see below) and other attacking techniques. The concept of a pre-emptive strike does not necessarily violate the "sacred" principle, because trained karateka can read the "tell" of an attack and are able to identify an opponent's subtle signals that "telegraph" an intended move. Hence, they will pre-emptively "block-strike" at the moment of an attacker's "tell." This could seem like a first attack to the untrained eye, but it is not.

Furthermore, it has to be pointed out that there is no "block" as such in Okinawan karate; every defensive technique is an offensive one at the same time. A simple "block" would allow an attacker to continue to attack, whereas a "block-strike" creates damage and has a chance to stop an attack.

To fully understand this concept, it has to be pointed out that the attack itself is the final point in a series of preceding intents, moves, actions, and "announcements," called "telegraphing" in combat karate. These occurrences constitute an "intent time line" (Hayes n.d., Vol. 14, Issue 1, p. 9f) during a real-life attack—be it on the street, in a bar, or in whatever other comparable situation—leaving an attacked karateka ample time and opportunities to act pre-emptively.

Example of an 'Intent Time Line' Developing During a Real-Life Attack

EARLY >>|>>>>>>>>>>|>>>>>>>>>>>>>|>>>>>>>>>|>>>>>>>>>>>|>>>>>>					**LATE**
first desire					attack launched
	anger	physiological signs; facial expressions	cursing; pointing	physical threats	pre-attack move(s)

Based on Hayes n. d., Vol. 14, Issue 1, p. 10; modified by the author

The graph above is just an example and not written in stone; karateka may modify the "intent time line" per their personal experience and may add or delete aspects as they encounter an opponent's signals in their own fighting experience. Plus, the shown spaces are not true to scale but illustrate a development. Nevertheless, if karateka wait until an opponent's attack is launched, they would irresponsibly sacrifice all their advantages in a desperate situation. "You would cede 90–99 percent of whatever advantage you may have had to the person who cares nothing about your life or the lives of those you are protecting" (Hayes n.d., Vol. 14, Issue 1, p. 10).

Motobu Choki Sensei, famous and cherished senior authority of *kenpo* and *Tomari-Te,* goes even further when stating that "unfortunately the phrase is terribly misunderstood . . . I simply don't believe that attacking first is wrong! However, in the same breath, let me also say that it's simply not *budo* spirit to ever attack anyone without just cause[14] . . . When you fight you must do so fiercely, otherwise the opponent could seriously hurt you . . . once it's been established that a fight is about to ensue the most important thing is to win. There is no other alternative to survive in a desperate situation" (quote in Chambers et. al. 2020, p. 121). His point definitely is to be taken seriously, and not only because he is a senior karate authority, but also because he was one of the few sensei in modern times with extensive serious combat experience, where he was forced to put his fighting skills (successfully) to the test.

Once it is understood that a block is at the same time a pre-emptive strike, the "no first attack in karate" principle becomes comprehensible. It is in this sense that it was understood by Okinawan karate masters, including Motobu Choki Sensei as quoted, Chibana Chosin Sensei, and others. Without this specification, the "no first attack in karate" principle would be an unrealistic artificial construct and not a logical derivation from the goal of self-protection in the genuine Okinawan martial arts. It would rather epitomize a political statement to create the view of karate being some kind of a disarmed "peaceful martial art," perhaps in order to support Japanese karatedo's recognition as sports-related, character-building, and meditative.

The described two-fold change of Okinawan karate, required by mainland Japan's martial arts institutions, became necessary not only for reasons related to sports and the education of youth but for commercial reasons. "Emphasizing non-combative personal benefits as goals of

---

14. Like Motobu Choki Sensei, Funakoshi Gichin Sensei legitimizes the use of force only for a just cause. The parallel to Augustin's Just War Doctrine in Christian ethics is amazing. The political connotation of Funakoshi Gichin Sensei's statement is, however, unveiled when he considers the actions of the Japanese Imperial Army in the Chinese-Japanese war as an example of righteous use of force (Meyer 2007, p. 36 n.17), whereas the Augustinian principle of just war allows violence only if the final goal to be achieved is peace, not colonialization, as it was the case then.

karate training made karate more appealing to new groups less attracted to fighting capabilities than to personal mental and/or physical improvements" (Kotek 2016, p. 69).

Genuine Okinawan karate is dangerous enough to cause real damage, but broken ribs, brain injuries, or possible lethal accidents would have ended the spread of karate as a sport and as a commercial product.

"Takeover" Attempts to Integrate Okinawan Karate into Japanese Karatedo

Compared to five-hundred-plus years of *Te* and three hundred years of *Shorin Ryu,*[15] Japanese karatedo with its more than ninety years of existence is a relative new development. However, Japan, the "*karate-reproducing*" country is—and used to be—the superior political power governing the "karate-*inventing*" and "karate-*cultivating*" region Okinawa, first as the occupying force of the Ryukyu kingdoms with its feudal structure, and thereafter as the central government overseeing Okinawa Prefecture.

(Mainland) Japan has its own, many centuries-old, even more than a millennium-old, martial arts *bujutsu* and *bushido* tradition. Combined with the hegemonic view of its own militaristic superiority and corresponding treatment of occupied territory, this may explain Japan's attitude, policies, and actions related to its attempt to claim karate as its own genuine Japanese martial art—which is of course correct in terms of its governmental sphere—but which is not correct in terms of subcultural heritage, and which fails to give appropriate credit to the "karate-inventing" and "karate-cultivating" region of Okinawa.

Moreover, traditional Okinawan karate was considered crude and "rural" by Japanese martial arts officials, compared to the centuries-old, elegant, and sophisticated Japanese *bushido* and arts of *koryu bujutsu,* and was therefore supposed to be socially acceptable on the mainland only after its conversion into its Japanized form.

---

15. Considering Takahara Pēchin Sensei (1683–1760) as one of the Okinawan *Te* pioneers in the *Ryukyus*—not to be confused with the earlier Hamahiga Pechin (born 1663), who demonstrated *Tode* (karate) and *Sai-jutsu* to the 5th Tokugawa Shogun (Quast 2015, p. 78)—and assuming Sakugawa Kanga "Tode" Sensei (1733–1815) as the progenitor of all *Shuri-Te* and thus *Shorin Ryu* styles.

On the other hand, it was explored how ". . . the stakes of war memory in Japan after its catastrophic defeat in World War II, [show] how and why defeat has become an indelible part of national collective life, especially in recent decades" (Hashimoto 2015, p. 3). It is the author's opinion that this collective shift away from hegemonic pre-war militarism also impacts the role and the view of martial arts in post-war Japan, redefining karate's intention into a spiritual way rather than self-protection, and redirecting its inherent lethal combat skills into sports.

In light of their long-term strategy to incorporate Japanese martial arts into the Olympic program, primarily for economic reasons, the actions of Japanese martial arts officials become transparent and explain why the Japanese karate umbrella organization early on tried to incorporate Okinawan karate: after WWII, martial arts officials in Japan decided to consolidate the various karate schools in Okinawa and Japan under one organization. Authorized by the Japanese government to promote anyone in any style to any rank (Bellina 2018, p. 28), Tomaya Kanken Sensei, who opened his first *Shudokan* dojo on mainland Japan in 1930 (ibid.), was assigned the task of unifying all Japanese and Okinawan karate into one overarching Japanese organization, the "Federation of All Japan Karate FAJKO" and made an effort to integrate Okinawan karate authorities as Japanese karate masters. He invited Okinawan karate masters to Tokyo to demonstrate their art, with the ultimate goal of being accepted as Japanese karate masters, though the other way round—having Japanese sensei recognized and accepted by Okinawan masters—would be historically, culturally, and rank-wise more accurate.

The background of this and comparable Japanese initiatives was to lay the groundwork for Japan's long-term strategy of having several martial arts accepted as an Olympic sport/discipline.[16] "Inclusion in the Olympic program is a fast-track to popularity with increased participation, television exposure, more sponsors, and amplified income; so it is hardly surprising that governments as well as sports organizations are keen to get in on the action."[17]

---

16. Until 1964, when Judo was included for the first time in the Tokyo Olympics, Asian martial arts were relegated to "demonstration sport" status. Judo was excluded again in 1968, returned in 1972, and has been a fixture since. Taekwondo became a full-medal sport from 2000 on continuously (*Encyclopedia Britannica*, https://www.britannica.com/story/olympics-martial-arts). Karate was to be included in 2020/21 and supposedly will be excluded again 2024.

17. https://www.businessinsider.com/this-is-how-sports-get-chosen-for-the-olympics-2016-7; retrieved 02/10/2020.

Beside its international popularity, one criterion for a sport to even be considered for nomination is its national representation by one single umbrella organization, a requirement that sheds clarifying light on the integration attempts led by (mainland) Japanese *budo* officials.

However, many Okinawan masters refused to come. "This concept did not sit well with them," explains 9th Dan *Goju Ryu* Kinjo Tsuneo Sensei in a CFA interview, "as they viewed karate on the mainland as a distant and very unsophisticated form of the karate that was born in Okinawa. Like a small grandchild in fact" (Kinjo interview 2020, p. 35).

The underlying sports- and politics-related reasons are explained by former FAJKO employee, author, and publisher, David Chambers, who legitimizes his statement by the fact that "I was working for FAJKO in Minato-ku, Tokyo, at that time (1975–1980) as an assistant to the General Secretary, General Eichi Eriguchi, and therefore know exactly what was going on." His explanation:

> FAJKO needed the Okinawans to join; otherwise, they could not comply with the rules of GAISF,[18] which was a necessary precursor to recognition as an Olympic sport. Olympic status was the ultimate aim of financier/industrialist Ryoichi Sasagawa, the president of FAJKO. The Okinawans were invited to the mainland, but only to be graded by their own, much less qualified students. To avail themselves of this honor, they also had to finance the trip and pay for their own grading, or at least that was the initial offer. Needless to say this was viewed as an insult, and to this day the Okinawan karate groups do not belong to the Japan Karate Federation, nor do they intend to join.[19]

Hence, the reason to reject oversight by FAJKO, which was founded around that time,[20] contradicts Shimabukuro Eizo Sensei's statement that

---

18. Global Association of International Sports Federation, founded 1967; its predecessor was the "permanent bureau of the international sports federations," created in 1922. "GAISF also acts as official sanctioning body for International Federations in the global sports movement" (https://gaisf.sport/mission-and-vision/) and collaborates with the International Olympic Committee (IOC). Its rules require, among other criteria, one national umbrella organization per country to represent a sport or discipline.

19. David Chambers, publisher of *Classical Fighting Arts* magazine, is director of the 'Publication Research and Production Group for the Inauguration of the Okinawa Karate Memorial Hall' within the Okinawa Prefectural Government Program as well as OPG Okinawa Goodwill Ambassador and sent this information in an email to the author on June 27th, 2019.

20. Sources mention different dates of the organization's foundation (overview in Bellina, p. 27f) as well as its name, e.g., "All Japan Karatedo Federation AJKF" (Bellina 2018, p. 27), "All Japan Karatedo League AJKL" (Shimabuku interview 1985), or "Federation of All Japan Karate FAJKO." The author chooses the last version, which is used by the Director General of Okinawa Karate Do Shinkokai, as well as by *Classical Fighting Arts* magazine (Kiyun Choko, interview 2018, p. 11), and by above-quoted publisher David Chambers.

the Okinawans did not travel to Japan because "they did not want to be embarrassed and known as failures" (Shimabukuro interview, 1985, n.p.) and sounds more reasonable than Shimabukuro Eizo Sensei's somewhat self-serving assumption.

After this rejection, Japan's "Ministry of Education lost interest and terminated their relationships with Okinawans"(ibid.). Instead, its focus became uniting the karate branches practiced on the mainland, eventually leading to the four major styles officially recognized by Japan's Karate Federation: *Shotokan, Wado Ryu, Shito Ryu,* and *Goju Ryu.* The first three are about ninety-year-old modified derivatives of *Shuri-Te, Naha-Te,* and *Tomari-Te,* and are not recognized on the Okinawan islands; the last one, *Goju Ryu,* is practiced in its Japanese form on the mainland and in its genuine form on the islands.

In contrast, it is highly unlikely, almost impossible, that there would be *four* officially recognized karate styles in Okinawa—it is three as stated earlier—due to an axiomatic subcultural principle on the Ryukyu Islands that postulates that "everything can be broken down into either three or five basic components" (see footnote 27).

In the 1960s, Japan's FAJKO and some style-specific organizations conglomerated into the Japan Karate Federation (JKF), which represents the mentioned four officially recognized Japanese karate styles, and—now as a member of the World Karate Federation (WKF) as well—continues its initiative to have Japanese martial arts accepted as an Olympic sport and discipline.

Officially Recognized Karate Styles in Mainland Japan and in Okinawa

Mainland Japan		Okinawa	
Style	Initiator	Style	Initiator
Shotokan	Funakoshi Gichin; around 1925	*Shorin Ryu*	Matsumura Sokon; around 1840 Itosu Anko around 1900 Chibana Chosin around 1930
Goju Ryu	Yamaguchi Gogen; around 1940 per Miyagi Chojun's assignment	*Goju Ryu*	Higaonna Kanryo; around 1870 Miyagi Chojun; around 1930
Shito Ryu	Mabuni Kenwa; around 1935	*Uechi Ryu*	Uechi Kanbun; around 1900
Wado Ryu	Otsuka Hironori; around 1935		

Countering the Japanese initiatives, Okinawans formed their own umbrella organization, initially containing *Goju Ryu, Uechi Ryu, (Kobayashi) Shorin Ryu,* and *Matsubayashi Ryu.* Several other style-specific as well as overarching organizations followed, until the formation of Okinawa Dento Karate-do Shinkokai in 2008 merged all earlier segmentations into one federation for all *dentou* Okinawan karate and *kobudo* (ODKS, n. d., n. p. "History" tab on that site).

Referring to Japan's intention to have karate recognized as an Olympic sport, Okinawan karate sensei couldn't care less. As summarized on *Classical Fighting Arts (CFA)* magazine's Facebook site:

> . . . we published an interview of Choko Kiyuna Sensei, at that time the Chairman of the Okinawa Karatedo Shinkokai . . . [author's remark: the interview was published in 2018, quoted earlier, and is listed in references]. It was clear from Kiyuna Sensei's words that the senior Okinawan teachers had little interest in Olympic Karate . . . They had tried to make some accommodations with the Olympic authorities. However, on two separate visits to the mainland, the Okinawan karate delegation had been told by the JKF and Ministry of Sport that (a) The Olympic torch would not come to Okinawa, (b) no karate events would be held in Okinawa, and (c) if Okinawan students wanted to compete in Tokyo, they would have to learn the *seitei gata* (contrived exhibition kata). Given that karate comes from Okinawa, I am sure that this seemed to the Okinawan karate people at least illogical, and at worst insulting. From that point, the movement to separate sport karate entirely from real karate seems to have gained momentum in Okinawa. (https://www .facebook.com/dentoukarate/ retrieved 03/26/2020).

To separate itself from Okinawan traditions, to create an artificial threshold for non-(mainland) Japanese karate, and to exclude Okinawan styles from their official karate tournaments, the Japan Karate Federation (JKF) created the *"shitei kata"* (mentioned in the quote) in the early 1980s. These kata were to be performed in a predetermined way, without allowing style-specific or individual deviations, and served as the precondition to attend official tournaments: *"shitei kata* . . . denotes a certain, specified, standard kata that every contestant in an officially sanctioned WKF/JKF tournament—no matter where in the world— needs to perform in the opening round(s) to qualify for the rest of the tournament"(Enkamp, n.d., n.p.).

This prerequisite remained in place until its "demise" in 2013, when karateka were finally allowed to express traditional katas in a way that is typical of the karatekas' specific styles.

Shitei kata are based on centuries-old katas of pure Okinawan *Shuri-Te* and *Naha-Te* origin (with Chinese martial arts impact of course), which were then "Japanized" in the 20th century, i.e., altered and adopted into the four official (mainland) Japanese karate styles:

- *Seienchin* from *Naha-Te* and *Passai Dai* from *Shuri-Te*; both now used in *Shito Ryu*
- *Jion* and *Kusanku Dai* from *Shuri-Te*; both now used in *Shotokan*
- *Saifa* and *Seipai* from *Naha-Te*; both now used in Japanese *Gojū Ryū*
- *Seishan* from *Naha-Te* and *Chinto* from *Shuri-Te*; both now used in *Wado Ryu*

This means that karateka from other styles, who are not familiar with the specifically required interpretations of these forms, were excluded—excluded at least from big official tournaments sanctioned by the WKF, JKF, or related federations.

It is important to note that the Okinawan masters strongly opposed the altered, "non-standard"—even considered "miserable"—Japanese interpretation of their sacred traditional forms. Letters between the Okinawa Karate Federation and the Japan Karate Federation "reveal that there was a dispute, a feeling that has lingered on till this day, as the rest of the karate world gradually moves away from its traditional Okinawan roots" (Enkamp, n. d., n. p.; source detail in footnote 22).

Nagamine Shoshin Sensei, president of the *Okinawa Ken Renmei* at that time, articulated the concern of Okinawan karate masters in a letter to *Zen Nihon Renmei* (i.e., JKF), signed by all twenty-one vice-presidents, advisers, and board members) as follows:[21]

". . . a total of eight kata were designated as shitei kata by the JKF . . . These appointed *shitei kata* were not only borrowed from us, but were also in a completely miserable condition . . . Okinawa is the birthplace of Karate. Therefore we, the Okinawan people, are proud of, and responsible for, maintaining the pure traditional kata and handing them down as such to our posterity" (ibid.).

---

21. Sensei Jesse Enkamp names the source of these letters as: "When my German friend Andreas Quast visited his late sensei, *soke* Nagamine Takayoshi *(1945–2012)* at his house and dojo in Kumoji in Naha, Okinawa, on a sunny day in 2011, he received a very special document as a gift (with the caveat that he had to translate it for the rest of the world). The document was a copy of a 1982 letter written by Takayoshi's father, the legendary Karate master Nagamine Shoshin (who at the time was the president of the Okinawa Karate Federation), to Takaki Fusajiro of the JKF—along with another letter with Mr. Takaki's reply from January 1983 to Nagamine Sensei" (Enkamp, n. d., n. p.).

The letter goes on to describe, acknowledge, and praise Japan's success in spreading martial arts as well as developing Japanese forms of sports karate—combined with regrets that the development of *kumite* and rules for competition took place without any input from Okinawan experts—and it ends with suggestions for how to proceed to resolve the issue along with a strong call: "We earnestly advise that you not only use the names of kata originating in Okinawa, but also the physical kata themselves as currently practiced in Okinawa, for future karate competitions throughout Japan" (ibid.).

Graph 1: Officially Recognized Karate Styles in Okinawa and Mainland Japan

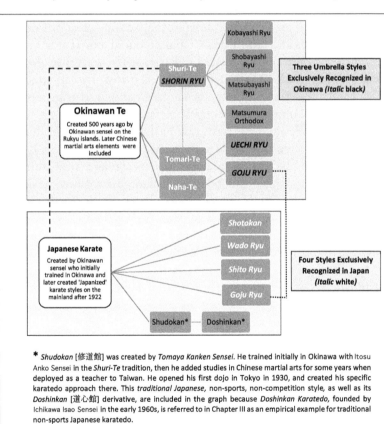

* *Shudokan* [修道館] was created by *Tomaya Kanken Sensei*. He trained initially in Okinawa with Itosu Anko Sensei in the *Shuri-Te* tradition, then he added studies in Chinese martial arts for some years when deployed as a teacher to Taiwan. He opened his first dojo in Tokyo in 1930, and created his specific karatedo approach there. This *traditional Japanese,* non-sports, non-competition style, as well as its *Doshinkan* [道心館] derivative, are included in the graph because *Doshinkan Karatedo,* founded by Ichikawa Isao Sensei in the early 1960s, is referred to in Chapter III as an empirical example for traditional non-sports Japanese karatedo.

The JKF response three months later was a short and even gruff rejection of any changes to current practices with the suggestion that ". . . we intend to have a discussion with you in the future for a satisfactory solution of the problem" (ibid.). This discussion never happened and leaves Okinawan karate and Japanese karatedo as two separated and relatively unbridged entities until today.

Worldwide Non-Okinawan-Karatedo "Inflation" after 1945

"Disarmed" versions of Okinawan karate accelerated the quick spread of karatedo into physical-education curricula for mainland Japan's youth. Large training groups at schools and universities replaced the Okinawan tradition of lethal techniques practiced in secret/private martial arts societies and family dojos[22] and produced a myriad of more or less qualified "instructors." Instead of karate sensei with their decades-long training background teaching the art, many physical-education school teachers were introduced to karate by means of truncated further education seminars to become "karate experts."

This approach of course has value in itself in that it introduces as many young people as possible to karate as quickly as possible. It actually was used on the Ryukyu Islands too, in accordance with Itosu Yasutsune Sensei's recommendations to include a modified version of karate into physical-education curricula. The fact that this is a modified and "disarmed" (sports) version of karate for schools kids, however, has to be stressed, and care should be taken to avoid confusing these physical-education karate derivations with *dentou* Okinawan karate.

As a result of this educational initiative, an estimated two hundred "wannabe styles" were active by 1955 on mainland Japan, in their majority taught by self-acclaimed instructors and many of them without sufficient qualifications (Kotek 2016, p. 61).

---

22. As an anecdotic example: "It has been said that [founder of the *Uechi Ryu* style, Uechi Kanbun Sensei's] teaching was based on the principle of hardiness and for handpicked students only. Pupils were allowed to attend only if they had a guarantor. It has been reported that only fellow pupils were allowed to watch the training in those days. Also it was strictly prohibited to do *enbu* demonstrations in front of other people" (https://web.archive.org/web/20080923052132/http://www.wonder-okinawa.jp/023/eng/009/001/index.html), retrieved 03/05/2020.

Institutionalization and integration of karatedo into the Japanese *budo* associations, however, allowed a regulatory framework not only for required curricula, etiquette, uniforms, ranking systems, sparring rules, and philosophical background of Japanese karate, but for required instructor qualification and instructor accreditation too. Consequently, hundreds of newly accredited Japanese karate instructors initiated a triumphal spread of "Japanized" karatedo in Japan as well as worldwide, strongly supported by Japan's karate associations sending these instructors all over the world to promote Japanese sports karate.

As stated above, this initiative was part of a long-time strategy to achieve karate's recognition for an Olympic sport; one criteria for that was its international popularity: in order to be accepted at the Olympic Games, "a sport must be 'widely practiced' by men in at least seventy-five countries and on four continents, and by women in no fewer than forty countries and on three continents"[23] and being represented by one national umbrella organization.

* * *

Separated from sports karate, a recreational, health-oriented, spiritual karatedo version with its implicit affinity to its non-sport, non-competition-related philosophical, psychological, meditative, and transcendental facets, fascinated rebellious young generations in Europe's academic and self-proclaimed "alternative" subcultures in the late 1960s to 1980s.

During this time, starting in Central Europe, traditional values and beliefs were opposed, authorities and "the establishment" in every shape and form were rejected, traditional social institutions (family; churches; military; educational, industrial, and political systems) were questioned and antagonized. Institutions converted, eroded, or even collapsed in the process. Rebellious generations distanced themselves from conservative values, traditions, and their representations and searched for new orientations instead, along with emerging new norms and values, symbolized in opposing lifestyles, haircuts, fashion, music, as well as in sexual liberation, gender roles, and other codes, symbols, and signs, which ensured nothing less than a complete revision to the existing cultural system and its traditions.

---

23. *Encyclopedia Britannica*, https://www.britannica.com/story/how-are-sports-chosen-for-the-olympics, retrieved February 9, 2020.

These angry young generations were disappointed by either the deeds or by the apathy of their parents' generation during WWII fascism in Nazi-Germany and Mussolini's Italy and by the following post-war "valueless" materialism. Many angry youths in Italy, France, and Germany turned politically to the left, hoping to find a fairer, more human political system in socialism instead of capitalism; more than a few became radicalized, and the well-educated among them started their "marching through the institutions" to change labor unions, educational, clerical, judicial, and administrative systems from within. They were quite successful, which, until today, is felt, for instance, in Italy's, Germany's and France's educational and judicial systems, and especially in universities and labor courts.

Others focused on environmental issues to start a "green movement" and created a new "green party," which became highly influential in Europe's political system over the following decades.

A third group of young people, motivated less by politics and more by "existentialism"[24] and the desire for self-discovery—a group, however, that later integrated many of the politically "left" and "green" motivated fractions—turned to Eastern philosophies in search of new insights, orientations, and alternative spiritual leaders. This started a considerable movement toward new beliefs and approaches that promised a new purpose and meaning of existence. This third group followed spiritual leaders teaching Hinduism and Buddhism rooted in experiential and literate knowledge, who they saw as guidance providing new values, as exemplars in life, and as inspirational sources to help their own spiritual evolution. This spiritual sub-movement prepared a high time of worshipping spiritual leaders, of cults, gurus, sects, and their closely knit worldwide communities of followers in the 1970s and 1980s. Many of those followers unfortunately did not realize that they simply replaced the traditional authority figures they hated with new ones, who not always had their best interests in mind.

Nevertheless, the common denominator tying all these developments together was the rejection of traditional values, beliefs, the representatives

---

24. Existentialism emphasizes individuals' experience, not merely as thinking subjects, but with all their emotions, actions, and feelings as constitutive of the nature of human existence. This philosophical conception, based on the philosophies of Søren Kierkegaard and—in some part—Friedrich Nietzsche, flourished in the 1940s and 1950s in Europe and rekindled in the 1960–70s through the writings of Jean-Paul Sartre and Albert Camus. It challenged mainstream, rationality-based philosophical approaches.

of those values and beliefs, and their institutions. New values, evolving from aspirations for peace, from experimenting with self-insight and self-development, from meditation and adoption of Eastern philosophies and their approaches like Zen-meditation, Yoga, and Tai Chi, add an additional layer to the explanation of the broad attraction that the spiritual, health-oriented version of karatedo quickly gained amongst young generations of new disciples in search of a new meaning of life and of "the way."

The spiritual way, the path, the *Do* [道], is connecting an individual with *Ki* (*Ch'i,* or *Qi* in Chinese), with the natural energy of the universe flowing through everything. The process of becoming part of it is called *Zen* and is achieved through meditation. It is essentially to reach a state of mind of being at peace with your own thoughts, being self-aware, balanced, and in acceptance of your place within the universe.

This meditative karatedo approach is linked to Buddhism; however, it looks like "the linking of Buddhism with karate is a modern innovation, and is an attempt, perhaps, to give to a deadly fighting technique the vestiges of a moral conscience" (Haines 1970, p. 105); this opinion is supported by other research: "After over thirty years of research into Chinese martial arts history, I have seen no clear evidence of Buddhist influence on the Chinese martial arts in general beyond names of some postures/forms and the possibility that some individual monks/others may have approached their martial arts practices from a Chan perspective. But this would have been an individual matter" (Henning 2007, p. 37). Non-relation to Buddhism is supported by Itosu Yasutsune Sensei as well, who in his introductory words to his famous "Ten Articles" on karate training, explicitly states that "karate did not descend from Buddhism or Confucianism" (text published in McCarthy 2016, p. 154).

Hence, we find two different point of views today, one connecting karate with Buddhism, another one rejecting this association (Hokama 2000, p. 16), and both claiming to be correct. This becomes reasonable considering the two different karate approaches: *dentou* Okinawan karate with its combat and self-protection orientation on the one side, and Japanese karate with its meditative, spiritual, and self-perfection orientation on the other.

"Creating maximal damage in the most efficient way" to an opponent, as intended in classical Okinawan karate, did not harmonize with the evolving peace-related new values of those generations, but "following a path of self-improvement and individual growth" did. In addition, it provided moral justification and an acceptable purpose to an initially lethal martial art.

The new spiritual and health-related philosophical underpinning turned karate's initial lethality into nonviolent, *Zen*-related meditative athletics and gave its followers the moral justification for doing what they were doing. This may explain why academically educated as well as alternative, pacifistic, "make love, not war" preaching subcultures were suddenly practicing deadly techniques, assuming it being health-related "traditional Japanese gymnastics with a martial twist" in support of meditation, which eventually would lead to the final answer to find oneself.

In the words of the JKA, the Japan Karate Association: "The result of true karate is natural, effortless action, and the confidence, humility, openness, and peace only possible through perfect unity of mind and body. This is the core teaching of Zen, the basis of bushido, and the basis of the JKA's karate philosophy" (JKA n.d., link "Philosophy" n.p.).

A partly comparable development supporting the health-related, spiritual version of karatedo is found in the USA in the late 1960s and 1970s, where this approach found broad acceptance in academic, alternative, and pacifist groups. In contrast to developments in Europe, the youth movements in the U.S. were not as much politically left-wing but rather represented a youth rebellion of antiwar sentiments and anti-authoritarianism.

Nevertheless, in conjunction with its European movement, these subcultures dedicated to peace, health, self-insight, and personal growth created a value-based, closely knit, and dedicated international "spiritual" karate community of respectable size.

It has to be pointed out that the health-improving effects of this spiritual karatedo is not just an assumption. Its therapeutic benefits "as a comprehensive approach to both physical and mental health" was already identified in the mid 1990s, attributed to the fact that "martial arts enhance self-esteem through the provision of physical activity and group experience, and the teaching of relaxation, concentration, assertiveness, and directiveness [*sic*] and honesty in communication" (Weiser et. al. 1995, p. 1).

* * *

Parallel to the "nonviolent," "spiritual" karate movement, another—completely different—movement contributed to the rising worldwide "karate inflation": American service members returning home after the Pacific and the Vietnam War, who had learned the art while stationed on

American military bases in Japan, were eager to build a living on their newly acquired skills in their homeland's new and promising markets.

Hence, "Americanization" of karate followed.

"Americanization" and Transformation of Karatedo into "Karate Commerce"

"Americanization" produced competition-oriented "American karate" that selectively borrowed features from Japanese karate and other Asian martial arts, and replaced the Asian approaches with ones that were closer to American sports-oriented values (Kotek 2016, p. 13)—kickboxing and mixed martial arts (MMA) being two of its popular representations.

Today MMA is the fastest growing sport in America. Fully "18.1 million Americans practiced a form of martial arts at least once between 2010–2011, comprising 9.4 million adults, 5.5 million teenagers, and 3.2 million children" (Connor 2019, n.p.), thus creating an industry of "$5 billion in total revenue in 2019, with 80,559 businesses" (Weller 2018, n.p.).

The spread was supported by the fact that in the 1970s and 1980s the film and TV industry jumped on the subject and created their fanciful karate-kung fu myth: their fairy-tale of incredible physical abilities and the super-human mental power of mystical masters and monks, which further popularized Asian martial arts. These pictures didn't really refer to specific historical facts or particular martial arts traditions; many were cheap mass productions intended to create revenue and favored spectacular action over credible information. It is an extremely rare occasion that a movie actually distinguished between Chinese and Japanese martial arts, let alone understanding Okinawan karate. Nevertheless, this fantasy world undoubtedly attracted numerous quick-win seekers into martial arts studios; i.e., students seeking to quickly master fighting skills without the need of investing the corresponding effort and sweat.

> ... since the 1970s, the easy availability of media and multimedia images, representations, accounts, and even manuals has taken control of the ability of martial arts styles to spread and transform. TV, film, print media, and multimedia have increasingly freed knowledge or awareness of martial arts styles from specific cultural contexts. In the process, martial arts have become increasingly deracinated and commodified. Deracination means that ethnic or cultural characteristics are "uprooted" and sometimes sanitized for external consumption; commodification means that goods or services that were never originally intended to be bought and sold are transformed into things

> that can be bought and sold. Thus, *traditional martial arts have been uprooted from their historical locations, new hybrid forms have emerged, and in the process, the places, roles, and functions of martial arts have changed considerably* (Bowman 2010, p. 2; italics are the author's).

It has to be pointed out, however, that there are many American karate sensei outside of the U.S. martial arts mainstream who promote and teach traditional karate with roots in either Japanese forms and fundamentals (this is the vast majority of instructors) or in genuine Okinawan karate (those constitute a minority).

It has to be underscored as well that some misunderstandings of the art in the USA were unavoidable, since "American service members were arriving and departing in great numbers but not staying long enough to develop skills beyond the 'shell' now more quickly given by their sensei" (Hayes 2018, p. 150), meaning that they could not dive into the second, let alone the third, level of understanding of kata and concepts.

Americanization of martial arts is not without consequences and creates a specific image—which is not necessarily a positive one—in Asia's traditional martial arts circles as well as in traditional "Western" ones. In its commercial dimension as well as in its training approach and its overall purpose, a large part of today's U.S. karate business differs significantly from traditional principles. This difference is the outcome of the combined impact of

(a) mind-sets formed and socialized while growing up in the American attention-and-acknowledgement seeking culture

(b) "Western" norms and values with their corresponding assumptions of individualism, equality, and related teaching and learning processes

(c) culture-specific assumptions about material/monetary minimum standards of living, about how to make a living and the resulting competitive orientations, which were developed and "imprinted" as habits through generations living in the US-capitalist market economy.

*   *   *

A sensei [25] in the old days used to make a living by working in a profession, a trade, or another core occupation in addition to developing a few,

---

25. "Sensei is . . . not a designation reserved for teachers of ikebana, karate, or a particular Japanese art. In fact, doctors, lawyers, and certain other professionals receive the same

maybe just one or two, *deshi* at a time in their humble *machi* dojo—or even in their home or backyard.[26]

Chibana Chosin Sensei points out the fundamental reason for this necessary distinction between earning a living and cultivating the art: "A martial person must make their living away from the martial arts so as not to contaminate it through the influence of 'making money' in order to 'make a living.' This is the Okinawan way" (quote in Chambers et. al. 2020, p. 45). Hence, the related fee was more a donation instead of a price for a service, to help sustain the operation of the dojo and to show gratitude to the sensei. The fundamental mind-set was stalwart dedication and respect for the art, its tradition, previous generations of sensei, and amongst each other.

Potential *deshi* asked whether they would be offered the privilege to be trained by the sensei and had to be accepted—accepted for a long path of hard training. The sensei's ultimate decision to accept or to reject a student was based on their character rather than on skills, and definitely not on money. This selection of only a few students tied sensei and *deshi* together with a particular bond of mutual responsibility.

It is a myth though that in the old days a karateka would have only one single sensei—many who became masters trained under two, three, or more. However, these sensei were not competing in a market, so there was no "market choice" for a student to pick a sensei or dojo out of an array of alternative moneymaking offers like today, where you have in every American town several dozen kickboxing, MMA, "karate" (in at least two or three style variations), taekwondo, "jiu-jitsu" and other fancy martial art-"studios," all competing with each other in their need for customers.

Because various forms of karate itself became the profession, the full-time activity—and the only income-generating activity of US-karate instructors, the initial sensei-deshi-relationship and interaction transformed completely over the last decades. Understandably, these instructors want to use their "karate businesses" to make a good living and not just a humble one. To create their personal brand, their marketing image,

---

designation. It's possible to suggest that a doctor, for example, is teaching the Way of medicine, but this understanding of teaching differs from that in the West" (Davey 2018, p. 10).

26. Full-time live-in students, *uchi-deshi* [内弟子], in many cases a family member, had the privilege to be taught all aspects and secrets of the art. They were the ones who conserved it, usually became the following head of the school after a master's demise, and passed the art on to the next generation. Students who lived outside a dojo were *soto-deshi* [外弟子].

and their individual market niche for themselves and their "style," many American instructor-entrepreneurs chose an eclectic assortment of impressive sounding and easy-to-sell techniques from a variety of styles and traditions as they saw fit.

In addition, many modern American instructors supposedly do not understand the core difference between Asian and American cultures in terms of teacher-student relations and, raised and socialized with the specific understanding of the American concept of "equality of man" in their native culture, confuse a sensei-deshi relation with a relationship in a social club, which is augmented by the fact that sensei and deshi are often of the same age group.

The Japanese sensei-deshi relationship is a unique and cultural specific one and should not be compared with the American Constitutional value of "equality of man." It is different, but it does not violate this legal Western value any more than day violates night, or yin violates yang. It is based on mutual respect of persons as well as on mutual respect of tradition, seniority, and a sensei's overall capabilities, combined with accepting the corresponding roles and social positions within the social structure or hierarchy of a culturally different society; e.g., reflected in the social structure of a traditional Okinawan family.[27] In this hierarchy a sensei may talk to a deshi, but it may be inappropriate for the deshi to address the sensei directly, without being spoken to by the latter. The word of the most senior authority is law, be it in a family or be it in a dojo, which explains to a certain degree the ongoing existence of parallel but different kata interpretations within the same style.

Hence, this combination of mutual respect, social stratification, and obligation to share knowledge in a traditional dojo seems incomprehensible to some American instructors and to many of their students. The relation between sensei [先生] and deshi [弟子] and between *senpai* [先輩, pronounced "sempai," i.e., a more senior [28] student] and *kohai* [後輩 i.e., a more junior student] does include elements of friendship,

---

27. The author is deeply thankful for clarifying conversations with Ms. Emi, a college instructor, who was born and raised in a traditional Okinawan family in the meager rural south of the island, before marrying and immigrating into the USA. Professor Emi's entire family has practiced martial arts for generations; its female family members mostly *Tai Chi* and the male members Okinawan *Te*. The insights gained in these conversations greatly helped the author's understanding of several Okinawan cultural specifics.

28. Seniority of *senpai/kohai* in Japan refers to membership in the same organization; it does not refer to age.

even brotherhood, and it does include the obligation to share knowledge and to truly develop a deshi, but it does not include trying to please a customer.

Though difficult to understand through the prism of a Western view, the traditional sensei-deshi hierarchy has nothing to do with autocracy and definitely nothing to do with the kind of militaristic bullying we find in some modern Western dojo that consider themselves "traditional." Quite to the contrary, it is a mentor-student relation based on mutual responsibility, deeply engraved into the Japanese culture, which sets the framework for the student's comprehensive personal development, physically, mentally, and spiritually.

The Asian way of teaching and developing a student differs greatly from the Western way. It is founded mainly on self-discovery and, hence, personal responsibility on the student's part. According to a cultural and philosophical principle we may call "from the inside out" (see footnote 27), the Okinawan path for students is to improve themselves first to be able to contribute to others in a better way. This path does not just include the art of karate itself; it includes developing spirit, attitudes, values, health, and even—in a more pragmatic sense—the kind of food and beverages one takes in.

The sensei will demonstrate the way, correct a student if needed, and the students would follow. In the old days there were no rewards or incentives, and there were only rare acknowledgements or encouragements. This was "unnecessary" in a certain sense because the students knew that if they fail, they would bring shame to their entire family (see footnote 27). In this context, the author will never forget the expression on Ichikawa Nobuo Sensei's face after he, as a young and naïve *deshi*, asked him during a summer camp in the 1980s, what he would suggest to do to remain motivated to train continuously at a high level. The puzzled look of complete incomprehension and deep irritation on the sensei's face was unforgettable and served as an invaluable early lesson for the author.

As long as the students maintain their efforts and continue on their path, being corrected by a sensei is not damaging a student's reputation, which does not match its possible implication in the Western/American culture, where a "mistake" may be supposed to show a sign of failure on the student's end. The author found this shortcoming-avoiding-attitude more than a few times in the business world, where mistakes were hidden from supervisors to fake a better performance impression when employees were managed with the guideline that "failure is not an option." Only in recent years we see in the Western business world the promotion of a different, new "flaw-culture," visualized on posters showing the slogan "make your daily mistake" in order to encourage employees to take risks and thereby enhance creativity—but these efforts seem more like the wishful thinking of consultants than the factual mind-sets of managers in charge. In karate training the "shortcoming-avoiding-attitude" shows itself by the frustrated grunts, groans, or even excuses of students when making a mistake—something we would never find in an Okinawan or a Japanese dojo. This Western attitude seems hard to change, and the author experienced his senseis explaining to students many, many times that "it is ok to make mistakes; we all make mistakes."

If a sensei were to correct a student continuously, an American student may feel picked-on. In a Western mind-set we want to achieve a goal—and never getting there would frustrate. On the contrary, when assuming a never-ending path, the need for correction never ends either. Hence, not correcting a student anymore in Okinawa would mean that the sensei does not perceive any more potential in this individual. So, contrary to American [Western] culture, where avoiding mistakes in order to avoid critique may become an individual goal, in Okinawan karate teaching, *making mistakes, recognizing them, and correcting them is an indication of a student's progress*, while no longer getting critiqued may be an indication that the student is not making enough effort.

True personal development on a sensei's end ultimately leads to not accepting any given level of a student's skills and to see more potential in someone than the person itself. It definitely will not award mediocracy, as it is done in some Western dojos to keep customers. Contradicting a Western mind-set, where "a goal has to be achieved," a sensei's never ending corrections oppose this acknowledgement- and attention-seeking attitude and may frustrate, even madden, a student.

Thus, true personal development bears the risk of losing a customer, especially one whose dedication was not firm enough to persevere on the path in the first place, which is expressed by the psychological concept of *ambiguity tolerance.* This concept describes a karateka's ability to persevere; it measures how comfortable an individual is when facing uncertainty. In plain English, it means "grit"; the ability to tolerate the pressure involved in straining to achieve a goal in the absence of certainty about how to achieve it—or even in absence of certainty that it

Image 4: Nakazato Shugoro Sensei Correcting Sensei Noel Smith in Okinawa, 1967

Photographs by Noel Smith

These historic images show an array of situations on the "never-ending path of corrections," where Nakazato Shugoro Sensei continuously corrects an already high black-belt carrying Noel Smith Sensei.

can be achieved at all. Thus it is a measure of how an individual persists and maintains the full capacity to act under pressure.

High ambiguity tolerance is a personality trait of utmost importance for athletes, warriors, leaders, commanders, managers, and comparable social roles, who all need to remain dedicated, persist, overcome frustration, and maintain all-out effort despite a seemingly endless path of baby steps and setbacks.

Another difference in learning and teaching is the mostly *cognitive* learning/teaching approach in Western culture versus *psychomotor-affective self-discovery* in Japanese martial arts training. In other words, "learning by asking" in the West versus "learning by doing" in Japan.

Socialized by Western culture, a U.S. student wants to know the "why" and the "how" of techniques to be motivated to practice. This may be different in Japan, where students are encouraged to find the answers indirectly by practicing and figuring it out on their own. Reciprocally, the role of a Japanese sensei is not to answer questions but to aid self-discovery.

The Japanese way of teaching changed gradually over time in Okinawa. Today we find a mixture of both teaching strategies in most Okinawan dojos, where—on the one hand—the specific Okinawan teaching approach is cultivated, and where—on the other hand—Okinawan sensei began to apply Western teaching methods after WWII in order to successfully train U.S. service members and later the tens of thousands of "karate tourists" visiting their machi dojo.

*   *   *

Nevertheless, as a result of its commercial dimension, its training approach, and its overall purpose, a huge change was initiated in the USA and other Western countries, *transforming the traditional path, the karatedo, into a product to be sold,* which inevitably led to fundamental shifts and a redefinition of basic karate principles:

- *Sensei* turn into entrepreneurs and sometimes even entertainers. This is in contrast to traditional sensei who are not selling and therefore do not have customers. "Sensei point the way by passing on knowledge and creating an environment where students are able to arrive at a direct understanding through their own efforts and motivation" (Davey 2018, p. 11).
- *Deshi* turn into customers versus in the traditional system where "students attend a class and expect to be taught. *Deshi* join a dojo to

discover and embrace a Way . . . Students seek information. *Deshi* make a commitment to undergoing transformation and gaining understanding" (Davey 2018, p. 12).

- *Dojo* turns into a sports club, "studio," or fitness center versus the original system in which "a dojo is not an enterprise designed to make money. It certainly can be run in a businesslike, professional manner, and . . . it may be prosperous. The fundamental intent of a dojo, however, differs from a business or school" (Davey 2018, p. 10).
- *Gi* and even *kobudo* weapons turn into fashion items.
- *Do* turns into marketing initiatives with "trial packages" containing a couple of training sessions, a uniform, and a certificate at a discounted price followed by preset, sometimes even guaranteed, promotions.
- Eroding etiquette, respect, humility, intrinsic commitment, and devotion are replaced by reward and incentive systems, badges, certificates, motivational celebrations, and applause even for mediocre performance.

"Most martial arts 'studios' in America run somewhere in between the two extremes of strict traditionalism and modernized fight club . . . that offers cardio kickboxing, kiddie ninja classes, MMA, karate, and 'jujitsu' classes around the clock" (Muramoto 2018, p. 7).

Of course we find traditional dojos in the USA and in other Western countries as well that uphold the traditional way, either in its traditional Japanese form (these constitute the majority today) or in its classic Okinawan form. How these traditional sensei master the difficult balance between running a business to make a living and maintaining the art in its genuine form is commendable. The difference, moreover, in demeanor, attitude, and overall charisma of sensei leading traditional dojos and their less traditional colleagues is palpable.

The downside of traditional sensei's humbleness in relation to American culture is their eroding popularity over the decades, perhaps allowing the art to be watered down. Younger generations of karateka, who never encountered these senior karate authorities (see, for example, Noel Smith, sensei, 8th Dan *Shorin Ryu, Shorinkan,* below) in their dojos, may not be familiar with the genuine forms and applications they teach, with their history, their achievements, and their deep knowledge. Thus, they unavoidably develop their own individual interpretations of kata and *bunkai,* which will not necessarily match the initial, traditional ones.

Of course karate changes slightly over time "because a teacher must continue to learn and add his personality to the teachings. There is an old

Okinawan martial-arts saying that states that it's much like a pond. In order for the pond to live, it must have fresh water" (Chibana Chosin Sensei quoted in Chambers et. al. 2020, p. 45). In this metaphor the "pond" remains the same pond; the pond itself does not change in spite of new water is flowing into it. This is comparable to the fact that changes in karate by following sensei generations never would change, let alone destroy, the essence or purpose of a form or style. The form or the style remain the same in its essence, in spite of changes, like the pond in the metaphor remains the same in spite of new water flowing in.

As in many other Eastern philosophical approaches, we find here the dichotomy of two equally important and simultaneously existing contradictory concepts: like night and day, *yin* and *yang,* one does not exist without the other, and one defines the other by contrast. The opposites of night and day together form one unit of time, thus forming an overarching entity of mutual determination. The opposites of *yin* and *yang* form one overarching unit, shown in its well-known circular symbol. Along the same line of argument, the opposites of preservation and change only exist together; one does not exist without the other. In other words, *change needs the presence of preservation, of a constant, to become change*: only when standing at a river bank (=constant) one can see the water move (=change); seeing the river from a boat hides the river's movement.

The constant in our application of this philosophical concept is *the essence of a kata or a style*, which is embodied in the "Principle of Never-Changing Kata," and which remains constant even if every sensei generation changes the style or form slightly.

Hence, if this Principle of Never-Changing Kata is not closely safeguarded with direct connection to its initial forms and masters in Okinawa, the *essence* of a style may change a little bit with every new generation, until after some decades it is not the same style anymore, and its original true purpose is lost. This would be like, in Chibana Sensei's metaphor, adding sand to the pond instead of freshwater.

Noel Smith Sensei, 8ᵗʰ Dan Shorin Ryu, Shorinkan

One example of a traditional, humble, and caring sensei in the USA—known today mostly or only to insiders—is the author's sensei, Noel Smith. He was trained by Nakazato Shugoro Sensei in Okinawa when deployed during the Vietnam War, living on the island for another year, and then visiting annually for training. When in Okinawa, Sensei Smith trained five to six hours per day, six days per week, during the daytime and in the evenings. His daily sixty-to-ninety minute "lunch-time" trainings allowed many one-on-one sessions with the master, who then would share *bunkai* and deeper aspects of concepts.

Sensei Smith is one of the so-called "Original Seven" black belts, directly trained by Nakazato Sensei and sent to the USA to spread *Shorin Ryu Shorinkan*. He devoted his life to maintaining, teaching, and to promoting *Kobayashi Shorin Ryu* in its initial form and purpose as it was taught to him in Okinawa. His dojo, opened 1968, was, and still is, an equivalent to an Okinawan *machi* dojo.

Sensei Smith on the one hand teaches *dentou Shorin Ryu* karate as, in his words, "it was intended to be," lethal and traditional. He has trained members of the Navy Seals and of the Virginia Beach Police's SWAT Team. On the other hand, he developed competition strategies based on this Okinawan style by adjusting controlled traditional techniques and concepts to specific tournament requirements. From 1973 to 1978, he served as head coach for the U.S. karate team, competing internationally, including in the world championships of 1975 in California and of 1977 in Tokyo.

His dedication, contributions, and successes were recognized in 1976 when he won the "Distinguished Service Award—Man of the Year" and was inducted into the USA Karate Hall of Fame. His way of approaching the art sets an example of how to combine—not to be confused with "to integrate"—*dentou* Okinawan karate with sports karate.

Today, in his upper seventies, though exposure to Agent Orange in the Vietnam War has taken a toll on his health, Sensei Smith still teaches his traditional, no-nonsense approach at his dojo and at training camps. He maintains his humble demeanor and the caring

Okinawan way of treating others, which formed him deeply during his time training and living on the island.

He never aggressively promoted or marketed his remarkable achievements and contributions to the art like many others did, who were conforming to the American commercial approach that involves forging an individual brand and creating a business. Hence, today, at training camps, some karate students do not know Sensei Smith and cannot therefore profit from his knowledge—a situation prone to be changed in 2020, when he, for the first time, started to teach and to share his knowledge online.

However, it was fascinating for the author to realize Sensei Smith's recognition in Okinawa during a training trip to the Shorin Ryu Shorinkan Honbu Dojo in 2019. Okinawans who encountered him in the past—former fellow students, now *hanshi* and *kyoshi* themselves, as well as sensei from other Okinawan dojos—were excited to meet him again. He will not be forgotten in Okinawa, and his contributions to the art will be conserved in the USA as well.

Photograph Noel Smith; cropped by the author

Chapter 2

Arguments to Maintain Okinawan Karate In Its Originality

Traditional Karate Is Okinawan Cultural Heritage

Throughout history, *cultural identity*[1] is affected, damaged, sometimes even destroyed by occupations, takeovers, annexations, and other means of oppression—often combined with feelings of superiority on the occupying force's side and such of inferiority in the occupied territory. This is because occupied territories lost battles and they definitely are powerless and at the occupier's mercy. Occupied territories are often exploited economically, and the occupying power usually imposes its culture on the conquered. This inferior and powerless position frequently leads to high sensibility[2] in an occupied territory about aspects of its own cultural heritage.

---

1. "Cultural identity can be understood as the experience, enactment, and negotiation of dynamic social identifications by group members within particular settings" (Chen/Lin 2016, p. 1). Or, in plain English, cultural identity is the feeling of belonging to a group and becomes a part of a person's self-conception and self-perception.

2. Cultural identity may be seen as a part of "social identity," where members of a subculture can "experience social identity threat when they think that their group is not sufficiently acknowledged as a separate entity with unique characteristics. Such group-distinctiveness threat is experienced when different groups of people are included in larger, more inclusive groups, nations, or organizations" (*Encyclopedia Britannica,* https://www.britannica.com /topic/social-identity-theory/Identity-threat, retrieved February 2, 2020).

We find this challenge in Okinawan history, where—within less than two centuries—the island was obtained and annexed by Japan, had its inhabitants assimilated and educated to become Japanese, was abandoned by the Japanese military in WWII, its population killed in battle in 1945, was then occupied by the United States for twenty-seven years, and was finally handed back to Japan.

Okinawa Maintains Its Subcultural Identity within Japan's Culture

Okinawa became part of Japan politically, but at the same time, culturally it was not, leaving a dichotomy of culture and citizenship. The process of Okinawa's assimilation into Japan's culture and political system is a complicated and unique one.

Okinawa was Japan's only new territory that was granted the status of prefecture in 1879. After a lengthy political process, Okinawans eventually received full legal citizenship in 1920, two years before Funakoshi Gichin Sensei introduced karate into mainland Japan. "This differentiates Okinawa from other occupied regions, e.g., Taiwan and Korea, which were colonies par excellence. They were never incorporated into the administrative system and social network of the Japanese state to the same extent as Okinawa" (Meyer 2007, p. 95).

The more recent history of the Pacific War molded another aspect of Okinawa's complex political experience. "In the spring of 1945 on the eve of the Battle of Okinawa, the Japanese . . . lawfully surrendered to the United States. Although the end of the war was reached, the emperor of Japan along with the military insisted on pressing on in an attempt to put off the inevitable occupation just a little longer" (Nielson 2006, p. 5). During the following battle an estimated one fourth of Okinawan civilians died.

After Japan's capitulation, Okinawa was governed under U.S. military rule. Restoration followed in 1972, and the island was given back to Japan. Okinawa Prefecture was reestablished and its current prefectural flag was adopted.

On the one hand, the experience of the battle with the USA led to initial resentments against Americans. On the other hand, suffering from being treated as inferior for decades as well as inhumane acts of Japanese soldiers during the battle of Okinawa[3] maintained some

---

3. "Unlike the Americans who were immediately perceived as the enemy and rightfully feared by Okinawans, the Japanese were to be the protectors of the civilians. Instead of shielding their

cultural boundary between Okinawa and Japan. This two-sided, bi-directional sentiment, aimed at the initial occupational force, Japan, as well as at the new one, America, prepared the re-enforcement of genuine Okinawan cultural symbols as well as peace-related values as important postwar and post-reversion aspects of Okinawan culture.

A witness at that time, Sam Athye Sensei, 7th Dan *Shorin Ryu, Shorinkan,* describes the general situation in Okinawa and his karate training experience in 1973, as[4]

> ". . . still suffering from an economic depression converting from dollars to yen, changing from the right side of the road to the left. There were still open sewers, few street lights, and no *gaigene* (karate tourists) wandering *kokusaidori* . . . I took day classes from Hanshi Yuchuko Higa. Night classes from Master Katsuya Miyahira.[5] I remember the class was filled (20+ old yudansha) [*sic*]; these guys had survived the war and the famine. We would do kata for fifteen minutes and a five minute smoke break you would follow [*sic*]. Half of Miyahira's dojo was open air. In both dojos, the younger guys my age would want to bang forearms, do ippon kumite, and ask me to do kata as a way to check me out. There were no military or *gaijin* at these dojos. They did not like white guys and were open about it."

The resentment toward foreigners soon changed, and over time Western karate tourists as well as U.S. service members were heartily welcomed in Okinawa and in Okinawan dojos.

Today, Okinawan hospitality toward American guests and caring for them is unmatched, and it is an extremely rare occasion—which the author himself experienced only once—that a fellow karateka shows some kind of resentment towards a *gaijin,* toward a non-Japanese outsider.

Until today, the Okinawans have not 100-percent assimilated into Japanese society. A boundary remains, and the dichotomy of culture and citizenship endures. Nothing indicates that it will disappear in the future.

---

brethren in battle from the common foe, they became the enemy while practicing horrific acts of violence and grand schemes of deceit against them. Japanese soldiers were commonly known to command Okinawan civilians to commit group suicide rather than surrender to the enemy. Okinawans who had found refuge from the battle by hiding in caves were killed by Japanese soldiers in order to use the shelters for themselves" (Nielson 2006, p. 6).

4. (https://www.facebook.com/groups/ShorinryuShorinkanGroup/?fref=nf). Sensei Sam Athye's reference to a *dojo* being "half open air" underlines the challenging training conditions in Okinawa's extremely hot and muggy climate for Americans accustomed to air conditioning.

5. Author's remark: both sensei trained under Chibana Chosin Sensei and are famous for their hard style fighting techniques, which were continuously used and practiced during *kumite* and sparring training sessions at that time.

Outwardly, the two societies are integrated, but the Okinawan people have proven masterful at the remaining cultural differences and attaching new importance to them (Meyer 2007, p. 316), genuine Okinawan karate being one of those cultural symbols.

Japan's commendable strategy of not destroying Okinawan traditions during centuries of occupation and control created favorable conditions for the reemergence of a culture that today represents the whole of Okinawa. We find this local culture for instance in the performing arts, in traditional rituals, and in celebrations: the music of sanshin, turtleback tombs, shiisaa [shisa] lions, the shiimii festival and other cultural constructs appropriated by the present-day narratives of Okinawan identity, were preserved against the expansion of Japanese culture" (Meyer 2007, p. 311).

"By debating and transforming Okinawan politics and values, and by creating a vibrant Okinawan music and literary scene, Okinawans are embroidering an intricate tapestry of Okinawanness. What it means to be Okinawan is being contested, redefined, and inscribed in the consciousness and praxis of Okinawa today" (Hein/Selden 2003, p. 1).

The island's culture and its implicit values are embodied in the peaceful, caring, easygoing personalities of the locals and their spirit of *yumaru* (i.e., helping one another).

Shisa lions are found all over Okinawa today, like the ones guarding the Shuri Castle entrance, as well as new modifications like the ones wearing *gi* and guarding the entrance of the famous *Shureido* karate gear store in the city of Naha in Okinawa.

Okinawan karate, however, unlike these tangible and other intangible symbols of Okinawan subcultural identity, was never "left alone" by Japan. On the contrary, Okinawan karate had to deal with several Japanese "takeover" attempts.

The fact that Okinawa is a prefecture of its former occupiers, and that mainland Japan is preserving its own, many centuries-old *bushido* and *budo* traditions, complicates things, because "while some maintain the autonomy and cultural rooting of karate as an indigenous art of Okinawa, those in the Japanese government view karate as a Japanese cultural tradition, as is consistent with their view of Okinawa as part of Japan both legally and culturally" (Johnson 2012, p. 62).

Image 5: Shisa Figures at Shuri Castle Gate

Image 6: Shisa Figures at Shureido Karate Gear Store Entrance

Okinawa Officially Promotes Karate as Its Cultural Heritage

Especially over the last two decades we find an ever increasing number of actions and strategies—with considerable involvement of the Okinawan Prefectural Government—proving that Okinawans *officially* consider karate as a major part of the island's cherished *cultural heritage:*[6]

- 1997: The Okinawa Prefecture declares *karate* and *kobudo* as Intangible Cultural Assets (http://okic.okinawa/en/local-network) and acclaims the first three famous and then still-active karate masters as Intangible Culture Assets Holders (see table below).
- 2005: The Okinawa Prefecture Assembly introduces October 25th as the "Day of Karate," which has been celebrated every year since. This is a day where thousands of karateka, inhabitants of the islands representing their Okinawan styles and dojos, often joined by their international karate guests, perform kata on Kokusaidori, which is Naha's main street. This impressive mass performance is complemented and highlighted by Okinawan masters demonstrating style-typical kata.
- 2008: Okinawa Dento Karatedo Shinkokai is established as the new umbrella organization for all traditional Okinawan karate and *kobudo* styles (http://www.odks.jp/en/).
- 2011: The Okinawa Traditional Karate Liaison Bureau (OTKLB) starts as a private project, funded by the Okinawan Prefectural Government as an "Okinawa Prefecture Culture and Arts Promotion–Industry Creation Support Project" (http://okkb.org/).[7]
- 2016: The Okinawa Governor announces the creation of the Karate Promotion Division within the Culture, Tourism and Sport Department

---

6. Cultural heritage is defined as an expression of the ways of living developed centuries ago, in this case on the Ryukyu Islands, and passed on from generation to generation (https://en .unesco.org/). As defined by UNESCO, it encompasses the two main categories: *tangible* and *intangible* cultural heritage. Karatedo falls into the second one:
    - *Tangible cultural heritage* is everything in "movable" form, like paintings, sculptures, coins, manuscripts, as well as "immovable' form," like monuments, archaeological sites, underwater wrecks, and ruins.
    - *Intangible cultural heritage* is oral traditions, the performing arts, and rituals.

7. Miguel Da Luz initiated and nurtured the OTKLB project. For many years he was a distinguished publisher and public relations representative of Okinawan karate, promoting Okinawan karate worldwide, and is now serving at the Okinawa Karate Information Center (OKIC).

Image 7: Days of Karate in Naha, Okinawa 2019: Okinawan Masters after Demonstrating Kata at the Karate Kaikan on Oct 24

Photographs by Vinh Dinh

of the Okinawan Prefectural Government (http://okic.okinawa/en/local
-network).

- 2016 The Okinawa prefecture creates the Okinawa Karate and
  Kobujutsu Preservation Society for designated intangible cultural
  assets.
- 2017 Opening of the Okinawa Karate Kaikan, a beautiful training hall
  and information center of Okinawan karate (see below) with its role

stated to be to "preserve, inherit, and develop Okinawan karate as a unique culture whilst telling people both in and outside Japan that 'Okinawa is the birthplace of karate,' and to be a facility that can be used as a place to learn the essence of karate" (http://karatekaikan.jp/en/).

- 2017 The Okinawan prefectural government establishes the Okinawa Karate Information Center (OKIC) to handle inquiries regarding karate and training requests for Okinawa as well as to promote Okinawa karate and *kobudo*. Supervised by the Okinawa Prefecture Government, the center is managed by Okinawa Dento Karatedo Shinkokai (http://okic.okinawa/en/).

- 1995–2018 Hosting international tournaments for Okinawan karate and *kobudo* independent from tournaments conducted by the Japan Karate Foundation JKF or the World Karate Foundation WKF (https://okinawa-karate.okinawa/en/history/):

  ➤ 1995: Okinawa Karatedo and Kobudo World Pre-Tournament (on the occasion of the fiftieth anniversary of the end of the pacific war and the Battle of Okinawa); three hundred participants

  ➤ 1997: Okinawa Karatedo and Kobudo World Tournament (commemoration of the completion of the Okinawa Prefectural Budokan); 810 participants

  ➤ 2003: Okinawa Karatedo and Kobudo World Tournament; 380 participants

  ➤ 2009 Okinawa Traditional Karatedo World Tournament (commemoration of the establishment of the Okinawa Dentou Karatedo Shinkokai); 646 participants.

- 2018 The first Okinawa Karate International Tournament with 4,087 participants[8] from fifty countries and with the stated purpose of "preserving and passing down correctly Okinawan Karate's skills and spirituality nurtured and systematized by its pioneers . . . with the aim of promoting traditional Okinawan karate and kobudo" (https://okinawa -karate.okinawa/en/schedule/).

---

8. Calculated by the author using official statistics in the tournament's report pp. 90–93, (https://okinawa-karate.okinawa/wp-content/uploads/2019/02/THE-1st-OKINAWA -KARATE-INTERNATIONAL-TOURNAMENT_Report.pdf).

The Governor's message on the report's opening page names '3,200 man-days' and 50 participating countries and regions ['man-day' is a unit of measurement, used especially in accounting and management, based on a standard number of man-hours in a day of work]. Miguel Da Luz at OKIC provided the link to the official report to the author by email on February 5, 2020.

- 1997–today Okinawan karate masters are venerated as Intangible Cultural Asset Holders by the Okinawan Prefectural Government (http://okic.okinawa/en/local-network).
- 2021–today The Okinawa Prefectural Planning and Coordination Division includes initiatives toward the registration of Okinawan karate as an UNESCO Intangible Cultural Heritage in its new promotion plan (http://okic.okinawa/en/archives/news/p4724). These efforts developed during the last decate and are not a bottom-up movement of local karate communities, but a top-down political act to promote a unique Okinawan culture within the prefecture, both domestically in Japan and internationally (Fuente/Niehaus 2020, p. 43).

All these demonstrative actions over the last two decades underline the importance government officials attribute to karate as part of Okinawa's cultural heritage. The fact that the Okinawan Prefectural Government took these actions and implemented policies is nothing less than an explicit and official political confirmation of the paramount role of karate as honored cultural heritage forming cultural identity. "Karate is a traditional culture that Okinawa is proud of. Even now, it has been carefully inherited as 'Okinawa Traditional Karatedo / Kobudo'" (http://karatekaikan.jp/en/history/).

In November 2017, the same year Okinawa Karate Kaikan was opened, officials of the Okinawan Prefecture Government (OPG) and karate masters opened a new international public relations dimension for traditional Okinawan karate.

Okinawan Karate Intangible Cultural Asset Holders 1997–2020

Year	Shorin Ryu (Shuri-Te)	Goju Ryu (Naha-Te)	Uechi Ryu	Kobudo/Kobujutsu
1997	Nagamine Shoshin Matsubayashi Ryu	Yagi Meitoku	Itokasu Seiki	
2000	Nakazato Shugoro Kobayashi Ryu Miyahira Katsuya Shido Kan Nakazato Jyoen Shurinji Ryu	Wakugawa Kosei Koshin Iha	Tomoyose Ryuku	
2013	Ishikawa Seitoku	Hichiya Yoshio Higaonna Morio	Uehara Takenobu	Nakamoto Masahiro Kobudo
2020	Morinobu Maeshiro Seikichi Iha	Masanari Kikugawa	Shintoku Takara Tsutomu Nakahodo	Kotaro Iha Kobujutsu

Creating the kaikan in itself was an astonishing symbolic act, since there was already the beautiful Okinawan *budokan* in place to be used as a training and events facility. The kaikan, however, shows a demonstrative (and successful) intention to separate *dentou* Okinawan karate from its Japanese sports-derivatives, for which the *budokan* primarily was used. The *budokan* roof is actually shaped to somewhat resemble a samurai's helmet, thus perhaps representing a Japanese symbol that does not have roots in Okinawa's martial arts traditions.

Referring to the new international dimension of *dentou* Okinawan karate, mentioned above, in November 2017 a delegation visited the USA under the Traditional Okinawa Exchange Program, sponsored by an official political agency, the Okinawan Prefectural Government, and the official karate/*kobudo* umbrella organization, Okinawa Traditional Shinkokai.

The purpose of this visit was to announce and to internationally promote The 1st Okinawa Karate International Tournament 2018, as well as to offer training seminars facilitated by the high ranking sensei in Okinawan karate.

Four karate masters and one *kobudo* master were sent to Virginia and Washington, DC, by the Okinawan Prefectural Government (picture below), who represented the three Okinawan karate styles *Shorin Ryu*, *Goju Ryu*, and *Uechi Ryu* as well as *kobudo*. The seminar itself was facilitated by Nestor Tadeusz Folta Sensei, 8th Dan *Uechi Ryu, Soke Shubukan*, one of the prominent U.S. *Uechi Ryu* sensei. He is a multiple world champion, who was introduced into the World Martial Arts Hall of Fame in 1996 and who lived in Okinawa for five years to study under the direct tutelage of Kanei Uechi Sensei, 10th Dan *Uechi Ryu*, the son of the founder of the *Uechi-Ryu* style of karate.

Almost ten times more participants (4,087) attended the following year at the 2018 tournament compared to the earlier four ones, and 150 U.S. karateka attended the training seminar in 2017 with the Okinawan sensei in Virginia (see picture below). This underlines the success and worldwide acknowledgement of this joint effort by Okinawan prefectural officials and Okinawan masters from Okinawa Dentou Karatedo Shinkokai.

During his speech at the seminar, Ahagon Naonobu Sensei, Vice-President of the Division for the Promotion of Okinawa Traditional Karate at the OPG, "emphasized the fact that Okinawa is the birthplace of karate and that Okinawan karate has been internationally shared to create and maintain foreign relations" (Yonaha-Tursi 2017, p. 25).

Image 8: Karate Kaikan and Budokan in Naha, Okinawa

Creative Commons

Creative Commons

Image 9: *Okinawan Masters Sent to the USA 2017 by the Okinawan Prefectural Government to Promote Dentou Okinawan Karate Internationally*

Hanshi Meitatsu Yagi, 10th Dan (Goju Ryu); Hanshi Naonobu Ahagon, 10th Dan (Shorin Ryu karate and kobudo); Hanshi Minoru Nakazato, 10th Dan (Shorin Ryu); Hanshi Masanari Kikukawa, 9th Dan (Goju Ryu); Kyoshi Harukichi Shimabukuro, 8th Dan (Uechi Ryu). Name spelling and honorary titles verbatim quoted from Yonaha-Tursi's article in the *Okinawan Times,* 11/25/2017.
Photograph by Sensei Nestor Folta, 8th Dan *Uechi Ryu*, organizer of the Okinawa Masters Seminar

When visiting the Japanese Embassy in Washington, DC, delegation member Yamakawa Tetsuo, director of the Karate Promotion Division of the Okinawa prefectural government, "made a clear announcement in a dignified manner about 'The Birth Place of Karate, Okinawa'" (ibid.).

As mentioned earlier, traditional Okinawan karate is taught in private machi dojo, whereas sports karate is taught in Okinawan high schools. These high school kids "unfortunately . . . have no idea about real karate, because they are learning from physical education instructors without much real experience or knowledge of karate. Few of them join private machi dojo, and therefore never experience the real karate that we have developed over the centuries here in Okinawa. The number of machi dojo is decreasing, and we worry about this" (Kinjo Interview 2020, p. 35).

On the other hand, starting in the late 1970s—and continuing into the 1980s and beyond—the development and availability of the World

Image 10: Okinawa Masters Seminar Attendants November 2017

All Attendees, First Day of the Seminar.
Photographs by Nestor Tadeusz Folta, sensei, 8th Dan Uechi Ryu, organizer of the Okinawa Masters
Seminar (front row on the right).

Black-Belt Training Group with Nakazato Minoru Sensei (front row, kneeling,
third from the left). Photograph by author.

Wide Web allowed dedicated karateka from all over the world to redis-
cover Okinawa as the birthplace and curator of *dentou* karate. Many
developed connections with machi dojo, came over to study authentic
karate at its roots, and started a movement which is known today as
"karate tourism."

The Okinawan prefectural government of course noticed its impact
on the local economy and, as the karate tourist movement exceeded ten
thousand visitors per year, decided to support this development.

There is some concern today that "the fact that the people from over-
seas were studying traditional Okinawan karate in *machi* dojo was lost
on the civil servants. They have tended to spend money on promoting

Japanese sport karate, therefore missing the point entirely" (Kinjo Interview 2020, p. 35).

This, however, is not completely the case for our above-described example: Okinawa Dentou Karatedo Shinkokai in conjunction with the Okinawan Prefectural Government kicked off and pursued an exemplary path of promoting Okinawan karate internationally as well as achieving financial sustainability for the effort. Though using the concept of a tournament, a sports competition setting, The 1st Okinawa Karate International Tournament was not promoting sports karate; it was a revenue-generating kata tournament for *Shuri-Te, Naha-Te,* and *Tomari-Te*–based genuine Okinawan kata. Additional seminars, workshops, and trainings, led by Okinawan masters, were offered in conjunction with the tournament. So, visiting karateka who succeeded in the qualifying rounds could participate in the competition, others could attend seminars, and others could visit solely as spectators. This initiative boosted international recognition, broadly reconnected American karateka with the Okinawan roots of their art, and enforced karate tourism—not just by inviting visitors and participants to the promoted events, but by stimulating future karate tourism and further training in machi dojo for years to come.

In addition to official prefectural policies and actions to reenforce Okinawan karate as cultural heritage, we find private business initiatives to connect Okinawan masters with foreign karateka for training as well, in this way establishing and promoting karate tourism.

Karate tourism seems to be the most promising and economically sound way to finance and maintain authentic Okinawan karate, since it connects karateka from all corners of the world with machi dojo, with the original local grassroots cells preserving the art. In fact, karate tourism may be economically of at least equal importance as cruise-ship tourism for the island because karateka stay on land during their trip, book rooms, buy food for several meals per day, and visit restaurants, whereas cruise-ship tourists may visit local restaurants for one meal, usually stay aboard for the night, and have their other meals on the ship.

Today there are several intitiatives designed to stimulate karate tourism, one being the Okinawa Karate Information Center within the Okinawan Karate Kaikan which, since its implementation, has successfully connected foreign karate tourists with training opportunities.

Another private initiative aimed at U.S. karateka (and from other countries) is *Classical Fighting Arts* magazine's yearly seminars in Japan and in the U.S. with Okinawan masters, going on since 2009. Though the most recent event was postponed in 2020 due to the COVID-19 outbreak, "our agreement with the Okinawan prefectural government runs until the end of this calendar year, so we will lose neither the practical benefits of their support nor the prestige it brings to our event. This is the third time they have supported our Spring Seminars in the last four years, which is very unusual given the number of applications they receive each year" (https://www.facebook.com/dentoukarate).

Finally, we find specialized karate-travel agencies in Okinawa itself,[9] businesses aiming at comparable target groups by offering training trips to machi dojo online, where foreign karateka can chose and book style-specific training arrangements, choosing from a list of several collaborating machi dojo.

*   *   *

There is also a non-commercial cultural initiative, not connected to karate tourism, to reconnect Okinawan karate with the native Okinawan language. Whereas the Ryukyuan state had appropriated written Japanese as the official language, the Ryukyuan innate language, *Uchinaguchi,* is commonly spoken by older Okinawans and understood by all Okinawans. Certain words and phrases are used today in everyday life by many.

Leading a project preceding her dissertation, Samantha May initiated the creation of an *Uchinaguchi*-focused Okinawan karate and *kobudo* handbook showing, among other content, the corresponding Okinawan-Japanese-English terms for techniques, concepts, and places (May 2016, pp. 210 ff.). Her intention is to encourage domestic and international *dentou* karate and *kobudo* dojo*s* and their instructors to implement native *Uchinaguchi* terms and phrases into their training practice. Though its impact remains to be seen, this initiative obviously

---

9. See for instance https://www.ageshiojapan.com/about-us. The group, which was founded 2017, lists as their three business activities for karate (1) travel service of Okinawan karate, (2) production of Okinawan karate goods, and (3) promotion of Okinawan karate.

Its Facebook site claims that "Ageshio Japan Co., Ltd, is the industry's first travel company specialized in Okinawa Karate services. Our main business activities include production of Okinawa karate workshops and events, introduction of Okinawa karate dojos, accommodation support, and so on. Our company wants to appeal the charm of Okinawa karate to the world [*sic*], and contribute to the development of Okinawa Karate" (https://www.facebook.com/ageshiojapan; retrieved 06/19/2020).

supports the view of *dentou* Okinawan martial arts as an essential symbol of the island's culture.

*   *   *

In summation, the sheer number of recent initiatives to promote *dentou* Okinawan karate as genuine cultural heritage speaks for itself, and the successful outcome of all this creativity in the last two decades is impressive: Okinawan karate is well on its way to being reestablished in the eyes of the world as an intangible local cultural tradition within the nation of Japan and it contributes significantly to the creation of Ryukyu's "collective identity" in the sociological sense (Giesen/Seyfert 2013).

Core Reasons to Maintain Okinawan Karate in Its Original Form

Okinawan karate adopted many of Dai Nippon Butoku Kai's formal requirements and changed its initial local practice. Students had not been specifically ranked but were either "beginners" or "advanced,"[10] no explicit training attire or outfit had been required, and kata had been individually assigned to deshi per a sensei's judgement.

Japanese conventions of white training uniforms, belt and rank systems, structured group training,[11] and kata curricula were implemented. Some dojo etiquette and terms were applied too, and some remained *dentou* Okinawan. Most importantly, Okinawan karate's essence, its original purpose of self-protection, together with its traditional forms, concepts, and techniques to assure the achievement of this purpose, remained unchanged.

---

10. At the time Sensei Noel Smith started his *shorin ryu* training in Okinawa in the early 1960s, there were only white belts, brown belts, and black belts in the dojo (see photos in Image 4), which represent the initial coherent system, introduced into iudo by Kano Jigoro Sensei in the early twentieth century to mark the level of his students. Later, Nakazato Shugoro Sensei adopted the colored belt ranking system used in Japanese martial arts, which most certainly was introduced in Europe, starting in England by Kawaishi Mikinosuke Sensei in the 1920s (Messner 2020).

11. "Whereas Japanese karate teachers are inclined to drill students in ordered lines up and down the dojo, in military fashion, in Okinawa the training is far less militaristic, and students often spend their time working individually or in small groups" (Clarke M. 2012, p. 1); an observation the author can, for the most part, confirm by his own training experience.

Peaceful Minds through the Study of Lethal Okinawan Karate?

One may dispute whether it is necessary at all to preserve a lethal martial art like Okinawan karate today. Shouldn't a changed world abolish such brutal techniques? Indeed, in a perfect world there would be no violence and no need for self-defense. But only ideals are perfect, not people, who remain as prone to violence as ever.

The Romans used to say, "si vis pacem para bellum"—"If you want peace, prepare for war." The *Pinan/Heian* kata series, which is taught in many karate styles, is rooted in the same thought process. It's name means "peaceful and safe."

In Miyagi Chojun Sensei's words, "Do not strike others and do not allow others to strike you. The goal is peace without incident" (quote in Chambers et. al. 2020, p. v).

This realistic view of human behavior and its correlated strategy of deterrence is not shared, let alone understood, by everyone—above all not by sheltered individuals who have had limited real-life encounters with ill-intentioned persons and no experience with physical combat, which does not make the approach less effective or reasonable in today's imperfect world as this metaphor explains.

As long as there are predators, being a sheep or acting like one doesn't prevent a predator's attack. To spin this metaphor further: only the teeth and the strength of a defender stop the predator, which leads one to think of the—unfortunately often misunderstood—phrase that "only persons capable of great violence may call themselves peaceful; persons not capable of violence are not peaceful, they are harmless."

How quickly people can turn to violence, even in today's so-called "civilized" societies, could be observed during the May/June 2020 protests and demonstrations throughout the USA, when a despicable act of deadly police misconduct created unpredictable ferocious riots and other disturbances within a few hours, which then went on for several weeks, even months in some places. Whether this violence was justified or not is seen differently by different stakeholders; it is not the author's intention to comment on it politically. His point is that an apparent powder keg of frustration, rage, hate, envy, and radicalism was touched off and that violence is not just an occurrence of the distant past, but a latent reality in today's societies as well.

On the other hand, life undoubtedly did change, at least in "civilized" societies. We no longer face constant violence; we no more fight numerous local battles, we are no longer engaged in hand-to-hand combat; and the vast majority of us are not permanently threatened by robberies, attacks, or oppression like our ancestors, and the ones of our Asian fellow karateka were during centuries of oppression, crime, unrests, and power struggles in ancient Japan—situations like the one described in the last paragraph excluded.

Hence, many mind-sets changed, and some martial arts training turned and went in another, "peaceful," direction—meaning that it became spiritual, meditative, and health oriented rather than combat oriented. That may end up in *budo* philosophies, in a different martial-arts *Do* for Japanized karate. But it doesn't change the nature of *dentou* Okinawan karate, which is a lethal martial art for serious violent encounters, one that has to be trained with utmost solemnity and as if in actual combat, envisioning bodily damage, even possible death, in every technique.

Still today, "karate is first a fighting art" as Doug Perry Sensei, 10th Dan *Shorin Ryu, Kensankai,* points out (Perry 2018, p. 286 ff) and at a training camp he further stressed that "there are no silver medals handed out in a life protection situation." Martial arts are *martial* arts, period, not "gymnastics arts"—though gymnastic exercises to stretch and to build up muscles and strength may of course be included in karate training.

In spite of its lethality, the purpose of *dentou* karate training is not the use of violence, it is *gaining self-control*, especially in situations loaded with threats and aggression, and where blood pressure and adrenaline levels are off the chart. Surprisingly enough, when seriously studying Okinawan karate and accepting its traditional self-defense goal, the indivisible combination of self-defense capabilities with physical, spiritual, and moral development increases the odds of students developing nonviolent mind-sets.

In this sense, studying lethal Okinawan karate *creates more peaceful minds*—even in the case of initially hair-triggered violent teens. Several prominent examples support this argument. For instance, there are Okinawan masters like Yamashita Tadashi Sensei, 10th Dan *Shorin Ryu, Shorinkan,* who used to be an angry and intense kid, and who changed during his training under Nakazato Shugoro Sensei. And there are

Western masters like Michael Clarke Sensei, 8th Dan *Goju Ryu, Jundokan,* born in Ireland and living in England for thirty years before immigrating to Australia, who, at the age of seventeen, was already a veteran street fighter doing hard time. *Shito Ryu* and *Goju Ryu* training turned his life around, a development he later describes in *Redemption–A Streetfighter's Path to Peace* (Clarke M. 2016). Along with many others, these karateka provide examples of the—perhaps surprising—fact that the training of *dentou* Okinawan karate creates peaceful minds. Peaceful minds are based on peace within oneself, and a peaceful mind constitutes the first basic prerequisite for a peaceful togetherness of people with different personalities, backgrounds, values, and opinions.

Dentou Okinawan karate training contributes to peace not only internally, within a society, but also in relations to other societies. When analyzing the role of karate-practicing communities as part of transnational cooperative structures, Samantha May from the University of the Ryukyus concludes that through this international conglomeration of kindred karate spirits "peace may be visualized . . . as an active, creative practice based on voluntary membership in a worldwide community" (May n.d., p. 1); this is supported by the fact that "'traditional' martial arts offer physical skills, moral codes, rituals, roles, and hierarchical relationships which, taken together, creates the perfect environment for psychological collectivism" (Partikova 2018, p. 49).

Comparable thoughts were already introduced in 1982 by Uechi Kanei Sensei in his "Letter to All Karateka of the World," where he expresses his strategy for peace through cultural exchange of karate, because in his view "karate can bring people together from different countries in a universal brotherhood and sisterhood similar to the ancient Stoic notion and contemporary cosmopolitan perspective, which asks people to consider others' well-being regardless of nationality" (Swift n.d., n.p.). Along these lines, eight Okinawan masters, representing all three Okinawan styles, visited the USA in 1999 to hold a series of special trainings under the motto of "World Peace Through Karatedo" (Hayes n.d., Vol. 3, Issue 2, *Summer*, p. 1).

The peaceful outcome of *dentou* Okinawan karate training was labeled as "possibly surprising" earlier, because based on the psychosocial theory of learning, one would assume that karate training increases aggression. This learning theory identifies *imitation* as one of the core factors of social learning, meaning that aggression is supposed to be learned through the imitation of violent, aggressive behavior—and karate training most definitely practices full-force violent techniques. Learning aggression through karate training, however, does not typically happen in traditional karate dojos.

Not just isolated case studies, but several experimental studies substantiate the fact that practicing traditional martial arts reduces aggression (Macarie/Roberts 2010). A comprehensive evaluation of scientific studies on the impact of martial arts on aggression (Martin 2006) clearly shows that a *traditional* karate training approach reduces aggression and "is an effective way of transmitting desirable values . . . and, over time, indoctrinates students with the idea of respect, a sense of consequence, a sense of personal responsibility, and a sense of connection to the self through a strong mentor" (ibid., p. 2).

However, according to the analysis, the *results are different for non-traditional martial arts schools.* Several scientific experiments show that aggression scores of students in these non-traditional schools did not change over time, while they went down for students at traditional martial arts schools (Martin 2006, p. 3ff). This may perhaps be attributed to the fact that "in modern sports karate . . . the fight takes place mainly in the attack and not as it once was, in the defense and counterattack" (Mudric/Rankovic 2016, p. 72).

Other scientific research goes as far as suggesting martial arts training "to be a legitimate form of therapy, for both 'neurotic' and some chronically mentally ill patients" (Weiser et. al. 1995, p. 1). The earlier mentioned concept of "psychological collectivism" "may provide one explanation for how non-Asian practitioners function in such training environments and how the traditional Asian martial arts can work as psychosocial therapies" (Partikova 2018, p. 49).

That aggression is reduced through training of traditional karate does not, however, come as a surprise to karateka who understand the true driving force behind and underneath inappropriate violent behavior: low self-esteem and a sense of inferiority, which usually go hand in hand with hidden aggression and anxiety.

This subconscious emotional state is the breeding ground of aggression, anger, hate, and envy. A statement like "because of fearing defeat I sometimes attacked more forcefully than necessary" (Oyama 1987, p. 116; translated by the author) unintentionally touches on the psychological explanation of the related and important psychological mechanism called *over-compensation"* (Dreikurs 1981, pp. 30ff.). The psychological mechanism of over-compensation explains why some unnecessary aggression is triggered in situations that could have been resolved differently, more constructively, and without the use of aggressive over-compensation. "Fear is the emotional correlate of feelings of inferiority; and thus a fearful, discouraged individual is dangerous" (Bayer 2000, p. 71; translated by the author) because of being prone to overcompensation, and, for all intents and purposes, prone to use "damaging physical violence in everyday life—and in the workplace producing emotional damage through degrading, scheming, or 'intellectual destruction'" (ibid. p 71).

The good news is that, when looking at it the other way around, this underlying and explosive combination of low self-esteem, feelings of inferiority, and hidden fear can be reduced by developing true combat skills. Through building up physical and mental strength, inappropriate overcompensating and aggressive tendencies lessen and eventually even vanish, since traditional karate training creates new self-definitions of capability and new self-perceptions of being able to successfully defend oneself and others. Unavoidably, self-confidence and courage eventually will improve and reduce feelings of inferiority.

As Fang Quiniang Sensei, the young Chinese woman who created the White Crane Gonfu style, puts it, as quoted in Article I of the *Bubishi*: "True power and wisdom come from within and are reflected without . . . This is the way to transcend ego-related distractions . . . People who truly understand the fighting traditions are never arrogant or unscrupulous, and never use their skill unjustly" (McCarthy 2016, p. 159).

#1: The Reason Not to Change Effective Techniques and Kata

The traditional self-defense goal of classic Okinawan karate—creating the most possible damage to an opponent in the most efficient way—requires minimizing time and distance in every move, as well as to maximizing body-weight/kinetic energy transfer. This optimization is based on—among other variables—physics, anatomy, and physiological fundamentals of the human body.

Using those fundamentals, offensive and defensive concepts were created many centuries ago to aid in surviving combat. During those violent times, the superiority of one technique over another was evaluated in terms of how much physical damage the technique could inflict when compared to another in real-life fighting. Once proven successful on the street and on the battlefield, superior techniques were honed to perfect efficiency and remained unchanged for centuries. Okinawa's classical martial art *Te* combined those techniques into kata, into encyclopedias of concepts and moves, and secretly passed the art down to following generations.

Based on these anatomical and physics-related factors, there is only one correct technical-mechanical way for a technique to minimize distance, maximize body-weight-power transfer, and to align bones at the moment of impact—taking *shuhari*, or an individual karateka's physiological variations with their resulting variation of moves, into account.

Hence, *once battle- and street-fight-proven, effective traditional moves were not altered* and kata remained essentially unchanged although each generation of sensei added some small alterations or individual modifications.

Such accepted feasible kata modifications are based on *shuhari*, allowing karateka some liberty, within narrow limitations, to develop their own way of executing techniques determined by their physical stature and their individual personality, but always based on correctly copying their instructor's techniques. Thus, within these limits, kata evolves according to Chibana Chosin Sensei's earlier-mentioned metaphor of karate being "a pond receiving fresh water" by each generation.

For the author's *Kobayashi Shorin Ryu* style, as practiced in *Shorin Ryu Shorinkan*, one example would be the higher chambered fist/hand position from *obi* (belt)-high to elbow-high, which was introduced by Nakazato Minoru Sensei after taking over the organization: whereas Nakazato Shugoro Sensei taught *obi*-high chambered fist positions, a modified, higher fist position was requested by Nakazato Minoru Sensei from the author during his visit at the Shorin Ryu Shorinkan Honbu Dojo in 2019.

This fist position is apparently used in other *Shorin Ryu* styles and schools too, and it matches the instructions in Article 1 of the *Bubishi*, which says that "techniques are executed forward and back from where the elbow meets the waist" (McCarthy 2016, p. 159).

"Techniques within a kata have more than a single application and are not intended to be used in self-defense exactly as performed in the kata . . . [they] are designed to suggest possible applications . . . As such, kata techniques are open to interpretation and even change of a

Image 11: Initial and Altered "Chambered" Fist Position in Kobayashi Shorin Ryu

Photograph by Noel Smith

Nakazato Shugoro Sensei's class in Okinawa in 1967 with Sensei
Noel Smith shows left fists obi-high.

Today, the left fist may be positioned
higher in Shorin Ryu Shorinkan.

special sort" (McCarthy 1987, p. 58)—with the important clarification of "when used in self-defense." When not used in self-defense, as in kata training, an unchanged approach is needed in the author's opinion. In a metaphor created by Bill Hayes, Sensei, 10th Dan *Shorin Ryu, Shobayashi Kan,* "No marine would maneuver on the battlefield the way a drill team marches" (Hayes n.d., Vol. 14, Issue 1, Spring, p. 9); however, both approaches are taught to marines and learned by them, the drill moves as well as the combat moves.

In terms of *shuhari,* the author's sensei, Noel Smith, points out some specific examples where initial *bunkai* needs to be carefully adjusted for a different physique between Okinawan and Western karateka. U.S. karateka are often taller and their limbs may extend farther compared to Okinawans, today as well as at the time kata were created. Hence, one or the other move in their original shape may not work properly for a taller physique in real combat.

For instance, the *mae-geri* kick after a *chudan-uke* middle block in *Pinan Shodan,* which is delivered from a *Nekoachi-dachi* cat stance may have to be adjusted accordingly. The leg length of many U.S. karateka may make it impossible to snap-stretch the kicking leg within the narrow space between the two opponents, but, instead, the attacker's knee would reach the opponent fittingly. Hence a forceful knee-kick instead of a *mae-geri* could suffice in combat reality for taller Western karateka.

However, when executing the form itself as kata training in a non-combat setting, the above quoted "change of a special sort" does not apply, and kata needs to be practiced in its initial *dentou* nature to maintain the essence of the form.

Another accepted change to kata was the result of hiding secret techniques when opening the art to new groups of students, whether to the Japanese occupiers or to non-Okinawan deshi. Again, all these were accepted alterations. Other kata modifications we see today were done by following generations of sensei over the last decades,[12] mostly in mainland Japan, and without approval from Okinawan masters. Some of these modifications were simply introduced to satisfy newly created competition rules without any reference to application in a real-life fight.

---

12. As a *deshi,* the author neither has the skills nor the authority to criticize kata alterations done by a sensei. He is only stating facts and references that can be verified by everyone.

One example of that statement is the inclusion of non-combat-related steps, even hops, to end a kata presentation exactly on the same *embusen* line or spot where it started, i.e., on the same "line at the floor plan of a kata," as requested by those rules, which is not necessary for *bunkai* in any genuine kata and which changes the initial combat-essence quite considerably.

The *Okinawan masters themselves did not change the essence of the old ways*, especially not to make a move "easier," usually meaning less effective in a fight;[13] as mentioned, this was done later, by following generations of sensei. In the words of Sensei Eddie Bethea, 8th Dan *Shorin Ryu, Shorinkan*, one of the "Original Seven," the first generation of US-students trained by Nagazato Shugoro Sensei (see footnote 2 in Chapter 3): "I trained directly under Hanshi Ju Dan [meaning 10th Dan] Shugoro Nakazato. Under him and for him I want the system to grow just as he conveyed it to me. Many times he would remind me *to always study and to never change anything*" (https://www.facebook.com /eddie.bethea.9; retrieved 01/31/2021 and italics added by the author). This necessity becomes even more transparent when we consider, as already mentioned, kata moves as something to be understood in its function rather than as a technique. The final kata position or technique is, in the words of Sensei David Colaizzi, 7th Dan *Shorin Ryu, Shorinkan*, the "destination" of a move; the "work" itself, the application, its impact on an opponent, happens throughout the move. If the final position, the "destination," is changed, the path toward this destination—the application and impact on an opponent—is altered as well.

Changing a kata move may even eliminate "hidden concepts," secret lethal techniques, visualized in an iceberg analogy below. These are non-apparent applications and impacts, covered by an obvious technique, which are only accessible with a deeper understanding of kata, which are severely wounding an opponent, and which were not broadly communicated by Okinawan masters to school kids, the Japanese, or to American or other Western students.

*   *   *

---

13. Chapter III exemplifies the hurtful consequences of changing *traditional*, narrower, and lower postures/stances/ positions into today's wider, deeper, or higher versions by analyzing these alterations using basic physics and mechanics.

The author suspects that "real" combat-related *bunkai* of kata moves is even today not shared with all students in Okinawa. This may impact the findings of brilliant martial-arts practitioner, researcher, and author Patrick McCarthy, Sensei, 9th Dan, *Koryu Uchinadi*, who mentions that he was not successful in his search "for a teacher, a style, or even an organization that could teach me the original and more functional combative application practices of kata and in a rational, coherent and systematized manner" (McCarthy 2005, n.p.). Going even further he states, "While there was certainly no shortage of excellent practitioners everywhere I looked, I found 'NO TRACE' of such teachings anywhere in Japan, or Okinawa!" (ibid.). This led Sensei McCarthy, after having studied several original martial arts systems in China and Japan, to develop his own system of effective and realistic fighting applications, based on the human body and its anatomy, on mechanics, and on realistic combat scenarios.

The author is not in the position to doubt the findings of Sensei McCarthy, who is a legend not only in the martial arts but for his research. If his findings are accurate, the art is in serious jeopardy of being watered down in its essence and genuine intentions. If it should be the case, however, that combat applications are not lost, but still not shared with all students, as the author was told by three of the so-called "Original Seven" black belts (see footnote 2 in Chapter 3) who were trained in Okinawa by Nakazato Shugoro Sensei in the mid-sixties, the "hidden concepts" in karate would be truly hidden. It is not claimed here that hidden concepts are kept a secret in Okinawan karate; according to many sources this is no longer the case today. However, there are certain levels of training, and the higher the level, the less the number of students these applications are shared with. It is up to the leading sensei of a style to choose the students, if any, to whom the deeper aspects of karate and kata concepts are introduced. According testimony is also given by Sensei Bill Hayes,[14] who reports that *Yudansha* in Shimabukuro Sensei's dojo changed their lethal combat training into some more moderate applications as soon as lower belts entered the

---

14. William ("Bill") Hayes, Sensei, 9th Dan *Shorin Ryu, Shobayashi-Kan,* is a retired U.S. Marine Corps major, director of the Okinawan Shorin Ryu Karate-do Research Society and the Shobayashi-Kan training group. He became one of Shimabukuro Eizo Sensei's trusted senior students and helped to spread the art of *Shobayashi Ryu* in the United States at Shimabukuro Sensei's request.

dojo in order to hide their initial approach and its related techniques (Hayes n.d., Vol. 3, Issue 2, Summer, p. 8).

Asking an Okinawan master to share lethal/hidden techniques may be an ineffective, perhaps even an inappropriate approach, born out of a Western thought process. As already mentioned, sharing these concepts works the other way round when a karate master chooses one individual or a small group of his students who then *in secrecy* are taught the deeper aspects of karate (Hayes 2018, p. 88). "The selection criteria used by a headmaster to pick those special students who will receive high-level training is a personal matter and those selected have no way of knowing whether or not they will ever receive full 'Okuden'-level instruction" (ibid., p. 89).

To be complete, it should not come as a surprise that these combat teachings in their classical forms that aim at protecting life are not found in mainland Japan's "disarmed" and altered karate derivations (see "Japanization" above), as Sensei McCarthy says in the above quote, because, as described earlier, many throws, joint locks, nerve suppressions, limb and head/neck manipulations, infighting, and ground-fighting techniques were eliminated in Japanized karatedo.

The training the author encounters in his dojo in direct lineage to Shugoro Nakazato Sensei's teaching of the 1960s and 1970s may be an indicator of the fact that "real fighting" was actually taught in Okinawa, whereas, in the words of one of the "Original Seven," kata today, as demonstrated in tournaments, "does not have any combat application whatsoever."[15]

As will be described in detail in Chapter III, the training the author has the privilege to attend with Noel Smith, Sensei, 8th Dan *Shorin Ryu, Shorinkan*, and with Yamashita Tadashi, Sensei, 10th Dan *Shorin Ryu, Shorinkan*, two of the "Original Seven," is based on the systematic development of fighting skills and use of realistic combat scenarios, partner drills, and free fighting without predetermined techniques (moves used by karate opponents as well as those used by street fighters), as well as the conditioning of limbs, bones, hands, and the upper and lower body. As far as the author is able to understand, Sensei Bill Hayes, who was trained directly by another karate legend, Shimabukuro Eizo Sensei, uses a comparable approach to teach the art in its classical life-protecting form as taught by his sensei. There are other sensei in the U.S. who were directly

---

15. Personal conversation with Frank Hargrove, Sensei 9th Dan *Shorin Ryu, Nakazato-Ha*, at his dojo in Newport News, Virginia, on 09/17/2020.

trained by Okinawan masters and who teach *dentou* Okinawan combat karate. All these trainings are definitely based on the anatomy of the human body and its related mechanics and physics, as will be explained in Chapter III in more detail.

It has to be pointed out, however, that this kind of systematic development of fighting skills and combat approach is not widespread in karate training today, neither in Japan nor in the U.S. nor in other parts of the world, which may be one reason why some MMA-fighters claim that, compared to their approach, karate does not work in combat and that karateka's refusal to fight them using their "too dangerous for the ring" argument is simply an excuse. Make no mistake: classic karate does work. "In fact, Okinawan Karate . . . is both efficient and effective. Its efficiency and effectiveness, however, lie in an arena in which few other more modern styles play. The arena of life or death!" (Hayes 2018, p. 114).

* * *

It is common ground in traditional karate circles to assume that every kata technique offers a concept for several different applications in *bunkai* and that no concept was ever created to have just one single application. The terms "concept" or "move" are used here instead of "techniques" to underline the fact that the art of karate is a dynamic and not a static one. Labelling moves as "techniques" creates the incorrect impression that karate would be a sequence of separate static positions, which it is not. Labelling moves as "techniques" was only done out of necessity to break the art down into learning objectives for physical education purposes during the Japanization of karate.

In the correct interpretation of kata as the dynamic flow of moves and concepts, there is always the obvious application, *omote* (surface) *bunkai*, usually a block, a strike, or a kick, which can be identified even with the untrained eye. Concepts below the surface, *ura* (hidden) *bunkai*, for the same technique, may involve preparing for a throw, breaking an opponent's limb or neck, grappling for nerve suppression, or grappling for extremity manipulations, just to name a handful. Finally, *honto* (essential) *bunkai* concepts are the very essence of a kata, when the form is stripped of all repetitions and "balancing moves": as Shimabukuro Eizo Sensei, 10th Dan *Shobayashi Ryu*, explains, the first one of repeated moves in a kata is the "real" one, the second one, the repetition, is intended to train the other side of the body for balanced development, and the third rendition of the technique is done to bring the karateka back into the same position as the first one. This consideration can be applied too when the same move is performed towards another direction, which trains the opposite side of the body after the first "real" technique. In other words, a *honto* kata is the condensed combination of essential concepts in this form, which all inflict severe damage on an adversary.

It has to be pointed out, however, that in combat-survival mode the simplest, fastest, and most direct move that makes use of muscle memory beats other "fancy" or possibly more "elegant" applications; this is supported not just by the author's personal experience, but by scientific research, where extensive measurements of efficiency and impacts of various techniques establish that "techniques of less complexity are shorter lasting and therefore safer for execution and implementation (Mudric/Rankovic 2016, p.72).

Graph 2: Iceberg Analogy of Kata Moves and Hidden Concepts

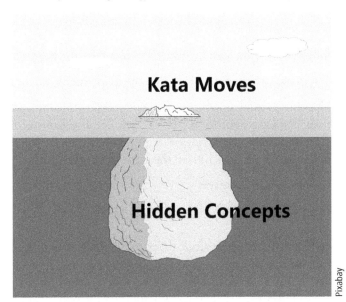

Pixabay

One relatively obvious example for a hidden concept in kata are some of the last moves in *Pinan Shodan ("Heian Nidan"* being its equivalent in Japanese *Shotokan).* What to the untrained eye looks like a sequence of blocks may as well be a throw, followed by a fatal neck snap—leaving aside the fact that there is no "block" as such in Okinawan karate; every defensive move is an offensive one at the same time, meaning that most preemptive strikes look like "blocks."

To repeat an earlier clarification: the concept of a preemptive strike does not violate the principle of "there is no first attack in karate." Since karateka can read an opponent's subtle signals that constitute "telegraphing" an intended move, they will preemptively "block-strike" at the moment of an attacker's "tell," which could seem like a first attack to the untrained eye but is not.

Part of the ending technique sequence in the *Pinan Shodan* kata is (the directions of "right/left" and "back/front" used are here defined by looking toward the karateka from *shomen,* i.e., from the front side of the dojo toward its backside):

a) right arm supported/augmented inside middle block (*morote chudan-uke*) to the back side,

b) 270-degree turn counter-clockwise with left low block (*gedan-barai/gedan-uke*),

c) followed by right arm high block (*jodan-uke*) to the same side.

At first glance, these moves look like the following:[16]

a) blocking a strong opponent's forceful middle punch from behind,

b) then blocking another attacker's kick coming from a different direction (from the right side), and finally

c) blocking a high punch from the same direction.

At second glance, however:

(1) the supported middle block (a) may be grabbing an opponent's jacket or *gi* top,

(2) then the turn with low block (b) becomes a hip or shoulder throw of the same attacker,

(3) followed by (c) snapping the same adversary's neck by placing the left hand over the face and quickly rotating the opponent's head by

---

16. This is, in fact, the *bunkai* explanation usually given (e.g. Wichmann 1998, pp. 27ff. in his illustrated explanation for *Shotokan).*

grabbing its backside with the right hand and utilizing a fatal quick torque when pushing the right arm up.

Since "distance is time," this throw concept instead of a low block *gedan-barai uke* actually seems to make more sense than wasting time and movement by counterproductively turning 270 degrees counterclockwise instead of simply turning 45 degrees or 90 degrees clockwise when blocking an attack from that direction.

Comparable hidden concepts in *Pinan* kata may as well apply to the spear-hand-blow *(nukite)* with following turn, where the counterclockwise 270 degrees turn toward another attacker from the left is taking way longer than a simple 45 or 90 degree when it is necessary to defend an attack from that direction.

The discussion about the appropriate *bunkai* for *morote-chudan uke* is ongoing; see, for instance, comments about the subject on Sensei Iain Abernethy's website,[17] where some statements support the interpretation in our example, others suggest something different, and some posts actually contradict each other.

All these different opinions are understandable and may all be accurate as well because, as mentioned, there is not just one correct concept for this technique; there are multiple applications that all are suitable, and in a variety of other kata miscellaneous hidden or open concepts are indeed used for the same technique. For example, *morote-chudan uke* applications at the end of *Pinan Yondan* may be (and are) different from the one at the end of *Pinan Shodan*, and both may be (and are) not the same as the application at the end of *Pinan Godan*.

In combat, many so-called "blocks" become parries anyway, especially when a sequence of multiple blows needs to be fought off. Chibana Chosin Sensei explains that "hard blocking is a sign of immaturity of technique. Soft blocking techniques show correct timing, maturity, and sophistication of technique" (quote in Chambers et. al. 2020, p. 37f). In addition, a block simply gives an attacker the opportunity to attack again and does not do much to end a fight. Consequently, hidden concepts may translate blocks into devastating preemptive strikes, nerve suppression, grappling, manipulations to break something, or preparations to throw and seriously wound.

In summation, a "simple" kata modification, like modifying arm positions or changing the angle for a technique, may destroy the initial

---

17. https://iainabernethy.co.uk/content/morote-uke; n.d.; retrieved 05/01/2020.

secret lethal concept and thus undermine the intentions of the Okinawan masters. That is why they did not change kata moves once proven successful in lethal fights and why they reject those changes still today our of respect for the Principle of Never-Changing Kata.

This principle comes to life in the teachings of the supreme Okinawan karate authorities, particularly Okinawan Intangible Cultural Asset holders like Nagamine Shoshin, Sensei, 10th Dan *Matsubayashi Ryu*; Yagi Meitoku, Sensei, 10th Dan *Goju Ryu*; Nakazato Shugoro, Sensei, 10th Dan *Shorin Ryu*, or Nakazato Jyoen, Sensei, 10th Dan *Shorinji Ryu*. The latter even "named (his) school Shorinji-Ryu, with the idea of getting back to the origins in every aspect, as a reaction to modern karatedom [*sic*] where kata have been changing one after another" (OPG 2003, n.p.).

Considerable kata modifications beyond *shuhari* were obviously introduced by following (often non-Okinawan) sensei generations, who—maybe intentionally,[18] maybe un-knowingly—defused original techniques by changing kata into competition showmanship, into something spectacular to look at, but without merit in combat. The sometimes-pathetic consequence of a kata modification in this sense is illustrated by the change of traditional mid-level kicks into modern high kicks.

Some mainland Japanese karate styles teach that in the *Pinan Shodan* kata (*Heian Nidan* being its equivalent in *Shotokan* karate) a front kick to the chest or to the head is followed by a middle punch. This does not work at all in combat: when kicked to the chest or head, an opponent bends back, stumbles backward, or even falls back, which is bringing him or her out of the reach of a middle punch. Therefore, the kick has to be *obi*-high or to the lower body, forcing the opponent to bend over forward. Now a middle punch reaches its target and can finish the fight.

This *Pinan Shodan* technique sequence, with its maximal *obi*-high kick, was taught to the author in *Kobayashi Shorin Ryu*. The exact same technique application is shown by Nagamine Shoshin Sensei, who kicks *obi*-high in his kata explanation for *Matsubayashi Ryu* (Nagamine 1976, p. 119).

The conclusion about the correct kick-level to prepare a middle punch has nothing to do with "styles"; it is the result of applying logic

---

18. We refer back to the "Japanization" of karate. It is a widely held, educated opinion that leading Okinawan karate masters, for instance Itosu ("Anko") Yasutsune Sensei, permitted some of their students to teach the secret art on mainland Japan, but advised them to change Okinawan karate and to keep specific techniques hidden.

and physics to the moves, instead of karate-style-specific interpretations. "Kicks are powerful, but the kicker is very, very vulnerable. High kicks simply had no place in oriental fighting until tournament rules made it illegal to kick the groin or grab the kicking leg. Then people started doing roundhouse kicks to the head. Note that the roundhouse kick leaves your groin wide open, not to mention all of your weight on one straight leg" (Clayton 2012, n.p.).

All these kinds of kata and technique changes may be understandable as *athletic optimizations* for the purposes of reaching physical perfection in sports karate or in athletic meditation, which is using physical activity as a medium to clear one's mind and to focus. If this altered purpose is not accepted, kata changes are not acceptable either, given the sacred Principle of Never-Changing Kata.

So, why kick head- or chest-high in the first place? Because it looks impressive to spectators during an athletic "kata dance" in a competition, but it has nothing to do with combat. A kata with realistic fighting moves is way less spectacular than sport karate's "dance moves"; some even call it boring.

Now, one may argue that karateka may use spectacular but combat-inefficient moves for showmanship in competitions and use effective ones in actual combat. Unfortunately, this does not work either: you do in combat exactly what you practiced to do in training, especially when being physically threatened, most certainly in pain, and definitely under considerable pressure. Anyone who has experienced the stress of physical combat will confirm that real fight conditions limit one's ability to think rationally, to see or to hear clearly—a condition retired army Lt. Col. Dave Grossman describes as "an altered state of consciousness" in his book on killing and combat (Grossman 2007, pp. 51ff.). In these situations, training kicks in, and karateka will have to rely on their muscle memory. Hence, if sports karate moves were trained, sports karate moves are forged into muscle memory, and sports karate moves will be used in combat.

It works the other way around too: practicing *dentou* Okinawan karate during training creates the correct muscle memory to succeed in real-life (lethal) combat. And, on the other side of the same coin, karateka who are proficient in traditional Okinawan karate are prone to successfully compete in sports karate tournaments at any time by using modified and controlled versions of their traditional techniques, as will be described in more detail in Reason #3 below.

#2: The Reason Not to Obscure an Intangible Cultural Heritage

Everybody knows that the original Eiffel Tower is located in Paris, France, and represents the country and its capital as an important cultural symbol. Everybody knows that there is an Eiffel Tower copy located in Las Vegas, Nevada, USA, as part of a hotel's theme that aims to create the impression of a French environment for Sin City tourists. Nobody ever confused the Las Vegas copy with the original French cultural symbol, which alone represents France's cultural heritage. That would be a violation of common sense. The original Eiffel Tower is, always was, and ever will be a *tangible* component of France's culture and no other country will ever take this from the French society—as should be the case with all cultural heritage around the world, tangible and intangible.

This Eiffel Tower metaphor refers to a *national* cultural symbol that represents the overarching culture within the political borders of a society and government, but the same thought process may be applied to *subcultures* within an overarching political system too. The sociological/ social borders of cultures and subcultures, and their unique symbols, assets, and heritage, do not necessarily match the political borders of governments—and, most importantly, their *subcultural heritage and symbols do not necessarily represent the overarching culture of a nation.*

Hence, a subcultural symbol, for instance Okinawan karate, may "from the outside" be incorrectly interpreted as a national Japanese cultural symbol, which it is not.

There are many parallel examples to support this argument. We use one that the author, as a former resident of Munich, Germany, for twenty-five years, is familiar with: the folk festival "Oktoberfest," which, almost everywhere in the word, is believed to be a "German" cultural symbol. However, it is not a German cultural symbol, it is a "Bavarian" *subcultural* symbol and part of that region's heritage.

Bavaria is a region and state in the southern part of Germany, which always was, and until today still is, proud of its cultural uniqueness. In social-cultural terms, reflected in cultural symbols like language and local dialect, traditional attire and costumes, Catholicism, architectural styles, folk music and its traditional instruments, economic structure, as well as in other important aspects of cultural heritage, Bavaria actually is much closer to the country of Austria, which is located to its south, than to the rest of Germany to its north. Non-Bavarian German citizens are still today called "Prussians" by Bavarian locals—and this is not meant in a friendly or appreciating way.

In Bavaria's capital Munich, the Octoberfest was created in the year 1810, when Bavaria was an independent and separate kingdom of its own, as an invitation to Bavarian citizens to help celebrate the wedding of the Bavarian crown prince and later King Ludwig the First.

This festival of 1810 was, per the decision of the Munich city council, to be celebrated yearly thereafter as a combination of folk festival and economic fair, especially exhibiting farming products. Later it became more a matter of festivity than about economics.

Hence, though being "German" in terms of today's governmental and political sphere, the two-hundred-plus-year-old *Oktoberfest is a Bavarian subcultural intangible heritage*, including all its genuine Bavarian—often imprecisely called "German"—components of "Lederhosen" and "Dirndl" costumes (which used to be the traditional clothes for rural Bavarians)—brass and folk music, the "Schuhplattler" dance (photo below), and traditional Bavarian food and beer.

Image 12: "Schuhplattler" Dance—Example of an Intangible Bavarian Subcultural Heritage within Germany

Creative Commons

The fact that today Oktoberfests are celebrated all over the word in modified, sometimes perverted forms centered on binge-drinking, and that Germany as a whole significantly profits economically as well as politically from this subcultural symbol, does not change its Bavarian origin and the fact of its indigenous subcultural heritage of Bavaria.

Extending this thought, we find Okinawan intangible subcultural heritage within the governmental and political sphere of the nation of Japan, and we find Ryukyu-specific rituals, oral traditions, the performing arts, and other symbols of indigenous subcultural origin, including karate. Most of these subcultural symbols were left untouched by Japan, but karate was not.

An example of "untouched" intangible Okinawan subcultural heritage in this sense is Ryukyu's traditional drum dance "*Eisa*," which has been performed on the islands for centuries (picture below). Today, it is not only demonstrated in Okinawa itself, but in other countries too, that have concentrations of ethnic Okinawans. *Eisa* may be sometimes modified to attract younger dancers, but nobody doubts its roots and the Okinawan originality of this dance. Japan, the political powerhouse governing Okinawa since mediaeval times, never aimed at integrating *Eisa* into its own rich and centuries-old culture of performing arts.

Image 13: "Eisa" Dance—Example of Intangible Okinawan Subcultural Heritage within Japan

Creative Commons

To "annex" such an intangible cultural asset like *Eisa* would be like offending—even attacking—a society's cultural identity and to fail to respect traditions that form a culture's identity. Again, trying to do that would look like a contradiction of common sense—*Eisa*, always was, remains, and ever will be of Okinawan origin and a component of

Okinawan cultural heritage. In this sense Japan is to be highly commended for tolerating some aspects of Okinawa's subculture in its prefecture for centuries without destroying it.

Unfortunately the situation with respect to karate is different. It is strange that Japan, with its own, thousands-of-years-old martial arts and *bushido* tradition, is so devoted to annexing Okinawan karate, which was practiced secretly in Okinawa, was genuine as it can be, and was unknown on the mainland for several centuries until recent decades.

Why is that the case specifically with karate? Or, the other way around, why is, in contrast to karate, noninterference with other forms of subcultural heritage like *Eisa* easier, leaving those symbols neither questioned nor disputed?

It is because karate is such an important and essential pillar of the Okinawan subculture. Integrating the Ryukyu Islands into Japanese culture was intended to create some kind of homogeneity between its martial arts traditions. "The Japanese government sought to assimilate the Okinawan people and enfold karate into their promotion of the imagined homogeneity of Japan" (Johnson 2012, p. 61).

Hence, besides commercial or sports and political considerations, the mind-set of Japan's martial arts and political officials seems to be that, because of its thousands-of-years-old martial arts tradition, its sophisticated and distinguished *koryu bujutsu,* its noble samurai tradition, and its elaborate *bushido,* this very tradition culminates in mainland Japan's assumed superiority in terms of martial arts per se, leading to the assertion by political and sports officials that mainland Japan's *budo* arts embody or represent *all* Japanese martial arts—including the "Japanized" versions from occupied territories.

"Compared to numerous other ancient societies, Japan has from antiquity viewed its martial aspects in a unique way, elevating its warriors' military skills to the level of art, and later in history combining these skills with meditative disciplines" (Davey n.d., p. 4). In this perspective, on mainland Japan traditional Okinawan karate may be considered socially acceptable as a martial arts discipline only after its conversion into its Japanized form.

Nevertheless, claiming karate as a Japanese martial art—though correct in terms of its governmental sphere but incorrect in terms of subcultural heritage—denies proper credit to the region that invented and cultivated karate, attacks a people's cultural identity, and lacks acknowledgement of cultural traditions. "Karate may be positioned within the constellation of Japanese martial arts, but can be represented as such only through the flattening of any difference between Okinawan and Japanese culture or through the modification of the practice itself. In order for karate to be considered a Japanese martial art, a shift of framing from the Okinawan culture and its traditions to those of main-land Japan—a cultural translation of the practice—was required" (Johnson 2012, p. 62).

However, the only legitimate people to deal with questions of cultural heritage are the members of the culture or subculture in question. Main-taining the subcultural heritage of traditional Okinawan karate is up to Okinawans and to nobody else; it is like maintaining a monument.

On a different note, when today one or another Western martial art-ist raises the question of why the style they developed is not recognized as "traditional," though their derivations may rooted in original funda-mentals and forms (see for instance Starr 2020), the author's answer to this question is two-fold. First, referring to the old saying that "a copy is never as good as the original," why create a new style in the first place? Since *all traditional styles are honed to perfection and are proven successful on the battlefield as well as in street fights*, altering optimized techniques—though possible—seems unnecessary. The inclination to make altera-tions raises the suspicion that some creators of such changed techniques are simply looking for a unique product to set themselves apart, maybe for reasons of individual prestige or maybe to create a niche in the mar-tial arts market. Second, and most importantly, what official Japanese—and, referring to our topic, official Okinawan—accreditation bodies declare *dentou* karatedo, should not be the concern of "Westerners" at all, because it deals with Okinawa's cultural heritage.

There are undoubtedly more than a few outstanding "Western" mar-tial artists who are well respected by their Asian counterparts, as the list of medal winners at The 1st Okinawa Karate International Tournament 2018 in Okinawa clearly shows (https://okinawa-karate.okinawa/en /result/, retrieved 03/19/2020).

Some other famous "Western" martial artists created their own style,[19] which may also be well respected in Asia; nonetheless these styles are not

---

19. For example, well-known actor Carlos Ray "Chuck" Norris created his *Chun Kuk Do* in the late 1980s; cherished martial artist Phillip Starr created his *Yilichuan Kung Fu* around the same time; and famous Lee Jun-fan, known as Bruce Lee, developed and taught his *Jeet Kune Do* in the late 1960s.

necessarily recognized as *dentou* styles over there, though developed out of Asian forms and fundamentals.

So what?

As soon as we all agree to see karate as an extremely important part of Okinawan *cultural heritage* (in addition to being a martial art combining self-defense capabilities with physical, spiritual, and mental development), then it becomes clear that only the members of the culture in question are able to rightfully deal with questions of cultural heritage.

When karate is a part of Okinawan (sub-) cultural heritage, no foreigner is in the position to decide on matters important to it, though there may be as many outstanding karate experts to be found outside of Okinawa in the West as on Okinawa itself. This is comparable to the fact that no foreigner is in the position to decide on the status of a monument in Italy as part of Italian cultural heritage, though there may be many outstanding experts on Italian culture to be found outside of Italy. All decisions should be up to the Italians. Foreigners may like what Italians do in this sense, or they may dislike it; they may research it and they may comment on it. They may have an opinion on it, they may agree with the Italians' decision or they may disagree. But the decision itself should be in the hands of the Italians. The same line of argument applies to Okinawan karate—even if non-Okinawans should claim to come up with a better decision or procedure than Okinawans themselves.

This is one of the author's philosophical, value-based axioms, comparable to the basis of international law, or, in politics, to the doctrine of nonintervention into foreign internal affairs. The author's position may not be shared by everyone. However, based on this maxim, all disputes about Okinawan karate-style recognition are to be resolved by Okinawans only.

On the flipside, the obligation of martial artists with non-Okinawan cultural backgrounds is to *understand and to accept karate as an aspect of Okinawa's cultural heritage* and its paramount role in forming Okinawan cultural identity, self-perception, and self-definition. Realizing karate's significance, the principle of non-interference and of not questioning Okinawan policies of karate development and style recognition should be indisputable. Then all possible and regrettable quarrels simply vanish. Better: they are revealed as symptoms perhaps of narcissism and definitely of business.

#3: The Reason Not to Call Sports-Karate Derivations a Martial Art

When *dentou* karate is a lethal martial art, and times today are more peaceful, wouldn't it be advisable to channel aggression into fun or sports competitions and to use its training practices for physical-education purposes?

Of course, this is, this can be, and this should be done; sports-related derivatives just should not be called "traditional martial arts," perhaps not even "martial arts" at all.

There is no reason to say any sports karate derivation should not exist, and there is no need either to create any philosophical superstructure for it, like there is no need to link today's sports of javelin or fencing to a warrior's combat education centuries ago. Javelin only assesses the distance of a throw; aiming accuracy and optimal penetration on impact is neglected. Fencing, similar to sports karate, only values speed to tag an opponent; maximal damage on impact is neglected, and uninterrupted follow-up attacks after a first hit, as well as grabs, neck-manipulations, back-leg sweeps, and many throws are even outlawed by "disarming" rules.

Sensei H. E. Davey, with Shudokan Martial Arts Association (SMAA), among others, clarified with their highly commendable work the origin and nature of traditional Japanese martial arts (not to be confused with the origin and nature of Okinawan *Te*) and explain that "*budo* are the modern martial arts of Japan. Examples of *budo* are judo, aikido, karate-do, iaido, and kendo. While these disciplines stem from ancient samurai military arts, or *koryu bujutsu,* they are not of ancient origin, having originated after the demise of the samurai in Japanese society" (Davey, n.d., p. 1).

First, this is incorrect for karate, which actually is of ancient origin. However, it does not stem from "ancient samurai military arts," but from secretly practiced indigenous Okinawan *Te*. Furthermore, in other martial arts disciplines there are actually different names for the Japanese sports derivatives that contrast with the names of their preceding combat forms, which is not the case for karate; here the same term includes both versions today, the ancient lethal origin as well as its modern sports derivatives.

Second, and historically correct, there was initially a clear separation of *connotation* and *meaning* between the two terms. *Jujitsu* or *bujutsu* was understood as "warrior skills" and the Japanese martial arts disciplines and their initial role were seen as arts of war. *Budo* was understood as the "warrior's way" of self-development and self-realization through the study of *bujutsu/jujitsu*. This changed and became confused when the term *Do* as "way" or "path" replaced the term "*jutsu*." This renaming ended up in today's confusing combination of "skill" and "way" in Japanese sports terminology, e.g., *judo* and *aikido*.

Nevertheless, in line with the above argument, it would be an easy solution to use the differentiation between *bushido* and *budo* to distinguish between Japanese traditional martial arts based on *bushido* versus Japanese modern sports derivations based on *budo*. Unfortunately, things are not quite as simple, as Sensei H. E. Davey points out: "While it's true that *budo* arts are not as effective as the classical *bujutsu* methods in classical combat, this represents combat in an ancient Japanese feudal context. It doesn't always correlate with civilian self-protection today. In truth, some forms of *budo*, having originated more recently, may be more effective for modern, non-military self-defense than certain forms of *koryu bujutsu*" (ibid. p. 17).

While this may be the case for *koryu bujutsu* and *budo* as stated in the quote, the author respectfully disagrees with Sensei Davey for *dentou* Okinawan karate compared to Japanese karatedo. Classical, "ancient" Okinawan karate is far more effective "for modern, non-military self-defense" than its "modern" traditional Japanese non-sports derivative, let alone its sports variation. This assertion is not just based on the author's own fighting experience, but on observations of fights between representatives of various karate styles, and lastly based on the laws of physics as well, which will be illustrated in Chapter III in more detail.

It may be the case that other traditional Japanese *bujutsu* did not work anymore with the evolution of new military weaponry, but bar or street fights and hand-to-hand combat did not change as much and allow *dentou* karate techniques to maintain their effective superiority.

There is one significant difference, though: contrary to Okinawan *Te*, neither Japanese *budo* nor *koryu bujutsu* were created exclusively for self-defense; ". . . they include aspects relating to Japanese history, philosophy, aesthetics, health maintenance, strategy, and yes, techniques that could be used for protecting yourself from danger" (ibid. p. 19).

Therefore both *budo* and *koryu bujutsu* differ significantly from traditional Okinawan karate, which stands unique and independent from both concepts as Okinawan martial arts per se—neither sharing the history of the Japanese *samurai* caste nor the binding concept of its *bushido*. Insofar as the further derivation of Japanese sports karate based on Japanese *budo* does not impact the independent role of genuine Okinawan karate at all, this sports-karate derivation is an exclusively Japanese development on the mainland (which later rolled back to Okinawa as well, of course).

In Chibana Chosin Sensei's words: "In the old days we trained karate as a martial art, but now they train at karate as a gymnastic sport. I think we must avoid treating karate as a sport—it must be a martial art at all times! . . . You have to think that if you kick, you try to kick the enemy dead. If you punch, you must thrust to kill. If you strike, then you strike to kill the enemy. This is the spirit you need in order to progress in your training" (quote in Chambers et. al. 2020, p. 49). This is a spirit expressed in the one-punch-kill, *ichigeki hissatsu,* mind-set.

Now, to avoid a possible misunderstanding, a karateka who is proficient in traditional Okinawan karate is of course able to successfully compete in sports karate events at any time. One example to support this statement is the author's Sensei Noel Smith, 8th Dan *Shorin Ryu, Shorinkan,* who was introduced earlier in Chapter I. Sensei Smith on the one hand teaches *dentou* Okinawan *Kobayashi Shorin Ryu* karate, lethal and classical. On the other hand, he developed competition strategies based on this Okinawan style by adjusting controlled traditional techniques and concepts to specific tournament requirements. As the head coach for the U.S. karate team from 1973 to 1978 he competed in Europe, South Africa, and Japan. Members of his dojo still successfully participate in tournaments today (the gray-haired author included).

The "challenge" *dentou* Okinawan karateka face in competitions is that they have to control their reflexes and readjust their muscle memory in order to avoid executing moves that would disqualify them.[20] In addition, they have to execute some "suboptimal" moves in terms of limiting their array of concepts due to competition rules instead of using more effectively damaging techniques, or limit their target areas, also due to these rules, when aiming at another target would be more advantageous.

---

20. David Colaizzi, Sensei, 7th Dan *Shorin Ryu, Shorinkan,* told the author that he once secured the bronze medal in a U.S. championship tournament instead of first place only because he received malus points for flashing double-punches, executed via muscle memory, when, according to the competition rules, he was required to stop after the first punch.

Because of these sport-specific restrictions, sparring training today is different from fighting training in Okinawa, as Sensei Noel Smith recalls. During his time there, *kumite* was serious combat training and not "disarmed" sports karate. Training was then broken down into its three segments of *kata*, *kumite*, and *kobudo*; there was no separation between these three mutually complementing pillars, and hence fighting *kumite* was a regular part of training sessions at Nakazato Shugoro Sensei's dojo in Okinawa.

In Nakazato Shugoro Sensei's words: "If you just practice *Te*, it is questionable if in battle you would be able to do well or not, and, on the other hand, if you just do freestyle fighting, there are many points there that are bad. We should not forget the meaning of why our sensais [*sic*] that have gone before us, have over their long experience talked about and developed *Te*. *In essence, we have to study both freestyle matches and* Te *in order to get the full meaning of things*" (Nakazato n. d., n. p.; italics are the author's).

Sensei Smith shared that after evening trainings Nakazato Shugoro Sensei would bow out and recede upstairs to his residence; all students would clean the dojo, close the shutters, and, thereafter, black-belt sparring took place. In these fights were no restrictions of techniques or limitations of target areas. In terms of protection, the fighters wore neither cups nor mouthpieces, let alone other padding gear; so, self-control and mutual respect were of utmost importance. As one can imagine, hurtful hits occurred regularly though; in Sensei Smith's words "we really used to bang bones then." However, in case a fighter lost sight of self-control and accidentally hit his opponent inappropriately, it was accepted when a sincere apology followed; if not, the other fighter would hit back accordingly—and the related learning process of mutual respect would quickly ensue.

When sharing his experience, Sensei Smith always points out the commitment, devotion, and full-force transfer of body-weight power Okinawan karateka would display in combat *kumite*, culminating in their fighting spirit of 100-percent dedication and how this changed over time into today's speedy "safety first" sports karate moves. "They came at you in full force," he stated several times, which requires a deliberate and solid "zone-defense-stronghold" to fend off these attacks, which led to his fighting drill mantra that "fighting starts with defense and ends with defense." A fighter needs to create a strong safeguard, a personal "fence" through "zone defense" from which "unannounced," "non-telegraphed" speedy and powerful attacks are to be launched. Sensei Smith's example illustrates that traditional karateka are well aware of the disparity between sports karate and *dentou* Okinawan karate and how to develop a path to combine—not to be confused with "to integrate"—these two variations.

Whereas karateka proficient in traditional Okinawan karate may successfully compete at karate tournaments, the other way round is not necessarily as successful: many empirical examples—personally known to the author—show that karateka who are practicing sports karate variations and join a classical dojo are—at least at first—overwhelmed in *kumite* by their counterparts, who are proficient in *dentou* Okinawan karate: these opponents do not "bounce around" like the competition adversaries they are familiar with, and they do not stop fighting when ineffectively tagged. Their sheer force of body-weight-power transfer; their relentless iteration of full-power techniques aiming at all kinds of soft tissue targets and nerve centers; and their use of an array of highly effective grips (excluded in sports karate, even prohibited), joint locks, sweeps, and throws can be overwhelming indeed.

Many sports karateka highly appreciate their new learning experience and their opportunity to understand the true intention of the art, and—sometimes for the first time ever—they start to think techniques through completely and replace their speedy fencing-type contacts with body-weight-power transfer, transferred through bone alignment at the moment of impact.

Hence, all such examples the author has encountered support David Chambers's experience that "when sport karate people experience real karate here in Okinawa, many embrace the origin of their existing style . . . *Shotokan* people change to *Seibukan* or *Kobayashi Ryu*. *Goju Kai* and *Kyokushinkai* to *Goju Ryu* and so forth. As sports karate kept only a small number of techniques, our seminar members are suddenly confronted with hundreds of locking, throwing, immobilization, nerve-suppression, and in-fighting techniques, all of which disappeared from 'modern karate' seventy or more years ago as the price of trying to make karate a commercial sport" (interviewer's comment in Kuramoto interview 2020, p. 19).

So, again, *sports karate is neither classical Okinawan karate nor martial arts.* It rather is the development of a new and fascinating modern sport with its own purpose and reason to exist, as was the case with other sport derivatives of other arts that had their origins in combat: javelin, fencing, archery, biathlon, and many others—without any need to create a special philosophical superstructure for it or to try to connect it with ancient combat.

In summation, we have three separated entities today in karate, all with legitimate but different reasons to exist, which should not be confused with each other; "classical" self-*protecting* Okinawan karate-jutsu, "traditional" form-only self-*perfecting* Japanese karatedo, and "modern" *sports* karate.

Chapter 3
Empirical Evidence and the Laws of Physics to Support the Sociocultural and Historic Arguments

This chapter provides empirical evidence for the socio-cultural and historic argumentation of Chapters I and II, illustrated by three examples[1] that are all taken from the author's training experience.

The first practical example compares a "disarmed," traditional, non-sports, and "form-only" Japanese karate variation, *Doshinkan Karatedo,* with a genuine classic Okinawan one, *Kobayashi Ryu.* Having trained with *hanshi* and *kyoshi* who were directly instructed by the originators of the two styles[2] increases the chance of identifying authentic forms and practices in both karate paths. This suggests the experienced

---

1. The three examples are partly based on earlier research papers by the author (Bayer, 2019a; 2019b; 2020).

2. (footnote continued on the following page) The author's first *Doshinkan Karatedo* sensei in Europe, Ichikawa Isao, Sensei, 10th Dan, *Shudokan,* started *Shudokan* training as Toyama Kanken Sensei's *uchi-deshi* in Japan in the 1940s. Soon after Tomaya Sensei's death in the late 1960s, Ichikawa Isao Sensei went to Europe and named his system in the *Shudokan* tradition *Doshinkan,* with its *honbu* dojo in Vienna, Austria. After his passing in 1996, his brother Ichikawa Nobuo, Sensei, 10th Dan, *Doshinkan,* became the new leader of the organization until he himself passed away in 2019. He was the author's second senior *Doshinkan Karatedo* sensei in Europe and in the USA.

differences as general representations of some core differences between Okinawan and Japanese karate.

Though the author trains *Kobayashi Ryu* as taught in *Shorin Ryu Shorinkan*, as a deshi he is neither authorized to speak for this organization in any official or unofficial capacity, nor does he intend to. Accordingly, as a *Doshinkan Karatedo sandan* he neither is in the position to officially or unofficially speak for this organization, nor does he intend to. The author's position is the neutral-analytic one of independent research.

The second and the third practical example illustrate the superiority of the Never Changing Kata Principle by applying physics, mechanics, and scientifically evaluated velocity measurements to kata moves. The specific illustrations used are two kata stances/positions, *Nekoachi-dachi* (cat stance) and *Naihanchi- (Kiba-) dachi* (straddled legs stance) in their traditional and their modern (altered) peculiarity. The laws of physics analysis of "modern" kata interpretations unveils some serious negative consequences of these modifications, namely *reduced body-weight-power transfer* into a technique in the first example, and a kara-teka's *increased vulnerability through delayed block-counters and damaging torque on knee joints* in the second one.

First Practical Example:
How Training Differences between Genuine Okinawan Karate and "Disarmed" Traditional Japanese Karatedo Lead to Contrasting Fighting Skills

The two different karate styles I use to study and compare here are *Doshinkan Karatedo*, one of the "Japanized" karate versions labeled "disarmed" in Chapter I, as the representation of traditional, non-sports, form-only *Japanese* karate. It was created in Japan by Ichikawa Isao

---

The author's *Kobayashi Ryu* sensei in Okinawa is Minoru Nakazato, Sensei, 10th Dan *Shorin Ryu, Shorinkan,* who since 2016 has lead *Shorin Ryu Shorinkan.* The author's senior sensei in the USA is Noel Smith, Sensei, 8th Dan *Shorin Ryu, Shorinkan.* Both were trained directly by Nakazato Shugoro Sensei, president of *Shorin Ryu Shorinkan* until his passing 2016.

Sensei Noel Smith is one of the so-called "Original Seven" black belts, sent to the USA by Nakazato Shugoro Sensei in the 1960s to promote *Shorin Ryu Shorinkan* there. These famous Original Seven are the two Okinawans Yamashita Tadashi (initially born in Japan) and Shiroma Jiro, and the five Americans Eddie Bethea, Sid Campbell, Frank Hargrove, Robert ("Bob") Herten, and Noel Smith (http://www.obikarateschool.com/lineage/shorinkan/our-lineage/).

Sensei and established in the early 1960s in Tomaya Kanken Sensei's *Shudokan* tradition.

The second one, classic Okinawan *Kobayashi Shorin Ryu*, developed from the centuries-old teachings of Matsumuro Sokon Sensei and, later, Isotu Anko Sensei. It was specifically honed and labeled by Chosin Chibana Sensei in the 1930s. Later, among others, his student Nakazato Shugoro Sensei spread it worldwide through his *Shorin Ryu Shorinkan* organization.

The characterizing terms we use are a modified version of the distinction introduced by Sensei Bill Hayes (Hayes n.d., Vol. 6, Spring, p. 10):

- "modern" *sport*-oriented karate
- "traditional" form-only self-*perfection* based karate-do
- "classical" form-, principle-, application- based self-*protection* karate-jutsu

Hence, *Doshinkan Karatedo* falls into the second category of "traditional" self-perfection based arts, whereas *Kobayashi Ryu* represents a version of the third category, a "classical" self- protection art.

Training in Okinawan *Kobayashi Ryu* is considerably less standardized or formalized than in Japanese *Doshinkan*; the latter mirrors mainland Japan's *budo* tradition with its militaristic roots and its preference for well-defined rules and narrow regime. This, however, does not mean that in *Shorin Ryu Shorinkan* respect for lineage and for honoring traditions would be less characteristic; it means that this respect and honor is accomplished there by internalized habits rather than through ordered rituals with detailed verbal commands.

In this sense, *Doshinkan Karatedo* is characterized by:

- synchronous moves of the entire training group
- ordered row switches from front to back throughout a training session with a particular protocol and etiquette
- predetermined rank positions at specific places within the training group
- elaborated rituals
- cultivated and upheld symbolism

In terms of symbolism, there is no *Doshinkan Karatedo* training session without the style's flag, showing logo and kanji, being displayed at *shomen,* or without meticulous opening and closing rituals (see below)—neither indoors in dojos, gyms, or rented rooms; nor, if trainings take place outdoors, in public spaces, as they often do, such as in parks, stadiums, or on beaches.

In addition, at training camps no session will start or end without an extensive and well-structured ceremony of chants and coordinated rhythmic body-conditioning slaps immediately preceding the opening and closing ceremonies. This is the derivative of an ancient Japanese ritual of counted rhythmic hand clapping to show gratitude, appreciation, and consent. The version used in *Doshinkan Karatedo* enhances group spirit and the social bond of a close international community, which may look to an outsider like the residue of a secret society.

The meticulous etiquette in *Doshinkan Karatedo* is only loosened for training attire, even in training camps with senior sensei, which is allowed to be surprisingly casual; T-shirts or tank-tops (or even no top at all) are permitted, whereas in *Shorin Ryu Shorinkan* training camps with senior sensei the standard white karate uniform is worn.

Contrasting *Doshinkan Karatedo's* rigid (mainland) Japanese etiquette, and representing the more relaxed Okinawan *Te* tradition, there are fewer and shorter rituals in a *Kobayashi Ryu* training group, fewer verbal commands, and more degrees of freedom, relying instead on internalized habits. A *Shorin Ryu* training group does not always stay together as one unit to move synchronously; it may be split up into sub-groups of students at comparable skill levels—sometimes supervised by a black-belt or color-belt *senpai*—where students may work on different assignments.

Rank positions in the training group are not fixed but appointed by the leading sensei; higher ranks may sometimes be requested to be in the front row(s) of the group and at other times in the back row(s), and the leading sensei may position lower color ranks at varying locations within the training group, depending on the intended learning experience for these students.

A *Kobayashi Ryu* kata is not started with the commands *"rei—kamaite"* for bow and following "ready-move," nor is it closed with *"naore—rei"* for finishing move and following bow, as is *always* the case in *Doshinkan Karatedo*—always, without any exception.

The distinguishable, less-formalized structure in *Shorin Ryu Shorinkan* is further mirrored in considerably different opening and closing rituals and their corresponding commands. Whereas in *Shorin Ryu Shorinkan*

Different Training Opening Etiquette in Japanese and Okinawan Karate

Doshinkan Karatedo (group always sitting in seiza)			Shorin Ryu Shorinkan (group always standing)		
Ordered by	Command	Meaning	Command	Meaning	Ordered by
Student	KIO-TSUKE	attention, line up	done routinely	automatic line up	Sensei
Student	SEIZA	get into sitting position	n/a	n/a	—
Student	SHOMEN NI-REI	bow to *shomen*/flag	REI	bow to shomen	Student
Sensei	MOKUTO	close eyes and focus	n/a	n/a	—
Sensei	NAORE	cease and open eyes		n/a	—
Student	SENSEI NI-REI	bow to sensei	SENSEI NI-REI	bow to sensei	Student
Student	KIRJITSU	stand up	n/a	n/a	—
Sensei	HAJIMEMASU	let us begin	n/a	n/a	—
All	ONEGAISHIMASU	Sensei, do us this favor	n/a	n/a	—

Different Training Closing Etiquette in Japanese and Okinawan Karate

Doshinkan Karatedo (group always sitting in seiza)			Shorin Ryu Shorinkan (group sitting or standing)		
Ordered by	Command	Meaning	Command	Meaning	Ordered by
Sensei	KOREMADE	up to here, let us finish	n/a	n/a	—
Sensei	DOZO	please line up	n/a	n/a	—
Student	KIO-TSUKE	attention, line up	n/a; done routinely*	automatic line up*	—
Student	SEIZA	get into sitting position	n/a; done routinely		—
Student	SHOMEN NI-REI	bow to shomen/flag			
Sensei	MOKUTO	close eyes/focus/reflect	MOKUTO	focus and reflect	Student
Sensei	NAORE	cease and open eyes	MOKUTO OWATE	cease reflecting	Student
Student	SENSEI NI-REI	bow to sensei	REI	bow to *shomen*	Student
Student	KIRJITSU	stand up	SENSEI NI-REI	bow to sensei	Student
Sensei	OWARIMASU	with this we finish			
All	ARIGATO GOZAIMASHITA	deepest thank you	ARIGATO GOZAIMASU	(and while bowing) deepest thank you	All

*Since every training session is ending with performing the *Naihanchi Ichidan* kata and some predetermined physical close-out exercises, falling into line for the following closing ritual does not require a specific verbal command.

the majority of the ritual is done without specific verbal orders but relies on internalized habits, and a few remaining commands are given by the most senior Dan student in the group, in a *Doshinkan* training group every single step is meticulously announced as a combination of alternating commands given between the most senior *Kyu*-rank present and the leading sensei.

In terms of *purpose*, at first glance both karate approaches, *Doshinkan Karatedo* and *Kobayashi Shorin Ryu*, seem to share the notion that karate is not a sport but a martial art designed for self-defense. For *Doshinkan Karatedo*, Ichikawa Isao Sensei wittily stated a couple of times during the author's trainings in Austria that "Kinder und Kartoffeln nicht verstehen," literally meaning "children and potatoes do not understand" this gravity of karate as a martial art. This phrase, jokingly used by him to label immature adult students, referred to a short-time European training attendee with the first name "Imo," meaning "potato" in Japanese, who displayed an inappropriate attitude and earned the questionable honor of being indirectly named as a negative example.

At second glance, however, purposes and their pursuits are completely different between the two styles. This difference is reflected in *major differences of training practices* between the two styles, leading to significantly different, even contradictory outcomes in terms of a student's fighting capabilities.

The meditative-athletic karate approach completely changed the original Okinawan training practice. During a personal conversation with the author, Sensei Frank Hargrove put it like this: "Today, people don't want to get touched." This makes sparring and fighting in self-perfecting, form-only styles obsolete, whereas acquiring lethal fighting skills is, always was, and always will be the intended goal of *dentou* Okinawan karate—whatever philosophical superstructure may have been created by following generations or by non-Okinawan karate adepts to justify what they are doing by adding a moral justification to a genuinely lethal martial art.

However, in spite of its lethality, and in spite of acquiring serious fighting skills in classical dojos, the purpose of Okinawan karate is not the use of violence, as mentioned earlier; it is *self-control* in combination with the confidence that comes from being prepared for all possible challenges.

We already listed scientific evidence for the fact (which, for the non-karateka, may be surprising) that seriously studying Okinawan karate and accepting its traditional goal of self-defense and the acquisition of combat readiness, go hand in hand with a peaceful mind. This is the result of an indivisible combination of increased self-confidence; reduction of fear, anxiety, and anger; and physical, spiritual, and moral development when acquiring fighting skills.

Changing classical Okinawan karate's initial purpose as a lethal martial art in Japanese *Doshinkan* karatedo leads to several *variances of training practices*, illustrated on the following pages, which in turn generate severely contradicting outcomes in terms of a student's fighting capabilities between the two styles:

Core Variances in Training Practices Between Kobayashi Shorin Ryu and Doshinkan Karatedo

Criterion	Kobayashi Shorin Ryu	Doshinkan Karatedo
General Training Approach	"The correct way and nothing else" as general training approach with non-verbal and verbal feedback.	Accepting individual differences as "personal *Do*" while learning exclusively through observation and imitation.
Curriculum and Rank Assignment	Defined curriculum of kata; progressing to the next kata only after sufficiently executing all previous ones. Belt testing and performance standards.	"Open system" of kata; all students are allowed to perform all kata at any time, regardless of skill level. Direct holistic rank allocation.
Bunkai Kumite Combat Training	Using *bunkai*, formal *kumite*, and combat *kumite* in its controlled and its free versions. In combat *kumite* no limitation of target areas or techniques used, but wearing some protective gear and with utmost respect for the training partner.	Neither formal *kumite* nor sparring *kumite*, let alone combat kumite is practiced. Sporadic controlled partner exercises may be spontaneously created and assigned by the leading sensei.

First Major Training Difference: The "Correct Way and Nothing Else" versus "Individual Approach"

The meaning and intention of some basic defensive or offensive techniques in karate may look obvious and self-explanatory. However, it is a misunderstanding that one would be able to understand the full meaning of moves and their intention, especially the more advanced ones, by simply imitating stances and techniques.

There are so many details at work in every move, that a difference of an inch or half an inch in a position, an angle, or execution of a technique can mean the difference between life and death. In addition, in *Kobayashi Shorin Ryu* every defensive technique is an offensive one at the same time, and vice versa. Hence, *repeating something many times incorrectly doesn't make it correct.*

"Keep your own *hara* and disturb the enemy *hara*—this is the essence of all martial arts" (Nitobe 2014, p. 100). *"Hara"* here means the center of the body, which is someone's center of gravity and thus balance. In a more comprehensive way, *hara* is also someone's center of life and individuality. To "disturb the enemy's *hara*," *creating maximal impact in the most efficient way,* is coming down to energy flow, physics, distance, and timing—or, in other words, to body-weight-power transfer, balance/posture, direct movement, locked joints, and bone alignment at the moment of impact.

In *Kobayashi Shorin Ryu* training it is "the correct way and nothing else": there is no training session without nonverbal or verbal feedback from the sensei to correct moves and to make sure that all students apply in their moves the basic principles of body-weight transfer, stance, balance/posture, direct movement, and bone alignment at the moment of impact.

The "correct moves" are correct in the sense that they are determined by the structure of the human body and optimizations of body-weight-power transfer, including the timing of the "explosion point" in every move.

During training, basic principles are demonstrated, verbally explained, and individually shaped in group and one-on-one instruction. Those basic principles are, just to name a few:

- **Posture/balance**: chest up, shoulders back and rolled down, rear back (i.e., locking the body to the arms by utilizing a specific position of the shoulder joint, and keeping the center of gravity centered)
- **Stances/positions**: foot, knee, elbow, and hand in line and "sitting low" (allows stability and optimal body-weight-power transfer; not to be confused with "sitting deep"—see later)
- **Balanced "C-steps"**: crescent leg move and no bopping up and down when stepping (avoids becoming unstable by lifting the body's center of gravity during the move and changing the angle of the hips)

- **"Foot then hand"**: a step has to be completed before a hand technique is executed to ensure anchored transfer of body-weight power into a hand technique, instead of using only the weight of an arm
- **"Elbow follows the hand," wrist flat**: forming a straight line without bending the wrist or elbow (transfers kinetic energy right to the tip-point of impact; bent wrist or elbow allows kinetic energy to "escape" upon impact at the bent joint)
- **Direct moves**: most blocks, kicks, and strikes are direct moves (using the most efficient path from point A to point B, where each move has a starting, ending, and explosion point), whereas most parries, throws, and limb manipulations are circular ones

Hence, the most frequent command *Kobayashi Shorin Ryu* students hear during their training is: "go back!" to repeat and to improve a previous move. This entire process of repeating every move correctly thousands of times creates the correct muscle memory.

During training at the Okinawan *honbu* dojo that the author attended, direct correction dominated as well: the leading sensei directly corrected a deshi's move or posture by naming the correct position while looking at the student, repeating a move while encouragingly looking at the deshi, or physically grabbing and moving a deshi's limb or torso into the correct position or angle.

This is the way the "correct way" is taught today in Okinawa, and it used to be exactly the same way it was taught there decades ago (see photos below); all corrections are clear, directly addressed, and deviations are not tolerated.

The author's training experience in Okinawa overall supports the earlier statement that there is a specific teaching approach in Okinawan dojos, which does not exactly match the traditional *indirect* Japanese way of teaching on the mainland. This mainland Japanese teaching approach is, however, cultivated in the other style we look at here, in *Doshinkan Karatedo*.

* * *

In contrast, *Doshinkan Karatedo* training follows an "individual approach" by exclusively providing "learning through observation and imitation." Neither Ichikawa Isao Sensei nor Ichikawa Nobuo Sensei explained to me the rationale behind a certain move, but always simply demonstrated it. Sometimes, but rarely, they showed the meaning of a

Image 14: Nakazato Shugoro Sensei Directly Correcting Postures of Sensei Noel Smith and Sensei Frank Hargrove

Photograph by Noel Smith

Photographs by Frank Hargrove

Image 15: Ichikawa Isao Sensei (right) and Ichikawa Nobuo Sensei (left) Demonstrating Defensive Moves 1988

move by choosing another high-ranking black-belt as a partner for a sporadic partner demonstration (example photographs above).

In the words of Doshinkan's Honbu website: "Through careful observation and imitation everyone is absorbing as much as possible to the best of their abilities."[3]

Hence, compared to my *Kobayashi Shorin Ryu* experience, there was very limited verbal instruction. In particular, neither basic posture/balance requirements nor bone-alignment at the moment of impact were ever expressly pointed out, and I developed some inefficient postures and moves, which I only (and painfully) discovered as being inefficient later during *bunkai* and sparring *kumite* in my Okinawan karate studies. Those suboptimal positions and moves—for instance, unnecessarily time-consuming and telegraphing head, shoulder, or hip movements, looking up or down instead of focusing on an opponent—were actually and honestly quite difficult to change, since after many years of training they became my "bad habit version" of muscle memory.

Obviously I was not the only one; during training camps we see *Doshinkan* karateka of comparable advanced rank in different postures for the same move; some chest up, shoulders back and down, others not; some using direct moves, others not; some keeping their wrists flat/ straight in line with their arms, others not; some transferring their body-weight power—by using their core energy or *hara*—others not. I never heard these kinds of differences being addressed; instead, the correct form was repeatedly demonstrated.

During this process, some karateka realize that their individual move or posture is not matching the sensei's model, but some don't. Using mirrors, as in the author's dojo, is unfortunately not common in *Doshinkan Karatedo*; however, mirrors provide indisputable "individual feedback" and help tremendously to detect blunders and mistakes in posture and execution of moves. The resulting differences are rather accepted as the outcome of a personal *Do* that is claimed to be "performed it its original sense," allowing one "to develop individuality without having to measure himself or herself with each other" (Bellina 2018, p. 191).

---

3. "*Durch aufmerksames Schauen und Nachahmen nimmt jeder so viel auf, wie er kann*" (https://doshinkan.or.at/; translated by the author).

This sounds like *shuhari*, however, and unfortunately more than a few of the observed substantial variations displayed in training groups the author attended were not even close to matching the instructor's model and instead looked like misunderstandings. Those significant variations cannot be explained by *shuhari,* by acceptable individual training variances within an acceptable range of possible interpretations. It rather seems like a possible lack of understanding of the underlying combat purpose and meaning of a technique. In a real fight, some of these variations would leave a karateka open to being damaged.

To clarify the implicit—and misleading—assumption in the last quote above: in genuine Okinawan karate it is not about comparison or measuring oneself against another either; it is about "correctness" of body-weight transfer, stance, balance/posture, direct moves, and bone alignment at the moment of impact in order end a fight and *to survive life-threatening situations.*

At *Doshinkan Karatedo* trainings, the karateka are filed in rows, where the front row, which is closest to the leading sensei, has the best opportunity to copy and to directly learn from the sensei. After some series of counted technique repetitions, "turn and move to the rear" is called; the first row bows and moves to the back of the group, allowing the next row to be the new front row and to practice close to the leading sensei.[4] To provide models and orientation in addition to the leading sensei, lower rank students are surrounded by higher ranks in whatever direction these Kyu ranks turn to or look at: *hanshi, shihan,* or *renshi* lead in the front of the training group; the next highest rank is covering the back, and the next higher ranks are placed at both sides.

Because of *Doshinkan Karatedo's* different *budo* approach, the execution of techniques to create maximal impact in the most efficient way is apparently not necessary in order to pursue an individual path of personal growth and character development, *and individual effort becomes the main purpose of training.*

---

4. Every move is repeated in a counted setting, which, as an interesting difference from other styles, today is a twelve- count series instead of the common ten- count series. During my trainings in the 1980s, it used to be a ten-series count too; the change to a twelve-series count seems to be Ichikawa Sensei's tribute to the growing number of U.S. *Doshinkan* karateka.

Second Major Training Difference: "Closed System/Curriculum of Katas" versus "Open System of Katas"

We may call *Kobayashi Ryu* a "curriculum-based kata system." There is a defined "closed curriculum system" of fourteen karate katas[5] and thirteen *kobudo* katas in *Shorin Ryu Shorinkan* designed to train specific muscle groups, which progressively include advanced techniques and concepts with increasing difficulty. These katas provide an encyclopedia of moves and concepts for all possible fighting challenges. In addition, there are a couple of basic technique drill-katas (three *Kihon* katas, three *Fukyu No* katas, and *Chi No* kata), which are taught during the first months of a new student's training and regularly performed thereafter.

Other *Shorin Ryu* substyles have comparable curriculum concepts. For example, there are twenty-three karate katas in *Shobayashi Ryu* (Hayes n.d., Vol. 14, Issue 2, p. 16); eighteen karate katas in Okinawan *Matsubayashi Ryu* (Nagamine 1976, p. 103ff); and nineteen in its U.S.-American *Matsubayashi Ryu* branch (Scummings/Scaglione 2002, p. 27). The same concept is used in Japanese karatedo, where Funakoshi Gichin Sensei introduces nineteen kata into *Shotokan* karate with the argument that "it is not necessary to study indiscriminately large numbers of them . . . since the purpose of learning kata is not just for the sake of learning them but for tempering and disciplining oneself" (Funakoshi 1973, p. 9).

In *Shuri-Te*-based *Shorin Ryu* and its substyles, kata is used to develop physical strength and to build up muscles, in contrast to the *Naha-Te* and *Tomari-Te* based styles, *Goju Ryu* and *Uechi Ryu*, where physical training is done before a student proceeds to practicing kata.

In *Shorin Ryu Shorinkan,* a student is promoted to the next kata only after being able to perform the previous one sufficiently with about three corrections left in "no count." This requires months and years of intensive training per kata before progressing to the next one, and improvement, of course, is never ending. This matches the general traditional Japanese understanding of "the path," the *Do*, where students endlessly repeat a move and apply their sensei's corrections.

---

5. Initially being a curriculum of fourteen katas, Nakazato Shugoro Sensei presented later a fifteenth *Shorin Ryu Shorinkan* form, *Gorin*, which he demonstrated at the 1996 Olympic Games in Atlanta.

According to a student's progress, *each new kata is taught by a high-ranking black-belt in a one-on-one setting* before the student joins the group practicing this kata. Every training session is run through the kata system, in counted and in no-count settings, up to the kata level of the leading sensei's decision. All students receive feedback from the sensei on their areas of improvement.

When the group is progressing to the kata above a student's current level, that student is excused from the group to work on his or her corrections, either individually or supported and guided by a higher rank. The student then may be called back later to perform the kata again in a one-on-one setting with the sensei, who, again, gives corrections. Additionally, the entire kata is explained, demonstrated, and practiced in *bunkai* and *kumite*.

Kobayashi Shorin Ryu kata emphasize the separation of moves by a split second to make every move equally strong; speed is achieved by minimizing time between moves without rushing.

Hence, a kata in *Kobayashi Shorin Ryu* is performed fluidly in a rapid, constant rhythm either in a counted setting (every move is verbally called by the sensei, executed, and the student waits for the next count to continue) and in a no-count setting (the sensei initiates the start and thereafter the student performs the entire kata without interruption). Separation of moves by a split second matches Chibana Chosin's philosophy of *doriyoku,* meaning total commitment in each movement, leading to "one technique, total destruction" (Chibana 2006, p. 20).

* * *

In contrast, *Doshinkan Karatedo* may be called an "open kata system." Tomaya Kanken Sensei never considered his *Shudokan* to be a "style"— his argument actually was that there are no "styles" at all in karate as there are no styles in sumo wrestling or boxing (Tomaya 2007, p. 56), but rather a setting to practice all forms of karate. Accordingly, "*Shudokan*" literally translates to "the hall for the study of the way" or, more figuratively, to "the institution for cultivating the way." His intention was to include all karate developments, and this perspective was perpetuated by his *uchi deshi*, Ichikawa Isao Sensei.

Hence, like *Shudokan*, its derivative, *Doshinkan Karatedo*, "absorbs" katas from other styles, and it developed its own forms as well, such as the *Kyoku* series of seven kata, which show some resemblance to *Shotokan's Taikyoku, Heian,* and the *Kusanku* kata series (Funakoshi 1973, pp. 42ff), and which are characterized by large, circular opening and closing arm moves that symbolize sunrise at the beginning (*kamaite*) and sunset at the end (*naore*) to synchronize physical activity, mental concentration, and breathing.

That kata are absorbed from different styles became obvious to me during my trainings in Europe as I personally worked on katas that are essential to a variety of different other styles. I worked on *Sanchin,* a basic kata in the *Naha-Te*–rooted *Goju Ryu* style. I worked on *Naifanchi [Naihanchi] Shodan,* the basic kata in *Shorin Ryu,* called *Naihanchi Ichidan* in *Kobayashi Ryu.* And I worked on *Ananku,* which is apparently named after a district of Fuzhou in China's Fujian province. But it is a kata with debated origin that is practiced in several traditional *Shorin Ryu* styles.[6]

The open *Doshinkan Karatedo* kata system allows the integration of limitless kata, so I am actually not sure about the total number in this style. During every ten-day summer training camp I attended, Sensei Ichikawa Isao or Nobuo introduced two or three new katas to the participants. So it seems like a safe bet that *Doshinkan Karatedo* consists of more katas than all Okinawan karate styles combined—especially since *Shudokan* founder Tomaya Kanken Sensei studied Chinese *ch'üan fa* in the mid-1920s during his teaching deployment to Taiwan and thereafter taught Chinese forms as well. Christian Bellina's educated guess is that "more than one hundred *karatedo* and *kobudo* katas are taught in *Doshinkan Karatedo*" (Bellina 2018, p. 194). This illustrates Ichikawa Isao Sensei's overarching kata knowledge, and allowed him to provide instruction (ibid., p. 194) on:

1. Many classical kata as well as some that have been lost over time, which today are only taught in *Karatedo Doshinkan* . . . learned from Tomaya Sensei
2. Kata that Ichikawa Sensei developed after Tomaya Sensei's death
3. Kata that Ichikawa Sensei modified from their classical format.

The author's position on changing or modifying traditional kata was explained earlier and will not be repeated here. It has to be pointed

---

6. Later I discovered that these traditional katas were modified, supposedly by Ichikawa Isao Sensei. I found out about the change to *Naihanchi* during my *Kobayashi Shorin Ryu* studies. That *sanchin* had been changed I realized during a training camp with the Okinawan *Goju Ryu* authority Yagi Maitatsu, Sensei, 10th Dan, who explained and demonstrated this kata in detail.

out, however, that based on physiological fundamentals and the laws of physics, to create the most possible damage to an opponent in the most efficient way, there is only one correct technical-mechanical way. Taking *shuhari* into account, this correct technical-mechanical use of a technique minimizes distance, maximizes body-weight-power transfer, and aligns bones at the moment of impact—which is inextricably part of the sacred Principle of Never-Changing Kata of Okinawan karate.

The different purpose of *Doshinkan Karatedo,* however, establishes a different path of character development, meditative athleticism, and spiritual health that apparently permits kata changes for a variety of reasons unrelated to combat. These fundamental changes separate this style from its Okinawan roots, from its initial purpose of self-protection and lethality. Hence students are not built up systematically in terms of combat skills, and it does not come as a surprise that all students are allowed to practice all kata at any time, regardless of their skill level and regardless of their current ability to follow the sensei's model.

Doshinkan Karatedo kata is taught in the above-described group setting, not in one-on-one instruction as in *Shorin Ryu Shorinkan.* Everyone follows the sensei's model to the best of their individual ability. Of course, the sensei may break the kata down into sequences that then are separately and repeatedly practiced.

In Doshinkan Karatedo *the most important learning objective is to internalize the pattern and flow of a kata*, though some application of moves may be trained separately in sporadic partner exercises, created and assigned by the leading sensei. However, I never saw kata application, *bunkai*, used systematically during my years of studying this style. All students practice all kata, and as soon as the flow is grasped, they move on to the next one, and their continuous optimization focuses on athleticism and on improving the health of body and mind.

In kata, moves are blended together into sequences, leading up to a final technique; speed is achieved by melting the preparing moves into the technique instead of separating them by a split-second. Hence, in Doshinkan Karatedo a kata is performed in a flexible rhythm with varying speed patterns in a setting where the count itself is not a steady rhythm, but one of varying speed.[7]

---

7. We see different counting conventions in the two karate styles: in *Kobayashi Shorin Ryu Shorinkan* for every count, the word "hop" is used; in *Doshinkan Karatedo* a continuous series of metric numbers is used.

Third Major Training Difference: Minimum Rank Requirements and Belt Testing versus Holistic Rank Allocation

In *Kobayashi Ryu*, performance standards are used for rank assignments[8] and minimum requirements exist for each rank. These requirements include being able to competently perform specific katas per belt; punch, kick, and strike sequences; block/counter, grappling, and sequences that involve breaking free from a hold; as well as throws, take-downs, etiquette, terminology, and history.

A test is administered to one single student at a time. All katas required for the rank in question as well as all basic katas are performed back to back, which not only allows the evaluation of a student's kata understanding but also to check their physical condition as well.

At the author's dojo, up to twenty defense sequences with one-, two-, and three-punch or kick counters, as well as with sweep-throw counters, are to be developed and shaped in detail by the student being tested, who needs to define and visualize attack situations, to think those through step by step, and to come up with proper blocks and counter moves.

In preparation for their test, the student being tested may ask fellow students, preferably *senpai*, to partner up to practice and to conduct dry-runs of what they have developed. The partnering *senpai* are not permitted to advise, teach, or point out flaws; they only act as "dummies"; the creations have to be completely developed and owned by the student.

During their examination, the student who is being tested must explain the attack or other situation they are being confronted with and demonstrate the techniques they will employ in response. Throughout this process, the testing sensei gives feedback and optimizes as needed. In addition to adequate body-weight-power transfer, the presented technique sequences are evaluated in terms of

---

8. At the author's dojo, rank is not as important as it seems to be in some other U.S. dojos, and rank requirements are rigid. For example, and this contrasts with other *Shorin Ryu* dojos, sufficiently performing all *Naihanchi, Pinan, and Passai* kata—i.e., the first ten out of the curriculum of fourteen kata total—results here in a 3rd *Kyu* rank (green belt), whereas this performance level at all other dojos known to the author results in a *Shodan* black belt. Accordingly, if a deshi performs all fourteen *Kobayashi Shorin Ryu* kata sufficiently, this results at the author's dojo in a 1st *Kyu* brown belt, in contrast to a higher black belt rank at this level in almost all other *Shorin Ryu* dojos. The brown belt itself is assigned for a period of several months during which deshi strengthen all fourteen kata, work on flexibility and smoothness, and hone timing, speed, and body-weight-power transfer into all moves.

- **logic** (Is the first technique used an appropriate reaction to an attacker's move? Are the following techniques fluid transitions from the previous ones?)
- **simplicity** (Are the shortest and most direct moves used, or is a student "overthinking" the situation and complicating the reaction?)
- **effectiveness** (What is the target area? Are distance and timing appropriate? Are sequences followed through up to a final technique to end the fight?)

Per a student's or a sensei's application, ranks issued by a non-Okinawan dojo may be re-evaluated by *Shorin Ryu Shorinkan* leader Nakazato Minoru, Sensei, 10th Dan *Shorin Ryu, Shorinkan,* at the honbu dojo for international recognition.

*   *   *

In contrast, *Doshinkan Karatedo* uses a holistic approach for rank assignment. There is no specific test situation created or technique demonstrated. Instead, a student's dedication, personality, and overall demeanor is holistically appraised.

Consequently, there are no minimum requirements, neither physical, nor for kata performance, nor for the execution of techniques; hence neither physical condition, nor execution of techniques, nor fighting capabilities are used for this rank assessment. The entire rank allocation process is based on a student's effort, dedication, and persistence instead.

One of Ichikawa Isao Sensei's first students, Albert Thai Sensei, remembers him underlining that "in the dojo, the beginner is the equal of a 10th degree master, in the sense that if the beginner does everything he can, if he gives it everything he has, then he can be sure that the master cannot do more than is possible for him" (https://www .toyama-book.org/blog). This means that individual effort indeed is the main purpose of training in this style, and ranking is based on individual dedication.

Since all students are allowed to practice all kata at any time, regardless of their skill level and of their current ability to follow the sensei's model, there is neither a specific curriculum to be followed for rank assignment, nor a specific set of katas to be satisfactorily performed for that purpose—though the use of five *Pinan/Heian* kata and seven *Kyoku* kata provides some kind of an implicit curriculum-related pattern.

Initially, until his passing, Ichikawa Isao Sensei exclusively assigned rank, and thereafter his successor, Ichikawa Nobuo Sensei, transferred the right to assign *Kyu* ranks to some local dojo and their leading *shihan*. Black belts, however, remain to be issued exclusively by the leading *hanshi*.

Fourth Major Training Difference: Bunkai, Formalized Kumite, Sparring and Combat Kumite versus Sporadic Partner Exercises

Miyagi Chojun Sensei says that "many people have a misconception that karate is only kata. However, there are four stages, *sanchin*,[9] kata training, pre-arranged sparring practice, then practical fighting training. *Since most people only learn to the second stage, they believe that karate is only kata training*" (Chambers et. al. 2020, p 155; italics are the author's).

Practicing kata techniques without understanding their meaning, intention, and applications are not what kata was intended to be. Techniques all by thesemselves amount to no more than athletic moves that together create a powerful "dance" to create a healthy body and mindset and, perhaps, a form of meditation. The application of kata moves to combat—in other words, *bunkai*—is essential. Without understanding *bunkai*, practicing kata becomes a physical gymnastic exercise, an athletic dance with beautiful movements. This is different from the purpose of what kata was intended to be: an encyclopedia of concepts for combat as laid out repeatedly throughout this text.

In Nakazato Shugoro Sensei's words: "By just practicing *Te*, you cannot learn skills that are needed to deal with the various conditions and changes that can be acquired by encounters with an opponent. These other skills are judgment and reflexes that have to be done promptly, and the position to take when an opponent first presents [*sic*], so that you can deliver the actions" (Nakazato n. d., n. p.). This means that in combat a karateka has to "read" an opponent instantly and correctly right from the start of the fight, and to act as soon as a "tell" of an intended move is recognized.

---

9. In *Goju Ryu, Uechi Ryu, White Crane,* and in some other styles, *sanchin* kata represents the most important fundamentals to synchronize breathing, focus, conditioning, moves, and body-weight transfer (Katekaru 2015, n.p.). "Regular practice of *sanchin* kata conditions the body, trains correct alignment, and teaches the essential body structure needed for generating power within all of your karate movements. Many karate practitioners believe that *sanchin* kata holds the key to mastering the traditional martial arts" (Wilder 2010, p. 1); this is an opinion that shows some parallels to the role of *Naihanchi Ichidan* in *Shorin Ryu*.

In Nagamine Shoshin Sensei's words: "Sticking to kata only cannot be called true karate. As I have always said, kata and *kumite* are like heaven and earth, like the sun and moon, like the front and the back side of things, which are perceived as dualities when in fact they are inseparable. And therefore kata and *kumite* must be studied complementary to each other. That is, the various techniques interwoven into the kata must not only be practiced theoretically against a 'virtual enemy in the air,' but specifically as an applied practice against an actual live human being. By way of trial and error, a personal combative experience is accumulated and finally brings about reflexive techniques of offense and defense at will. This is the final goal of karate as a *bujutsu*" (Nagamine Shoshin, translated by Andreas Quast 2016b, n. p.).

Without realistic *kumite* and *bunkai*, it is impossible for a student to develop an appropriate feeling for timing, distance, or efficiency of moves, nor does it allow one, as mentioned earlier, to identify an opponent's "tells," the subtle signals telegraphing an intended move—let alone the competency to control a fight or to "mentally guide" an opponent.

Beyond kata, and parallel to sparring practice and fighting training, karateka want to strengthen and harden the parts of their body that forcefully connect with an adversary: especially fists and feet, but also fingers, elbows, toes, and arm and leg bones. This is achieved by—among other approaches—conditioning partner drills and by striking and kicking *makiwara*, strong but flexible tapered wooden boards, which are anchored to the ground.

Makiwara is assumed to be a uniquely Okinawan training tool, since the "Chinese book Bubishi makes no reference to the use of training equipment similar to *makiwara*" (Nagamine 1976, p. 250).

The effect of using the *makiwara* on a karateka's fist is amazing: the photos below show hands and fists of two martial artists of about the same height and physical stature, both trained in their traditional styles for several decades, one in Okinawa, the other one in the USA, and both are personally known to the author. We see at about the same wrist diameter a size difference between the two hands and fists of at least 30 percent, where the fighter with the darker skin continuously used the *makiwara* for decades and the other one did not.

Like the founders of Okinawan karate, following senior Okinawan karate authorities—for instance, Intangible Cultural Asset Holder Nagamine Shoshin Sensei—demand that karateka "study and practice *kumite*

Image 16: Karateka Hands and Fists with and without *Makiwara* Conditioning

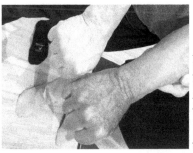

Photographs by Vinh Dinh

(formalized and free fighting) . . . to acquire *ma-ai*, to develop the martial-art sense of reading the opponent's movements, and to develop *kiai* and stamina, which cannot be fully attained through the practice of kata alone" (Nagamine 1976, p. 29; where *ma-ai* means distance and timing, and *kiai* means focus and power).

Performing techniques and kata in a counted setting is a first step to fighting because the count represents an opponent's action, triggering the student's move as a reaction. But, of course, it is not enough to succeed in a fight. "Kata without *bunkai* has no fight at all. And if one can only kick, punch and block, karate offers very little advantage. A larger and stronger person can probably kick, punch, and block harder, even with no martial arts training. Only through a proper study of *bunkai* can kata actually be used for self-defense" (Goodin 2006, p. 18).

In *Kobayashi Shorin Ryu* at the author's dojo, *bunkai*, formalized *kumite*, and a realistic form of *combat kumite* are essential parts of the training. Punching bags are used for practicing strikes and kicks, and the *makiwara* is used according to students' individual preferences. Instruction on the Okinawan way to use the *makiwara*, with specific attention to conditioning hands and knuckles, proper posture, and punching techniques, are given during training camps (pictures below).

Bunkai is demonstrated and practiced in the dojo and during regional weekend training camps. At the author's dojo, Sensei Noel Smith explains and demonstrates the purpose and intention of defensive and offensive kata moves, as taught to him in Okinawa, explains their start, stop, and explosion-points, and emphasizes how defensive moves become devastating blows and offensive moves are defenses at the same time.

Image 17: Sensei Doug Perry Instructing Makiwara Use

Photographs by Annie Banh

Dropping weight when punching was new information for many attendants.

Shifting body weight to put pressure from various angles onto the first two knuckles.

Photographs by Annie Banh

Students work together to understand and to stage the multiple-attack concepts during a kata, thus allowing a fellow student to develop the timing and most efficient technique to block and counter.

As mentioned earlier, the author's Sensei Noel Smith points out that some *bunkai* need to be adjusted for differences in physique between Okinawan and Western builds. U.S. karateka may be taller and their limbs may extend farther compared to Okinawans, both today as well as at the time kata were created. Hence, some kata moves have to be adjusted accordingly for combat. In addition, a taller U.S. karateka faces a comparable need for an adjustment when fighting smaller Okinawan (or other small) fellow karateka; in this case, a lower center-of-gravity is essential, leading to Nakazato Shugoro Sensei's mantra "the lower you are, the stronger you are," which has been repeated by Sensei Smith countless times (it will be proven to be correct through the lens of the laws of physics covered in Chapter III).

A yearly "Okinawan Karate and Kobudo Winter Camp" focuses on eye-opening *Shorin Ryu* kata *bunkai* and concepts, as well as on *Te Waza* and *Te Gumi* techniques. In these training camps, organized by Clint Green, Sensei, 7th Dan *Shorin Ryu, Shorinkan,* twenty to thirty (mostly) *Shorin Ryu hanshi, kyoshi,* and *renshi* from all corners of the U.S. (picture of thirty instructors at the 2018 camp below) teach and share their knowledge.

Other high-ranking *Shorin Ryu* sensei offer other training camps all across the U.S. to teach *bunkai* interpretations, as is done in other traditional Okinawa karate styles too, of course. One famous example is the "Okinawan Karate and Kobudo Summer Camp," informally known as "Little Okinawa," and facilitated by Doug Perry, Sensei, 10th Dan *Shorin Ryu, Kensankai,* initially as a *Shorin Ryu Shorinkan* event, later under the patronage of *Shorin Ryu Kensankai.* Another well-known example are camps facilitated by Neil Stolsmark, Sensei, 8th Dan *Shorin Ryu, Shorinkan,* who for some reason is not shown as an instructor in Image 19, though he regularly teaches at this winter camp.

All *formal Yakusoku kumite* was created to teach students timing and distance in a controlled setting. Presumably, these exercises were introduced later by Chibana Chosin Sensei's students, since he himself "never seemed to teach formalized kumite techniques" (Noble 2019b, p. 22). The author can verify this assumption as a fact for

Image 19: Instructors Okinawan Karate and Kobudo Winter Camp 2018

Photograph by Annie Banh

Left to right
Front row: Jeff Brown, David Colaizzi, Noel Smith, Doug Perry, Clint Green, Pat Haley,
David Ahrens, David K. Johnson.
Middle row: Jay King, Dieter von der Markwitz, Mel Meibers, Peter Polander, Eberhard
Welch, John Carria, Christian Estes, MD, Sean Riley, Paul Cote, Amy Green, Chris Licciardello.
Top row: Tom Ward, Michael Madden, Chuck Harris, Kevin Pleasant, Gene Corbo, Troy Price,
Patsy Callahan, Sam Athye, Thomas Harris, Chris Estes, Michael Kiefer.

Chibana Sensei's student Nakazato Shugoro Sensei, who created and taught both drills, formalized and free fight *kumite*, to the author's Sensei Noel Smith during the latter's studies in Okinawa mid-1960s to mid-1970s.

Formal *kumite* in the sense of formalized partner exercises, is practiced as

- *"Gohon-kumite,"* a traditional structured series of five attacks and corresponding block-counters
- *"Juhon-kumite,"* a traditional, structured series of ten attacks and corresponding block-counters (as Sensei 6th Dan *Shorin Ryu* Raymond "Gene" Adkins told the author, this initially used to be a series of twenty-five exercises taught by Nakazato Shugoro Sensei)
- *"Minoru Yakusoku Kumite,"* a newer series of seven basic and seven advanced attacks and block-counters, developed by Nakazato Minoru Sensei.

One issue to be aware of, when evaluating formal *Yakusoku kumite* drills under the lens of combat, is that these are "developing our ability to be consistently behind the curve in life-protection situations" (Hayes n.d., Vol. 14, Issue 1, Spring, p. 9). They suggest that karateka know what will happen next, and they drill them to wait and to react instead of acting pre-emptively. On the other hand, these drills provide repetition and conditioning and can be an excellent tool to minimize reaction time and to diagnose an opponent's "tell" as early as possible.

In addition to the listed three formalized forms, at the author's dojo *"Suikendo kumite"* is also practiced. This is an arrangement of multiple attacks, parries, blocks, and counters, using *Kihon* and *Naihanchi* kata moves as well as various techniques from advanced kata and combining everything into an "endless" sequence of powerful techniques. Yamashita Tadashi Sensei[10] created these exercises as a training method within his famous fighting style *Suikendo (*"fists flowing like water").

Image 20: Yamashita Tadashi Sensei Teaching Suikendo at OBI Okinawan Budo Institute 2019

Photograph by Noel Smith

Yamashita Sensei (middle) with Sensei Aaron Sumpter (right) and Sensei Clint Green (left).

---

10. (Footnote continued on next page) Yamashita Tadashi Sensei studied *Kobayashi Shorin Ryu* under its senior authorities Chibana Sensei and Nakazato Sensei. For several years he trained together with the author's sensei, Noel Smith, under Nakazato Shugoro Sensei. At that time

Suikendo kumite focuses on iterate, flashing but powerful hand techniques, to be executed with speed, power, and accuracy to hit an opponent multiple times within the blink of an eye, often followed by a final takedown with a lethal punch. The beauty and challenge of these exercises is that "correct" positions (e.g., blocking/striking hand and leg on the same side) are intentionally and quickly altered, which forces a karateka's mind to open up completely and to act efficiently in all conceivable positions. Another important learning objective in these techniques is optimal hip movement to support every technique with full body-weight-power transfer as the result of effective minimal hip torque.

Sparring *kumite* "is the part of karate in which a student trains against an adversary, using the techniques learned . . . the goal is to test yourself against another by putting what you have learned to practical use" (Virginia Shorin Ryu Shorinkan Karate School, n.d., n.p.). This is done in a particular fighting stance allowing unlimited mobility in every direction and "zone defense" for head and upper and lower body through specific arm positioning.

Sparring *kumite* is either trained as combat fighting using full power and speed for advanced karateka, or at 50 percent or less power and speed, allowing lower-belt students to respond, to see a move clearly, to think it through, and to understand timing, distance, and an opponent's "tells," the subtle motions telegraphing an opponent's intention and next move.

The fight itself is not done in the fencing, tagging, and restricting form of modern karate competitions, but in a realistic combat form, where both partners are allowed to use all their empty-hand weapons with no restriction to target areas or techniques—however, with utmost caution so as not to cause any injury. Strikes must be controlled and utmost respect for the sparring partner must be shown (gloves and mouthpiece are mandatory; cups and additional protective gear may be worn voluntarily).

---

both were taught real-life fighting applications. Yamashita Sensei later developed his own fighting approach and became famous for his explosive open hand techniques, combining iterative fighting tactics with traditional karatedo, resulting in his system "*Suikendo*" ("fists flowing like water"). This unlimited sequence of fluid, quick but powerful moves allows karateka to simultaneously block and strike opponents multiple times with speed and accuracy within the blink of an eye. The system is spread worldwide by Yamashita International Budo Association.

As far as the author knows, Yamashita Sensei is one of today's rare senior sensei with extensive real-life combat experience, forged in numerous serious encounters during his employments in the private security field.

This almost matches the way Sensei Noel Smith learned sparring and combat *kumite* in Okinawa in the early 1960s, which was trained there as serious freestyle combat exercise and not as "disarmed" sports karate. Freestyle fighting was a regular part of Nakazato Shugoro Sensei's training sessions; these fights were not restricted to specific techniques or target areas. In those days, the fighters did not wear cups or mouthpieces as it is the case today; so, self-control and mutual respect were of utmost importance.

The goal of free-fighting *kumite* is to learn how to control the "chess game"-like process of a fight, how to set up adversaries, how to use combinations of techniques, including fake-moves, and, most importantly, making opponents do what you want them to do and when you want them to do it in order to finish the fight with one final technique. Thus free-fighting *kumite* best matches the reality of a life-threatening situation.

Just to clarify a potential misunderstanding: what we call a "real fight," combat, or the "reality of a life-threatening situation" does not have "rules" and the differentiation between "fair" and "unfair" fighting does not apply anymore. Fights on the streets are not "fair." The inherent necessity to succeed in such a situation creates a strategy of "the end justifying the means." As soon as any kind of rules are implemented in a fight, an artificial "game," a sport, or sparring situation is created that has nothing to do with life-protecting combat.

At the author's *Shorin Ryu* dojo, students are carefully built up with sparring exercises limited to the use of specific attacking, defensive, and counter techniques and in an "offense-defense" setting before being allowed to fight in the described unlimited freestyle form. In this kind of training setting, one student acts offensively, the other one reacts defensively but can only react with one block or parry and some kind of counter to his offensive partner, either in full power/speed mode or in reduced power/speed mode.

Scientific research supports the great importance of sparring *kumite* to build up superior fighting skills with the necessary "elasticity": the energy needed for a karateka to regain full potential for the next move after a strenuous previous one, which is called "metabolic power," is more effectively trained when exercising sparring *kumite* than when practicing kata (Doria et. al. 2009, p. 1); hence, only by practicing sparring or free-fight *kumite* may a karateka acquire the necessary mental and physical "bounce-back capability" for combat.

Not all *Shorin Ryu* dojos practice sparring or free-fight *kumite*, but the ones led by the sensei generation that was directly instructed by Nakazato Shugoro Sensei do. Only sparring and free-fight *kumite* settings allow the "feel"—the direct experience—of the utmost need for strong postures, for "zone defense," for distance, for timing and speed without rushing a move, and for optimal transfer of body-weight power into a technique to survive combat.

*   *   *

In contrast, in *Doshinkan Karatedo* no effort is made to generate fighting skills. Whereas some *kumite* (in the sense of sporadic partner exercises individually created by a sensei) is applied, but neither formalized *kumite,* nor *bunkai,* nor sparring or free-fight combat *kumite* are practiced. The outcome is two-fold: in sporadic partner exercises students may develop some feeling for timing and distance; however, and as I myself found out the hard way, it does not prepare one at all for the reality of fighting—not even in its "disarmed" sports or sparring form.

Starting in May 2019, a new development may evolve, as *Doshinkan Karatedo* in the USA offered a training camp focusing on "Efficiency in Movement, Effectiveness in Application" (Doshinkan 2019). June Pilcher, Sensei, 8th Dan, *Doshinkan*, who taught at the camp, wrote to the author on April 24th, 2019: "I have worked on applications in kata for close to ten years now. A few others do, but probably not many."

Only time will tell whether this indicates a sustainable development under *Doshinkan Karatedo's* new leadership of Fujimoto-Stock Masako, Sensei, 10th Dan, *Doshinkan,*[11] or whether it will remain another of a few rare occurrences.

Again, based on *Doshinkan Karatedo's budo* approach, it may be possible to grow individually and to improve health, self-awareness, self-understanding, and relationships with others by pursuing a form of athletic and meditative *Do* without any *bunkai* or sparring, or free-fight kumite.

You just will not be able to succeed in a fight.

---

11. "Hanshi 10 Dan Nobuo Ichikawa passed away March 6th, 2019. Sometime before his death, he chose Shihan Masako Fujimoto-Stock as his successor as Hanshi 10 Dan. Receiving the red belt in a ceremony on March 31st, 2019, she became the new head of *Karatedo Doshinkan"* (Doshinkan, n.d.; use of honorary titles as quoted).

Image 21: Systematic Supervised Development of Kumite Skills in Kobayashi Ryu

Photographs by Noel Smith

Sparring-Techniques Are Introduced by Yudansha to Deshi at White Belt Level. Postures and Applications Are Systematically Further Developed Under Supervision.

Conclusion: The Two Ways Lead to Opposing Combat Skills

Genuine Okinawan karate, like *Kobayashi Shorin Ryu*, is intended to maintain peace through an implicit strategy of deterrence, articulated two millennia ago as "si vis pacem, para bellum," and to prepare students to successfully use its techniques in real-life combat while restricting usage of the art to a just cause and developing the superior self-control of a peaceful mind. In contrast, "disarmed" Japanese Karatedo, like *Shudokan* and *Doshinkan*, is intended to develop character, spiritual and physical health, and to optimize personal growth, resulting *in extremely limited capabilities to control an opponent in a real-life fighting challenge*.

Hence, using these two karate styles as representatives of classical Okinawan self-defense-oriented karate and traditional (non-sports) form-only Japanese self-perfection-oriented karatedo, the two should not be regarded as equivalent or as leading to the same outcome. The end results of the two alternative ways are not at all identical; they are significantly different, even contradicting.

Two quotes may shed final light on the author's position on this difference:

1. "When exploring your training, it is important to recognize and accept the weaknesses and strengths of each training method.

- *Sparring* [author's remark: here used in the sense of sports/competition, as "disarmed" fighting with rules] provides contact, but lacks the deeper aspects of karate.
- *Kata* teaches strength of body, mind, and spirit in addition to a full system of advanced techniques . . . but also involves hitting a lot of air. Simply understanding the details of kata is not enough to make a complete martial artist.
- *Freestyle kumite drills can bridge that gap* if both students have enough control.
- Prearranged *Yakusoku drills* can provide conditioning and repetition, but run the risk of teaching students the bad habits of waiting for attacks and relying on knowing what will happen next" (Apsokardu 2010, n.p.; italics added by author).
2. "Though a hazardous fight is legally outlawed, one cannot understand the severity of martial arts before experiencing such a fight . . . martial arts enthusiasts who never fought this way cannot claim the very purpose for their art as it was intended to be" (Oyama 1987, p. 71f.; translated by the author).

It is conceivable that the ambiguity between classical Okinawan karate and traditional (non-sports) Japanese karatedo will someday evolve into a new overarching unity. This would mean that the two approaches would no longer be mutually exclusive, but they could *define each other by contrast and create a new holistic entity together*, like night and day together create a unit of time, *yin* and *yang* together create a unity visualized in its circle symbol. If that could be achieved, then, depending on a student's personal goal and intentions, either of the two options may represent the appropriate path, mind-set, and perspective.

This only happens, however, when both approaches maintain their intended purpose of lethality. Unfortunately this is not the case today; different paths underpin the contrast of "disarmed" Japanese self-perfection karatedo derivatives versus genuine Okinawan karate that aims at protecting life. These two different approaches today should not be confused with each other in spite of numerous attempts to label traditional (non-sport) Japanese karatedo as genuine, classical Okinawan karate.

It is not.

Second Practical Example:
Modern Nekoachi-dachi Modifications Prove
the Superiority of the "Never Changing Kata Principle"

In traditional Okinawan karate styles and their associated Okinawan dojos—as well as in some associated international dojos—sensei who learned the art of fighting directly from Okinawan masters continue to teach the classical self-defense goal of Okinawan karate and reject "modern deviations." In this fighting philosophy, kata alterations are at least questionable and are likely to increase a karateka's vulnerability. The *Nekoachi-dachi* (cat stance) analysis offered in this section illustrates the fact that a "modern" stance or position alteration indeed increases a karateka's vulnerability in bunkai and in combat.

In conducting the following analysis, unbiased laws of physics and mechanics are applied to block-counters. Hence, our approach shares the approach other authors have used to shed light on underlying mechanical-physical concepts when explaining karate techniques and impacts; for example, Albrecht Pflüger in Europe/Germany in the mid-1970s (Pflüger 1975), or Jason Thalken and John David ("JD") Swanson in recent years in the USA (Thalken 2015; Swanson 2017).

To prevent a possible misunderstanding, some implications of the following text need to be stressed here at the beginning:

a) *It is not the author's intention to criticize modern kata modifications*: as a deshi he neither has the competence nor the authority to valuate an alteration made by a sensei, and there are various ways to interpret kata concepts and bunkai. The approach used here, the application of basic physics, allows an option for every reader to reevaluate our findings and to conduct their own analysis.

b) Our results are subjective, as all evaluations tend to be. However, *the objective unbiased "givens" are the laws of physics and the structure of the human body.*

c) Based on these givens, *karateka may use our approach to re-evaluate our results* by executing the stances and steps as explained, measuring their steps, which are based on their individual physiological condition. Hence, all interested readers may conduct their own measurements, do the corresponding calculations, *and then they will be able to draw their own conclusion.*

How Changing the Traditional Low Nekoachi-dachi in Modern Kata Interpretations Weakens Block-Counters

First, it has to be pointed out that *there are no "stances" or static postures in karate*. Chibana Chosin Sensei, senior authority of *Kobayashi Shorin Ryu*, preferred calling them "steps" instead of "stances," referring to the footwork that ends up in postures that most people would call "stances." These fluid positions, focused on hara with all muscles flexed in a blink of an eye, give karateka the physical foundation, the base of support and anchor, to optimally transfer body-weight power into a technique. *To include this dynamic view in our argument, we use the combined term "stance/position."*

There is an ongoing discussion amongst *Shorin Ryu* adepts about whether this style utilizes higher stances/positions compared to other karate styles. A considerable number of opinions point out that in this style, indeed, higher stances (in some cases referred to as "natural stances") are taught and used.[12]

However, in the author's dojo it is continuously stressed how "sitting lower" in a stance/ position transfers more strength and body-weight power into a technique. This seems to contradict the statements calling for higher stances/positions.

* * *

To resolve the contradiction by using the benchmark moves of senior karate authorities, *shuhari* has to be taken into account, especially when watching video clips recorded at a sensei's high age. Referring to our subject, it may well be that eighty-year-old karate masters are not able to bend their knees as much anymore as they used to do in their earlier years. This may lead to misinterpretations by younger instructor generations, who did not personally train with these masters decades ago and now promote higher positions based on those videos.

In this sense, we indeed find a noticeable difference for the same stance/position when comparing Nakazato Shugoro Sensei in his early fifties to his late seventies, early eighties as shown in the photo on the right below.

---

12. https://www.facebook.com/groups/ShorinryuShorinkanGroup/1141276369391137/
?comment_id=1141278946057546&notif_id=1565794718983033&notif_t=group
_highlights; comparable opinions can be found in printed publications (e.g. Clarke, C.
2012, p. 173) and online (e.g. Wikipedia https://en.wikipedia.org/wiki/Sh%C5%8Drin
-ry%C5%AB, or USADojo https://www.usadojo.com/kobayashi-Shorin Ryu/).

Frank Hargrove Sensei, 9th Dan *Shorin Ryu, Nakazato-Ha*, one of the "Original Seven" black belts, actually sees this difference as the core reason for today's "weaker" karate, explaining that "the general quality of the karate grew progressively weaker until now," because "there is one significant difference between the *Shorin Ryu* of the people imitating an eighty-year-old Nakazato (who, after 1999, most have only seen perform on the video tapes), and the strong bujitsu karate of the forty-five-year-old Nakazato" (Hargrove, n.d., n. p).

Image 22: Nakazato Shugoro Sensei Demonstrating *Nekoachi-Dachi* at 53 Years and at almost 80 Years of Age

Photograph by Noel Smith

1973 at OBI Okinawan Budo Institute during Sensei Shugoro Nakazato's visit.

Sensei Shugoro Nagazato close to 80 years of age on a VCR tape.
Photograph taken by the author from a 20+ years-old analog VCR recording.

Hence, in the *Kobayashi Shorin Ryu* style we are referring to, the most authentic training or advice a *Shorin Ryu Shorinkan* adept can receive today in the USA—and in Okinawa as well, of course—is from a sensei who was directly trained *by Nakazato Shugoro Sensei* at the peak of the latter's physical abilities, and, in the USA, who represents the "first sensei generation," called the "Original Seven" (listed in footnote 2).

Five of these legendary masters still teach today in the USA;[13] these are the two Okinawans Yamashita Tadashi Sensei and Shiroma Jiro Sensei, as well as the three Americans Sensei Eddie Bethea, Sensei Frank Hargrove, and Sensei Noel Smith.

Comments to the author by these senior masters, the representatives of the first *Shorin Ryu Shorinkan* sensei generation in the USA, suggest that succeeding generations unfortunately too often neglect the opportunity to ask them for advice or clarification.

These younger sensei now themselves hold high ranks and perhaps developed their own techniques and interpretations of kata and bunkai—with the unfortunate result that traditional postures and bunkai are in jeopardy of being lost in the USA.

*   *   *

Back to the initial considerations on high versus low stances/positions and to our analysis. The statements calling for higher cat stances/positions in some of today's USA *Kobayashi Shorin Ryu* dojos not only contradict the advice we receive from the "Original Seven"; interestingly enough they also contradict the postures/stances/positions common in Okinawa itself, illustrated by the photo below showing a low *Nekoachi-dachi* stance/positions at the 2019 Day of Karate. However, during the author's training at the Shorin Ryu Shorinkan Honbu Dojo in 2019, Nakazato Minoru Sensei continuously emphasized the use of what he called a "natural" stance/ position, and his interpretation of "natural" obviously does not contradict the low stance/position displayed by his student Sayuri Iha Sensei, 7th Dan *Shorin Ryu, Shorinkan* in the photograph below. Hence, the suspicion arises that there may be a potential misunderstanding between the Okinawan and the Western interpretation of a "natural" stance/ position.

Sayuri Iha Sensei[14] shows a *Nekoachi-dachi* shape in 2019 (center of the front row of the photo) that matches Nakazato Shugoro Sensei's position in the 1973 photo above. The similarity underlines that this

---

13. Sensei Sid Campbell passed away in 2008 and Sensei Robert ("Bob") Herten followed in 2020. May they both rest in peace; they will never be forgotten.

14. Sayuri Iha, 7th Dan is the first female karateka promoted to 7th Dan in *Shorin Ryu Shorinkan* history ever. Later, in 2015, 7th Dan Rocky Stolsmark followed as the second female karateka to receive this honor; at the same time embodying the first ever female 7th Dan *Shorin Ryu Shorinkan* karateka in history in the USA.

"low" stance/position does not contradict the requirements for a so-called "natural stance" as requested in the Okinawan honbu dojo. Hence, when referring back to the dispute between high versus low stances/positions, our suspicion of a potential misunderstanding between Okinawan and Western interpretations of "natural" stances seems substantiated.

Image 23: 7th Dan Shorin Ryu Sayuri Iha and other Yudansha Performing at 2019 Day of Karate

Photograph by Vinh Dinh

In other words, the controversy between high and low stances/positions looks like—at least in part—the result of confusing a "low" position/stance with a "deep" one.

The Difference between a Low and a Deep Stance/Position
"Low" positions/stances do not necessarily mean "deep" stances/positions; these two postures are completely different.

To execute a "deep" position/stance, karateka set their feet wide apart and drop their body into a—sometimes artificial—deep posture (see images below; the lower photo shows *Kiba-dachi* and the upper photo shows a deep *Jigo-dachi*).

In contrast, in "low" position/stances, the feet do not need to be set as wide apart (hence they are often called "natural" stance/positions)

Image 24: Artificial Deep Stances/Positions in Kata

and the knees are in a line positioned over the big toes with knee joints bent as much as possible.

The following images of *Jigo-dachi* (horse stance) below may illustrate this difference further. In the more narrow horse stance on the left (knees placed over the big toes), Nakazato Shugoro Sensei is pushing Sensei Noel Smith's hips vertically down to get lower in this stance/position without altering his foot position.

The deep horse stance with feet wider apart on the right is used for maximal stretching during warm-up exercises:

Image 25: Low Versus Deep Jigo-dachi (Horse Stance)

Photograph by Noel Smith

More narrow low horse stance.
Okinawa, 1967, at the Shorin Ryu Shorinkan
Honbu Dojo.

Wider Deep Horse Stance.

To ultimately resolve this dispute between high versus low stances or positions, the author uses the laws of physics and mechanics to clarify how the location of the center of gravity and transfer of body weight combine to make an effective karate technique.

Insights from the Laws of Physics into Higher Versus
Lower Stances/Positions

We apply the laws of physics to an arm middle block/counter, *chudan-uke,* in the *Nekoachi-dachi* (cat stance), as used, among other applications, in the *Pinan Shodan* kata. The image below visualizes the application.

It shows a karateka who has achieved equilibrium by securing the appropriate posture, balance, and locked joints/bone alignment for maximal body-weight transfer into the blocking technique at the moment of impact.

Graph 3: A Karateka's Body in Equilibrium as a Lever Delivering Maximal Strength into a Block/Counter*

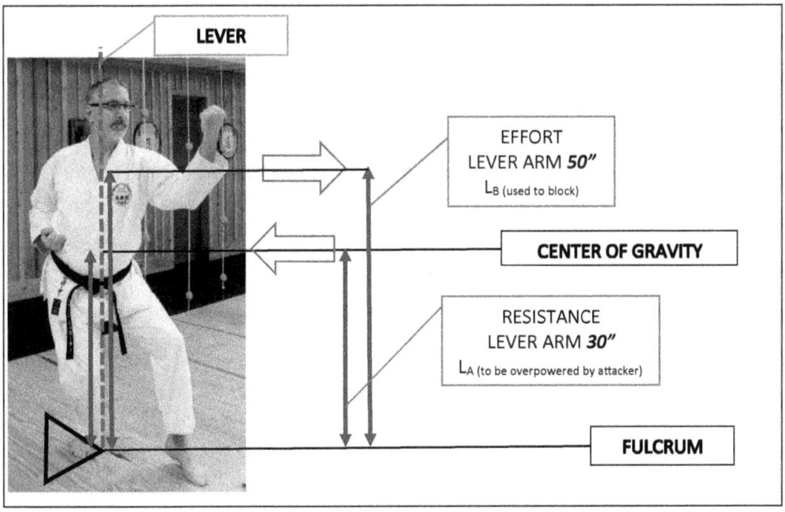

*Explanations of physics terms used in this image are provided in the box on the next page. The assumed lever arm lengths of 30″ and 50″ will be explained later as well.

As soon as the karateka is in equilibrium, both lever parts, "resistance lever arm" and "effort lever arm," are variable through lifting or lowering the position of the karateka's center of gravity via higher or lower stances/positions. All other variables remain constant.

Maintaining balance and keeping the equilibrium undisturbed is the core component, because the entire purpose of the defender's blocking

Explanation of Terms Used in the
Law-of-the-Lever Analysis

Lever : a rigid object transmitting and modifying force or motion when forces are applied at two points.

Applied to karate, the lever is the karateka's body itself. When using the laws of physics, this lever is represented as the imaginary vertical axis through the center of the karateka's body.

Fulcrum: the support, or point of rest, on which a lever pivots. A "class 2" and "class 3" lever's fulcrum is located at one of their end points (like a hinge).

Applied to karate, the fulcrum is located at the bottom of a karateka's feet, making his body a class-2 lever, where the load or weight moves in the same direction as the effort.

Lever arm: the distance between the point of application of a force and the fulcrum. There is an "effort arm" portion and a "resistance arm" portion of a lever.

Applied to karate, the lever arms in play (both representing sections of the imaginary vertical axis through the center of a karateka's body) are:

- the effort arm, used by the defender, from the ground up to the height of the blocking arm's midpoint
- the resistance arm, to be overpowered by the attacker, from the ground up to the center of gravity.

Equilibrium : a state of an object where all the forces that act upon this object are balanced.

Applied to karate, a karateka's body is balanced with appropriate posture and locked joints for maximal body-weight transfer into the blocking technique.

Center of Gravity : the point in a body where all different forces exerted on that body balance each other and its weight concentrates. The gravitational force pushes vertically down onto the base of support.

Applied to karate, the center of gravity lies in front of a karateka's second sacral vertebra, close to two inches below the navel.[1] In a stance/position, the base of support is the space from the outer edge of the feet and the space between the feet.

---

1. A NASA website provides detailed information about humans' center of gravity, used for space ship design with different sized people: http://msis.jsc.nasa.gov/sections /section03.htm.

technique is to maintain posture, balance, and control, whereas the attacker's purpose is to break the defender's equilibrium, balance, and posture (numerous examples in Thalken 2015, pp. 3ff).

Karateka maximize stability to keep their equilibrium in a *Nekoachidachi* by minimizing the leverage an attacker uses. This is achieved by lowering their center of gravity and by enlarging their base of support. The base of support increases by spreading the feet into what Sensei Noel Smith calls a "long 45 cat stance," which simultaneously lowers the center of gravity.

This posture has the body and shoulders turned at a 45-degree angle, shoulders back and chest up, front foot in line with back foot heel, feet set apart rather than close together, knee over the big toes and bent, back hip pushed backward. Another detail: in *Shorin Ryu* the front foot heel is not lifted as high as in some other styles.

Second, bending the knees as far as possible (and then some) will lower the center of gravity even more. The combined result of these stance/position optimizations require a higher force (more weight in motion) delivered by the attacker to be able to break the defender's equilibrium—or, the other way round, the combined result of these stance/position optimizations leads to a "mechanical advantage" on the defender's side, to a stronger block.

This explains our earlier comment about Nakazato Shugoro Sensei teaching free fighting to the author's sensei, Noel Smith, under the premise of "the lower you are the stronger you are." Applying the laws of physics verifies that "sitting low in a natural stance" results in stronger postures, optimal transfer of body-weight power, and speed.

Examples and Mathematical Proof:
The Lower You Are, the Stronger You Are
Here is the empirical evidence and the general mathematical proof to support our statement. We use the well-established "law of the lever" formula that states that at a lever in equilibrium, "resistance arm times weight = effort arm times weight":

[1] $L_A * W_A = L_B * W_B$ *(the letter A is referring to the attacker and B to the blocker;*
  - *hence L_A and L_B represent the two lever arms;*
  - *W_A and W_B are the two weights in motion)*

[2] $W_A = (L_B * W_B) / L_A$ *Equation [1] transformed for attacking body-weight-power to maintain equilibrium*

For formula [2] let us observe the equilibrium of the same karateka in optimal *Nekoachi-dachi* posture for three different center of gravity locations. Let's assume that this center of gravity is initially located 30 inches above ground (L_A), the effort lever part from the ground to the karateka's blocking arm midpoint measures 50 inches (L_B), and the blocking karateka is transferring 100 pounds of body-weight-power (W_B) into the block.

That gives us the "matching" attacking body-weight-power (W_A) in order to maintain the equilibrium. Hence, to break the block, W_A has to be higher than the calculated result (the attack needs to be stronger). The calculation below on the left uses these example figures; the ones to the right are for "sitting lower" in the stance/position, with the center of gravity lowered by two or by four inches, shortening both levers accordingly by two or by four inches:

Impact of Different Center of Gravity Positions on Block Strength

Center of Gravity 30" above ground	Center of Gravity 28" above ground	Center of Gravity 26" above ground
$W_A = (50'' \cdot 100 \text{ lbs.})/30''$ $= 167$ lbs. *Attacking body-weight* *power to break the block:* **$W_A > 167$ lbs.**	$W_A = (48'' \cdot 100 \text{ lbs.})/28''$ $= 171$ lbs. *Attacking body-weight* *power to break the block:* **$W_A > 171$ lbs.**	$W_A = (46'' \cdot 100 \text{ lbs.})/26''$ $= 177$ lbs. *Attacking body-weight* *power to break the block:* **$W_A > 177$ lbs.**
Mechanical Advantage $= 50/30 = 1.67$	Mechanical Advantage $= 48/28 = 1.71$	Mechanical Advantage $= 46/26 = 1.77$

In order to break the defending karateka's equilibrium/posture/balance—more force (more transferred body-weight power)—is necessary the lower the defender's center of gravity is located. Or, the other way round, *the lower the defending karateka is sitting in a* Nekoachi-dachi, *the stronger the block.*

Since in the law-of-the-lever formula, the defender's weight W_B remains constant and the levers come to be shorter by lowering the center of gravity ($L_{B \text{ lower}}$ and $L_{A \text{ lower}}$), the attacking force W_A has to compensate in the formula for these lever reductions; in other words, *the lower you are, the stronger you are* indeed:

$$L_A * W_A = L_B * W_B \quad \Rightarrow \quad W_A = (L_B * W_B) / L_A$$

$$\text{If} \quad L_{B \text{ lower}} < L_B \quad \text{and} \quad L_{A \text{ lower}} < L_A$$

$$\text{Then} \quad W_A = (L_{B \text{ lower}} * W_B) / L_{A \text{ lower}} > (L_B * W_B) / L_A$$

Based on the fact that this calculation gives us the mathematical proof in its general form, the general conclusion can be drawn *that this is true for all stances/positions*, because it is lowering the karateka's center of gravity in all of these.

> "The lower you are the stronger you are" is true for
> all positions/stances.

Low stances/position, however, must not to be confused with deep stances/position: the optimal posture is only to be achieved by aligning the bending direction of the knee joints with foot position vectors, which is, in short, placing "knees over the big toes." This aligns the bending directions of both joints, knees, and ankles without creating any harmful torque on knee joints when getting lower (photographs in the last section of this chapter).

Conclusion and Solution:
Sitting Low in a Natural Stance/Position

As already pointed out earlier, the term "natural stance," though it sounds simple, needs clarification. At the beginning of this chapter it was stressed that a natural *low* stance/position is not to be confused with a *deep* stance/position. Artificial deep stances/positions significantly reduce a karateka's flexibility and ability to move smoothly into another stance/position, compared to the continuous flexibility and ability to move quickly all the way through natural low stances/positions.

The distinguishing factor between "low" and "deep" stances/positions was identified as the knee-bending angle for "low" and the distance between feet placements for "deep."

Secondly, there is not one single "natural stance/position" as such; there is only a variety of "natural stances/positions," depending on a specific situation; for instance, a "natural" fighting stance/position is different from a "natural" forward stance/position. Both differ from a "natural" horse stance/position, a "natural" cat stance/position, and so on. The three common denominators in Okinawan karate compared to modern Japanese derivations in all these natural low stances/positions are:

1. **More narrow foot positioning**—in some cases, especially in *kobudo*, "semi" forms like "semi forward" or "semi horse" stance/position;

2. Placement of the **knees over the big toes**, i.e., paralleling the bending direction of knees and ankles
3. **Knees bent** as far as possible.

At the beginning of this chapter we mentioned that the online discussion among karateka about this difference between higher versus lower stances/positions did not result in a clear majority in favor of lower stances. This is now explained partly, but only partly, by the confusion of low with deep stances/positions. The other part of the controversy results in the simple deviation of today's teachings and kata interpretations from classical versions; in other words because of violations of the "Never Changing Kata Principle."

Neglecting to drop weight by sitting low in today's stances is mirrored in the image below, which shows straight or almost straight back legs instead of bent back legs in *Nekoachi-dachi*. The photo shows black-belt karateka from various U.S. dojos performing kata at a karate training camp, all neglecting to drop weight by sitting low. Instead, all of them display *high Nekoachi-dachi* stances/positions, which today is obviously the most common and most widespread kata interpretation.

Image 26: Today's Common High Cat Stances with Straight Back Leg

Photograph by Annie Banh

Image 22 above showed Nakazato Shugoro Sensei teaching at OBI Okinawan Budo Institute, Virginia Beach, and demonstrating the correct low cat stance/position, with feet apart, knees over the big toes and knees bent as much as possible. His position, which we call "sitting low in a natural stance," is supported by the laws of physics and by our calculations. Students at this dojo today are still referring to his benchmark and show a remarkable difference from the high stances presented in the image above.

Image 27: Yudansha in "Low" Cat Stance at OBI Okinawan Budo Institute

Photograph by Noel Smith

Yudansha Percy Santos, Glen Graves, Sean Schroeder (left to right).

Third Practical Example:
Modern Naihanchi-dachi Modifications Prove the Superiority of the "Never Changing Kata Principle"

Whereas our previous empirical example shows that a defending karateka's block/counter is weakened by a modern kata alteration, our next example will show that with another modern kata alteration the defending karateka has no chance at all to even initiate a block/counter before an attacker's full-blown punch finds its target.

Since the *Naihanchi* kata series (see "Remarks on *Naihanchi* Kata" at the end of this chapter) was taught to the author as "the heart of *Shorin Ryu* karate," his specific interest to look into stance/position variations in this kata arose when observing different postures during kata performance displayed by karateka from several dojos at various Okinawan karate training camps in the USA.

As the two example pictures below show, throughout the performance of *Naihanchi* kata, only two color belts in the front row (on the left in both images) show the traditional *Naihanchi* stance/position

Image 28: Naihanchi Ichidan Postures Displayed at a Training Camp 2020

Naihanchi-dachi with bent legs only at front row left
All other legs straight in Naihanchi-dachi.

Hachiji-dachi instead of Naihanchi-dachi at all rows on the right.

Photographs by Annie Banh

with toes in, heels out, and knees bent, whereas all black belts (to the right of and behind the color belts in both images) display straight or almost straight legs with feet not as much turned inside (with only one exception, a female karateka in the second row on the right with footwear)—even ending up in using *Haichiji-dachi* (far right in both photos) instead of any kind of *Kiba-dachi*.

Further inquiry—communicating with high-ranking black belts from a variety of karate styles, watching numerous video clips of *Naihanchi* kata performance (*Tekki* being its equivalent in Japanese *Shotokan* karate) posted on the internet, and watching black-belt contestants at martial arts tournaments—revealed a broad spectrum of deviations from the *traditional Naihanchi-dachi* stance/position in today's interpretations of this essential Okinawan kata.

The sheer variety of displayed leg-spreads and foot positions, with corresponding variety of distances to be covered when stepping sideways, further sparked the author's desire to analyze how these stance/position variations may impact a karateka's vulnerability in bunkai, because at his dojo it is stressed that only the traditional stance would allow optimal flexibility, speed, and body-weight-power transfer into a technique.

To answer this question, once again basic physics, mechanics, and, this time, scientifically evaluated velocity measurements were applied to punches and steps—which led to the result that modern *Naihanchi* stance/position alterations indeed increase a karateka's vulnerability in bunkai, in a real-life combat simulation.

Repeating the comment posted at the beginning of the first example, the author again wants to point out that *there are no "stances" or static postures in karate.* Karateka fluidly use flashings of positions to optimally transmit body-weight power into a technique.

How Changing the Traditional Naihanchi-dachi in Modern Kata Interpretations Increases a Karateka's Vulnerability

Following Chibana Chosin Sensei's benchmark, who continued to teach *Naihanchi* as the first forms to beginners, when many other styles started with the *Pinan* kata series (Noble, 2019a, p. 44), this series is taught as the first kata at the author's dojo as well—which is an American traditional machi dojo associated with *Shorin Ryu Shorinkan*. One specific traditional stance/position for the entire *Naihanchi* kata series is trained there and variations of this stance/position are not tolerated.

The foot position is shoulder width, with toes angled inwards, heels angled outwards, knees bent inwards, paralleling the feet angle, and "sitting low," thus shaping a specific *Naihanchi-dachi* as a slightly wider form of an *Uechi Hachiji-dachi*. The *Naihanchi-dachi* foot position may be a little wider than shoulder-width, up to the "length of shank plus width of fist" as Nagamine Shoshin Sensei explains (Nagamine 1976, p. 65). This specific position/stance combines:

(a) ensured balance and stability throughout the kata
(b) utmost body-weight-power transfer and strength due to a low center of gravity
(c) optimized flexibility, speed, and low center of gravity when stepping sideways while distributing weight evenly between both legs throughout the entire stepping sequence—hence in the cross stance as well.

Chosin Chibana Sensei, embodiment of the *Kobayashi Shorin Ryu* style in the *Shuri-Te* tradition since the 1930s, shows his specific stance/position in a video clip while performing *Naihanchi Ichidan* (https:// www.youtube.com/watch?v=mkSr5-iM-BI). His benchmark serves here as a first indicator for the correct traditional posture in *Kobayashi Shorin Ryu Naihanchi* kata, and Chibana Sensei's stance/position matches what the author was taught in his dojo.

To further verify whether a possible alteration/modification was introduced into *Shorin Ryu Shorinkan* at its honbu dojo, the author evaluated the same karate practices at its source, in Okinawa.

Confirming Traditional Naihanchi-dachi in Okinawa 2019

On October 24, 2019, the author asked the two oldest *Shorin Ryu Shorinkan* authorities known to him for clarification. Both senior *Kobayashi Shorin Ryu* sensei, both close to eighty years of age, Genka Noritsune Sensei, 10th Dan *Shorin Ryu, Shorinkan* and Asato Sezaburo Sensei, 9th Dan *Shorin Ryu, Shorinkan,* trained under Chibana Chosin Sensei in their youth and later, for another five decades, under Nakazato Shugoro Sensei. Today they run their own dojos and work with Nakazato Minoru Hanshi, 10th Dan *Shorin Ryu, Shorinkan,* who now presides over the international *Shorinkan* association.

Image 29: Nakazato Minoru Hanshi, Genka Noritzune Hanshi, and Asato Sezaburo Kyoshi at the Shorin Ryu Shorinkan Honbu Dojo

Nakazato Minoru Sensei
Chairman Okinawa Ken Karatedo Rengokai
President Okinawan Karatedo Shorin Ryu
Shorinkan
President Okinawa Kobudo International
Federation.

Genka Noritsune Sensei (left)
and
Asato Sezaburo Sensei (right).

Both sensei explained and demonstrated the traditional stance/position to the author with toes in, heels out, and knees bent low, which they called *Naihanchi-dachi.*

In addition, the author observed the exact same stance/position on October 25, 2019, during a *Naihanchi Ichidan* demonstration at the "Okinawan Day of Karate," where dozens of *Shorin Ryu* sensei and their deshi from various Okinawan dojos all showed this identical stance/position as taught to the author at his dojo (photo below).

The author had the same experience when training with Kinjo Kempo Sensei, 10th Dan *Shorin Ryu, Shorinkan,* and Kinjo Satoshi Sensei, 9th Dan *Shorin Ryu, Shorinkan,* two other senior Okinawan *Kobayashi Shorin Ryu* authorities, in their Okinawan *Shorin Ryu Shorinkan Yaese* family dojo in November 2019.

And last but not least, during several training sessions the author attended in Okinawa in October and November of 2019 at the Shorin

Image 30: Traditional Naihanchi-Dachi in Okinawa October 25th, 2019
and at OBI Okinawan Budo Institute

Ryu Shorinkan Honbu Dojo, Nakazato Minoru, Sensei, 10th Dan *Shorin Ryu, Shorinkan* as well as the other Okinawan *hanshi, kyoshi* and *renshi* attending these trainings, displayed this identical shape/stance/position.

The combined result of the author's inquiries in Okinawa is shown in the image below, visualizing the feet position in the traditional *Naihanchi-dachi,* derived from *Soto-hachiji-dachi.*

The correct feet distance for the latter results when

(1) turning feet 45 degrees from *Heisoku-dachi* into *Musubi-dachi,* then
(2) turning heels out, pivoting on the balls of the feet, and
(3) pivot feet on their heels to bring toes outward into *Hachiji-dachi.* After
(4) turning feet on their balls parallel into *Heiko-dachi,*
(5) turning toes in and heels out (two separate moves) settles into the traditional *Naihanchi-dachi,* which is performed shoulder-width and up to the length of the shank plus the width of a fist.

Graph 4: Traditional Naihanchi-Dachi Through Heisoku-Dachi and Hachiji-Dachi

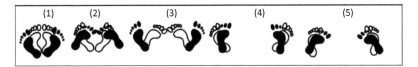

To avoid confusion, we will use the term *"traditional Naihanchi-dachi"* for this stance/ position as explained to the author in the Shorin Ryu Shorinkan Honbu Dojo, where it was called *Naihanchi-dachi* by Nakazato Minoru Sensei, Genka Noritsune Sensei, and Asato Sezaburo Sensei.

In contrast, we will use the term *"modern Naihanchi- (Kiba-) dachi"* for today's altered positions/stances, into which this *traditional Kobayashi Shorin Ryu* stance/position is converted:

Modern Naihanchi- (Kiba-) dachi Variations
The author found those variations in non-Okinawan karate styles, where the traditional stance/position is changed into a wide *Kiba-dachi,*[15] a modified horse stance (image below). The foot distance for this "modern" stance/position is shank-length plus foot-width (not fist-width), considerably wider than the traditional *Naihanchi-dachi,* and is achieved when turning the feet parallel from *Jigo-dachi.*

Graph 5: Modern Naihanchi-dachi as Kiba-dachi from Jigo-dachi

This stance and kata modification is a wide, as well as wide and deep, *Kiba-dachi,* especially in American and Japanese karate-do; one example being *Shotokan,* where the *Naihanchi* kata is called *Tekki.* In his famous book *Karatedo Kiohan—The Master Text,* Funakoshi Gichin Sensei calls this *Kiba-dachi* stance/position "horse-riding-stance" (Funakoshi 1973, p. 20) and uses it in all of his illustrated explanations of *Tekki* kata (ibid, pp. 120ff).

The same *Kiba-dachi* is found in American (*Matsubayashi*) *Shorin Ryu.* Today's (*Matsubayashi*) "Shorin Ryu Karate USA" leader, Robert Scaglione Sensei, who authored the *Shorin Ryu Okinawan Karate Question and Answer Book,* explains that *"Naihanchi-dachi* [straddle-leg stance]" is "the same as *Jigotai-dachi* [wide open-leg stance] . . . but with feet parallel instead of forty-five degrees" (Cummings/Scaglione 2002, p. 71).

---

15. It looks like the term *Naihanchi-dachi* is the Okinawan term and form, whereas the term and stance/position *Kiba-dachi* is the Japanese one: https://www.thekaratelifestyle.com /list-of-karate-stances/#anchor5.

This American *(Matsubayashi) Shorin Ryu* stance/position differs from Nagamine Shoshin Sensei's description of *Naihanchi-dachi* in Okinawan *Matsubayashi Ryu* (Nagamine 1976, p. 65) and was most likely created in the USA by Ueshiro Ansei Sensei.[16]

The picture below shows the most common *Kiba-dachi* stance/position used in non-genuine Okinawan styles to perform *Naihanchi* kata on the right, contrasting with the traditional *Naihanchi-dachi* on the left.

Image 31: Traditional and "Modern" Position/Stance in Naihanchi Kata

Traditional Naihanchi-dachi.   Modern Wide Kiba-dachi.

With the longer distance to be covered when stepping sideways, it is indisputable that all these wider stances/positions have consequences in terms of the time needed when stepping sideways to block/counter an attack, compared to the traditional *dachi*.

---

16. The author bases his conclusion on the fact that the mentioned publication provides a synopsis of Ueshiro Ansei Sensei's teachings, who was sent to the USA in the 1960s by Nagamine Shoshin Sensei in order to promote *Matsubayashi Ryu* there, but separated from his teacher some time later. Though displaying a clear *Kiba-dachi* shape (Cummings/Scaglione 2002, p. 71), this stance/position is called *Naihanchi-dachi* in the American style.

The question is whether this time difference is negligible in a fighting/bunkai situation, or whether the resulting block/counter delay significantly impacts a karateka's vulnerability when using one of these modern variations.

As we will show in the following evaluation, the latter is the case: modern *Naihanchi- (Kiba)-dachi* variations[17] significantly increase a karateka's vulnerability.

Block/Counter Delay When Using Modern Kiba-dachi Variations Instead of Traditional Naihanchi-dachi

For our analysis, we look at a sequence of two steps to the side into a side block, which is from *Hachiji-dachi* with body facing forward and looking to the right (the same sequence would apply when stepping and blocking to the left side instead):

(a) stepping with left foot to the right into a cross stance, then

(b) stepping right with the right foot into the final *Naihanchi-dachi* stance/position in order to block *Haito-uchi* or *Soto-uke* sideways with the right arm.

In our measurements, the width difference between the narrower *traditional Naihanchi-dachi* and the wider *modern Naihanchi- (Kiba-) dachi* was 25 to 30 percent, depending on factors specific to karateka's physiology. This figure should be seen as raw data rather than a confirmed result, and karate-savvy readers are encouraged to use their own measurements to evaluate their personal step difference.

In other words, with the longer distance to be covered, it takes a "blink of an eye" longer to complete the steps to the side when using a wider modern *Naihanchi- (Kiba-) dachi*.

How many milliseconds is this "blink of an eye"? And is its result, a block/counter delayed by these milliseconds, negligible or does it increase a karateka's vulnerability?

To conduct the calculation, we first need the difference in stepped distance (Δ *distance*) between the two stances, where cross stances as

---

17. The author found one more modern *Naihanchi-dachi* variation in some non-Okinawan *Kobayashi Shorin Ryu* dojos and in other *Shorin Ryu* substyles. This variation shows the traditional feet distance, but feet outside parallel instead of toes in and heels out. This specific variation will be commented on at the end of this chapter.

well as the distance stepped is different, as shown below. Using the traditional *Naihanchi-dachi*, this step sequence covers a total distance of forty-three inches in our measurements. Using the modern *Naihanchi-(Kiba-) dachi* for the same step sequence by the same karateka, it covers a total distance of fifty-five inches.

Graph 6: Step Sequence to Side Block with Naihanchi-dachi and Kiba-dachi

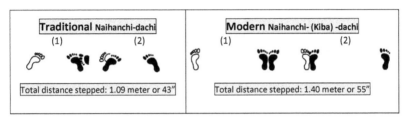

At this point physics comes into play. We are using the well-established *velocity formula*, which is "distance per time," in order to calculate the "blink of an eye" within the parameters explained in the box on the next page. The stepped difference in distance between the two stances is 0.31 meters or 11.8 inches.

> Since "distance is time" when fighting, the first negative consequence of widening the traditional *Naihanchi-dachi* to modern *Kiba-dachi* variations is that it takes longer to step, ergo it takes longer to block/counter.

The delayed defender's reaction time to block cannot be successfully reduced because the block to the side should only be thrown after the defender's foot hits the floor: "foot, then hand," is a basic principle ensuring anchored transfer of body-weight power into a technique, instead of using only the weight of an arm. Arm weight alone in a blocking technique cannot stop a punch from hitting its target when this punch is carrying the opponent's body weight.

Parameters to Evaluate "Distance Per Time"

Points of measure on the karateka's body

Since we only need relative measurements, or step differences (symbol is Δ *distance* in the formulas), it does not matter whether we measure feet inside, outside, or midpoint; we just have to make sure to always use the same points for all measures.

Punch velocity

We use scientific research results presented in academic publications when converting distance differences into "time needed to cover a distance when stepping." These published results are listed in the table below, with the ranges of measured low punch speed up to maximum punch speed.

Punch Technique	Velocity m/sec	Velocity foot/sec	Publication
Front punch forward	5.7–9.8	18.7–32.2	Wilk, McNair, and Feld, 1979
Front punch forward	6.2–11.2	20.3–36.7	Băițel and Deliu, 2014
Front punch forward	About 7–8	About 23–26	Walker, 1975
Hammer fist down	10.0–14.0	32.8–45.9	Wilk, McNair, and Feld, 1979

Confirmed forward punch velocity

Twenty-three to 26 feet per second is the first officially published measurement (Walker 1975) and was later scientifically confirmed by other research. Since there were velocity measurements up to 11.2 meters (36.7 foot) per second, we'll use 8 meters (26 feet) per second in our calculations as a plausible speed for a forward punch. This kind of punch by an offender of average weight (70 kg or 155 lbs) exerts the energy of more than 330 joule (Roy/Ashwin 2014, p. 587), which is in physical terms more than the "work" needed to lift a 70 lb. (32kg) dumbbell from the ground onto a 3.3 foot (1m) high table.*

Concluded step velocity

There is no scientific research available measuring side-step velocity as such, hence we need to plausibly estimate it by using the available results for punch velocity: it is a biological fact that a human arm represents about 5 percent of total body mass, whereas a human leg carries around 20 percent of total body mass (Singh, p 3). Hence, it is safe to assume that a step is not quite as fast as a forward punch. Based on the respective body mass to be moved, common sense suggests that step velocity would be one quarter of forward punch velocity, but since there are different muscle groups at play, we will use the more realistic assumption of step velocity being half the punch velocity, which is half of 8 m/s (see #3), or 4 meters (13 feet) per second.

---

*Work = (mass) times (distance) times (earth gravity) = (32kg) * (1m) * (9.80665m/sec^2) = 314 joules.

The difference in the distance stepping between the two stances is 0.31 meters or 11.8 inches. That gives us, based on our above parameters (step velocity being 4 meters per second):

[1] $step\ velocity = \dfrac{\Delta step\ distance}{time}$ *Transformed for time calculation:*

[2] $time = \dfrac{\Delta step\ distance}{step\ velocity} = \dfrac{.31m}{4m/s} = 0.077$ *seconds* = **77** *milliseconds*

Our empirical result for using the modern *Naihanchi- (Kiba-) dachi* instead of the traditional *Naihanchi-dachi* shows a delay of the block by the "blink of an eye of 77 milliseconds" at the completion of a two-step sequence to the side. What is happening during these 77 milliseconds? One possible bunkai concept of the step/block sequence is to counter a punch to the head, *Jodan-zuki*, thrown by an opponent from the side. The karateka is starting to move into the side-step sequence as soon as he or she realizes the "tell" of the opponent's punch. Before the block hits the opponent's arm, the attacking punch travelled 77 milliseconds, representing a distance of 24.4 inches or 0.62 meter, as shown here:

[3] $punch\ velocity = \dfrac{\Delta punch\ distance}{time}$ *Transformed for Δ distance of*

the opponent's punch:

[4] $punch\ distance = punch\ velocity * time = 8\dfrac{m}{s} * 0.077s = 0.62$ meter

$= 24.4$ *inches*

The block/counter delay when using a modern *Naihanchi- (Kiba-)dachi* variation results in an attacker's fist hitting the defender's head at full force before the latter's block touches the attacker's arm, thus considerably increasing the defender's vulnerability. In contrast, when using the traditional *Naihanchi-dachi*, the karateka's block/counter starts to move 77 milliseconds earlier at the time the opponent's punch is starting, telegraphed by its "tell," the subtle signal allowing a trained karateka to read the intended move.

Other karateka-specific variables do not have any impact on this result, because by using only differences in distance for the same karateka means that we achieve *ceteris paribus*—all other variables remain constant and can thus be neglected.

Our assumption about step velocity may be challenged since we used forward punch velocity to estimate side-step velocity. Hence, we show alternative calculations below for quicker steps (up to assuming steps not taking longer than a forward punch), which all support the argument.

A wider *Kiba-dachi* does not only delay the defender's block/counter, but "the lower you are, the stronger you are" applies in this stance as well. Aligning the bending directions of knee and ankles in the traditional form allows a lower stance/position, which means dropping weight, and thus brings down the center of gravity along the imaginary vertical axis through a karateka's body. The lower this center of gravity, the shorter the "lever" from the ground to the center of gravity, reducing the leverage an opponent can use to break a karateka's balance when hitting the blocking arm (see especially section "Examples and Mathematical Proof: The Lower You Are, the Stronger You Are" in the last chapter).

Based on the fact that our calculation in the last chapter gives us the mathematical proof in its general form, the general conclusion can be drawn that it is true for all stances/positions. In other words, this applies to *Naihanchi-dachi* in its traditional form as well and confirms its superiority over modern, higher stance/position variations

Unfortunately, there is an additional negative consequence of altering the traditional *Naihanchi-dachi* to its modern *Kiba-dachi* variations: damaging tension in the knee-joints.

Alternative Calculations for Higher Step Velocity

For moving a leg, 20 percent of body mass has to be moved compared to 5 percent when moving an arm, which suggests that a step is not as quick as a punch. Just to cover all angles, though, the table below shows alternative calculations, from our starting assumption (step velocity = ½ punch velocity) up to assuming steps not taking longer than a forward punch at all, which still supports our point:

Step Velocity & Reaction Time		*Opponent's According Arm Extension*	
Side-Step Velocity being	*1/1000 sec. to block*	*Meters*	*Inches*
1/2 Punch Velocity	77	0.62	24.4
3/4 Punch Velocity	52	0.46	18.1
Equal Punch Velocity	39	0.31	12.2

Even in the not-quite realistic case of a side-step being exactly as fast as a forward punch, the attacker's arm is dangerously close to the defender's head and will reach its target before the block starts to move when using the modern *Naihanchi- (Kiba-) dachi* instead of the traditional *Naihanchi-dachi*. The attacker's punch already travelled more than one foot, meaning that it has reached its maximum acceleration (Ionete et.al. 2011) at about 80 percent arm extension, thus significantly increasing the defender's vulnerability—even in this hypothetical scenario.

Knee Joint Damage When Using Modern Kiba-dachi Variations Instead of Traditional Naihanchi-dachi

The second shortcoming of changing traditional *Naihanchi-dachi* to its modern variations is that karateka may destroy their knee joints—at least in the long run—when using these modern stance/position variations.

Generally speaking, as soon as a karateka's thighs are pointing in a direction other than that of the same leg's foot, force is transferred along the direction the thigh is pointing and force is transferred along the direction the foot is pointing. Hence, the two forces are angled, pushing into different directions and an unhealthy torque strains the knee joints as soon as these joints are bent. A force pushing into a direction is visualized as an arrow, called a "vector" in physics, and we can use such "vectors" to illustrate the extent of a damaging torque on the knee as shown in the images on the following pages. The extent of the damage done to the knee joints depends on the angle between the vector (arrows in the images below) pointing in the direction of a karateka's thighs in relation to the one pointing in the direction of the foot. The larger the angle, the more damaging the torque will be when bending the knee. However, when the thighs and feet of the same leg are pointing in the same direction ("knees over the big toes"), both forces ("vectors") are pushing in the same direction; bending the knees follows the knee joints' natural forward-bending direction, and bending is effortless, neither harmful nor painful. This fact has absolutely nothing to do with karate styles or kata interpretation; it is solely determined by anatomy and by the law of physics.

In the traditional *Naihanchi-dachi,* the toes are pointing inward, heels outward, knees are bent inward, placing the knees over the big toes as it should be in all stances/positions, thus *allowing karateka to drop their weight as low as possible* by using the natural forward—in this case, inward—bending direction of the knee joints. Being as low as possible in this stance allows lowering the center of gravity, thus reducing the leverage an opponent can use to break the karateka's balance—as well as securing an immediate explosion point when side-stepping by pushing with the stepping foot. This combined effect provides maximal transfer of kinetic energy.

Modern *Naihanchi- (Kiba-) dachi* variations apply a (damaging) outward torque upon the knee joints, contradicting the natural-bending direction of these joints, and limiting how low a karateka can "sit" in this stance/position. Hence, lowering the center of gravity in these modern variations is often achieved by sitting deep instead of low through keeping the feet widely spread, as described earlier and shown in the images below.

The outward torque on the knee joints in these wide stances is quite severe, with 50- to 60-degree angles between the vectors/arrows showing force being transferred along the direction the thigh is pointing and the force transferred along the direction the foot is pointing (lines in the image below).

In contrast, we see parallel vectors and arrows in traditional *Naihanchi-dachi* (lines in the image below)—that is, parallel alignment of thighs

Image 32: Damaging Torque Angle between Knee-Bending Direction and Foot Placement in
Modern Kiba-dachi (upper photo) vs. Natural Bending Direction
in Traditional Naihanchi-dachi (lower photo)
Modern Wide Kiba-dachi

Damaging torque angle about 50 degrees.

Traditional Naihanchi-dachi

No damaging torque angle.

and feet equals paralleling the direction in which the knee joint bends and the direction in which the ankle bends. There is no damaging angle at all in this traditional stance/position.

Similar conditions in terms of a damaging angle are in play in our example when taking the first step to the side into a cross stance. With the outsides of the feet parallel in modern *Naihanchi- (Kiba-) dachi* versions, the structure of the human body completely prevents the karateka from bending the knees to get lower. Hence the cross stance in modern *Naihanchi- (Kiba-) dachi* versions is almost upright, with considerably less weight on the stepping leg.

In contrast, the traditional *Naihanchi-dachi* distributes weight evenly between both legs throughout the entire stepping sequence— hence in the cross stance as well—and the karateka is able keep his weight dropped, or low, relatively effortlessly by keeping both knees bent inward throughout the step sequence using the natural bending direction of the knee joints.

If the modern *Naihanchi- (Kiba-) dachi* is changed into a *Jigo-dachi* (horse stance), as is the case in some karate styles (see photo below), knees can be brought outward over the feet and toes too, allowing one to "sit" low and deep without the damaging torque on the knee joints, shown as black arrows.

The distance to be stepped, however, in combination with the depth of the stance, reduces the ability to move as quickly to the side as in the *traditional Naihanchi-dachi*, so the above calculations about block/counter delay apply to this variation as well.

In addition, the cross stance here remains completely upright too, with almost no weight on the stepping leg (Wichmann 1998, p. 113).

As mentioned earlier (footnote 17), the author observed one more stance/position variation, called *Naihanchi-dachi* by its practitioners too. This variation places the outsides of the feet parallel instead of toes pointing in and heels pointing out (see image 34). It is found in some American *Shorin Ryu Shorinkan* dojos as well as in other styles, and it actually looks like another, not quite as wide, *Kiba-dachi* version. Whereas its stance width matches the *traditional Naihanchi-dachi*, foot positioning and consequently the position of the center of gravity differ between the two forms.

Both positions create a damaging torque on the knee joints, though less dramatically as in the wide *Kiba-dachi*, especially if the karateka

Image 33: Jigo-dachi Version in Naihanchi Kata

bends the knees inwards (right photo below), because the vectors of thigh and foot are not parallel. If the knees are placed over the big toes and not bent inwards, the angle between the thigh and foot vectors even increases (photo below left).

The stance/position on the left in image 34 shows some similarity to a historic image of Motobu Choki Sensei (available at https://en .wikipedia.org/wiki/Karate). Hence, again, and in all earnest, the author as a deshi is neither in the position, nor does he have the competence, nor does he have the intention to question a karate legend. He is simply referring to the unbiased laws of physics, because in this variation it is, again, not possible to drop the center of gravity without creating the damaging outward torque of about 30 degrees on the knee joints (lines), counterproductive to the natural direction in which they want to bend. This limits how low a karateka can "sit" in this stance/position, which may be not quite as low as in the traditional *Naihanchi-dachi*. The

Image 34: Modern Naihanchi-dachi Variations with Feet Straight

| Knees not bent inwards. | Knees bent inwards. |
| Damaging torque angle about 30°. | Damaging torque angle about 15°. |

unavoidable result would be that—though in this stance/position variation there is no delayed block/counter due to stepped distance—the impact of a differently located center of gravity on transferred bodyweight power is likely.

Secondly, in a stance/position with feet parallel, the structure of the human body prevents the karateka from significantly bending the knees in a cross stance as well, leaving the cross stance in this modern version more upright, paralleling this situation with the above-described other *Kiba-dachi* variations.

The author does not have the competency or skill level to understand why this stance/position replaces the traditional *Naihanchi-dachi* in some American *Shorin Ryu Shorinkan* dojos even though the traditional form is still used in the Okinawan *honbu* dojo.

One may argue that the resulting difference in stepping time is negligible; however, we look at "milliseconds"—a couple of 1/1000ths of a second—it takes for an attacker to hit a target full force with a forward punch.

Remarks on Naihanchi Kata

Naihanchi is viewed as one of Okinawan *Te's* first and most original forms. While the composer of this kata is unknown, many say that Matsumura Soken was the creator, who is assumed to have learned it from a Chinese martial artist named Ason. This, however, is speculation, because, comparable to other aspects of Okinawan *Te*, historic documents concerning *Naihanchi* do not exist. In other words, almost everything we find today is oral history. The most reliable sources seem to be:

- Sensei Scot Mertz of *Ryuho Ryu* (*Naha-Te* related karate style) has researched documents in Okinawa for ten years and found that Ason was a guard for the Sapposhi visit in 1838 and taught the kata to Ufu Giko and others. Ufu taught the kata to Matsumora Kosaku, who then continued to teach it. This may actually explain the name confusion with Matsumura Soken. Sensei Scot Mertz provides the evidence to support his finding on Sensei Bob Young's website (https://www.karate4theheart.com/2020/01/nerd-life-origins-of -naihanchi.html; retrieved June 8th, 2020).
- Sensei Scot Mertz interviewed Nakazato Shugoro Sensei in 2012, who states that "Ufu Giko learned Naihanchi from Ason, it was called *Daipochin*. This was in 1838" (ibid.).
- According to Mabuni Kenwa Sensei's statement, who is one of Itosu Yasutsune ("Anko") Sensei's students and who later developed *Shito Ryu*, "We can be certain that Itosu changed *Naihanchi* from an older version" (Chambers et. al. 2020, p. 29).

One view today supposes that *Naihanchi* was initially one single kata and was broken down later into three separate ones (e.g., Donelly n.d., p. 1). This view is not supported by historic evidence either.

Others assume that Itosu Sensei created the *Nidan* and *Sandan* versions and gave the original kata its *Shodan* suffix (Abernethy 2010, n.p.). This view claims that the two newer forms were specifically designed for teaching in high schools (comparable to the *Pinan* series), and hence do not contain the more dangerous techniques of the original first one. Again, no historic evidence is to be found for this view, and it is interesting that Chibana Chosin Sensei considered the third one, *Naihanchi Sandan*, to be the most important *Naihanchi* kata (Noble 2019a, p. 44) in terms of flow, lethality, and controlled hip movements.

"As opposed to some of the romantic stories that seem to float around, *Naihanchi* was never intended for use when a practitioner's back was up against a castle wall. Nor was it intended for self-defense on a boat or between rice patty fields . . . the simple *embusen* of *Naihanchi* that goes side-to-side can be used effectively in three dimensions against an opponent who in all statistical probability will be approaching you head-on" (Apsokardu 2010, n.p.; author's remark: apparently "directions" are meant here rather than "dimensions").

Referring to the term *Naihanchi* itself and to its meaning, Sensei Andreas Quast comes up with an interesting interpretation (http://ryukyu-bugei.com/?tag=naihanchi) which would directly link the kata-name to the traditional term for Okinawan *Te* and thus supports its Okinawan origin:

"As I noted earlier and in fact already back in 2005, the honorific term for *ti* [Te] 手 (ティー) in the Okinawan language was *'nchi* ンチ. Now, usually the syllables of Naihanchi have always and unanimously been considered to be *Nai* | *han* | *chi*. But what if it is *Nai* | *ha* | *'nchi*? It so might be a corruption of the Chinese **Nèif'a** 内法, meaning as much as "inside method" plus *'nchi* ンチ (手), meaning "(martial) skill." *'nchi* means *ti* 手.

"In any case, while it is impossible to prove this right, it is also impossible to prove this wrong. However, as long as it cannot be proven wrong, logic says it is also impossible to prove any other option to be solely right." (Quast 2017, p. 1; bolded by the author).

So, in summation, if a stance/position increases a defending karate-ka's vulnerability in any way, it is hard to make an argument for techniques that carry this vulnerability, and to adhere to the Principle of Never-Changing Kata seems to be the better option.

Consolidated Deduction from Empirical Evidence and Final Thoughts

The difference in purpose between self-/life-protecting classical Okinawan karate and traditional (non-sports) self-perfecting Japanese karatedo leads to training and emphasis differences, which were illustrated by comparing and contrasting *Doshinkan Karatedo,* as the representation of a traditional, "disarmed" Japanese non-sports approach, and *Kobayashi Shorin Ryu,* as the representation of classical, genuine Okinawan karate.

The analysis shows that modifications of Okinawan karate in Japanese karatedo do not only alter purpose, philosophy, kata, techniques, and lethality of genuine Okinawan karate, but that they actually increase a karateka's vulnerability in non-sports-real-life combat and that they are counterproductive in a real fight.

Applying the laws of physics shows that today's higher, wider, and deeper (not to be confused with "lower") stance/position variations not only violate the battle- and street-fight-proven Principle of Never-Changing Kata, but that they rather serve the purpose of athletic-gymnastic exercises or competition showmanship instead of being successful applications in combat, thus contrasting with the lethal Okinawan karate's purpose of self-protection.

These variations of techniques support the philosophical approach and purpose of Japanese karatedo, i.e., character development and self-perfection, specifically health-related self-perfection. Though (mainland) Japanese karate may provide spectacular moves at karate tournaments, many of these moves are ineffective, hazardous, and self-damaging in combat.

Increased vulnerability as one outcome of modern technique modifications is empirically verified by elementary physics and mechanics, which are applied to two standard karate stances/positions. Though the presented approach is not the only way to look at kata alterations, based on the given laws of physics, on mechanics, anatomy, and the given of their individual body structure, every karateka may use our approach to evaluate their personal physiological condition, may conduct their own measurement of stances/positions and steps, do their own calculations, and will be able to draw their own conclusion to verify our reasoning.

The combined results show the superiority of the Never Changing Kata Principle in Okinawan karate over modern karate kata alterations and modifications.

The two karatedo paths of self-protection and self-perfection may complement each other, which was emphasized by many karate masters in history, because in all martial arts training honing techniques and physical development is closely related with—and cannot be separated from—mental and spiritual development. Surface contradictions between these two karatedo paths may form a new overarching unity, not mutually exclusive but defining each other in contrast to create a new holistic entity together. This only happens, however, when both approaches *maintain their intended purpose of lethality*. Unfortunately this is not always the fact today; different paths underpin the contrast of "disarmed" Japanese karate-derivatives versus genuine Okinawan karate, and result in the fact that, in spite of numerous attempts to claim *dentou* Okinawan karate as Japanese martial arts, Okinawan and Japanese karatedo remain two relatively separated entities today—which is an unfortunate situation without an easy resolution in sight.

The purpose of classical Okinawan karate as a *lethal martial art, and therefore its original intention*, should not be sacrificed for the artificial creation of new techniques or kata modifications which then are incorrectly declared as being traditional and original.

However, modern karate developments, like form-only-based self-perfection karate as well as sports karate, do have their own benefits and merits, and there is no reason to question their existence and role. There is no need either to create new philosophical superstructures for these modern derivations, like there is no need to link today's sports of javelin or fencing to a warrior's combat education centuries ago.

In contrast, *dentou Okinawan karate's origin, tradition, and genuine form*, as part of the island's sub-cultural heritage and sub-cultural identity, *is embodying value in itself as a cultural symbol*.

Hence, we face three entities in today's world of karate, *each one with legitimate, but different reasons to exist*, which should not be confused with each other (based on Hayes n.d., Vol. 6, Spring, p. 10),

- **"modern"** sport oriented karate
- **"traditional"** Japanese karatedo as form-only based *self-perfection* arts
- **"classical"** Okinawan karate-jutsu as form-, principle-, and application-based *self-/life-protection* art

Hence, it would make sense to alter the current practice of using the same term "karate" for all its three variations, and to assign different terms to these three karate variations.

LIST OF ABBREVIATIONS

AAU	Amateur Athletic Union
CFA	*Classical Fighting Arts* magazine
et al.	Latin, meaning "and others"; used to shorten a lists of co-author names when referencing
FAJKO	Federation of All Japan Karate (predecessor of JKF)
GAISF	Global Association of International Sports Federation
ibid.	Latin, meaning "same location"; used to reference an immediately before quoted source
i.e.	Latin, meaning "that is"; used to introduce an elaboration on something that has already been stated
IOC	International Olympic Committee
JKF	Japan Karate Federation, aka. Japan Karatedo (or Karatedo) Federation
ISKA	International San Ten Karate Association founded by Sensei Vincent Cruz 1979
MMA	Mixed Martial Arts
n. d.	"No publication date available"; used when referencing (internet) publications
n. p.	"No page numbers available"; used when referencing (internet) publications
OBI	Okinawan Budo Institute—Old School of Martial Arts, Virginia Beach, VA, USA
ODKS	Okinawa Dentou Karatedo Shinkokai; or "Okinawan Traditional Karatedo Association"
OKIC	Okinawa Karate Information Center within the Okinawan Karate Kaikan
OPG	Okinawan Prefectural Government
OTKLB	Okinawa Traditional Karate Liaison Bureau
publ.	"Publishers"; used to distinguish authors from publishers in references

sic	Latin, meaning "thus"; used to indicate that something unconventionally written is intentionally being left as it was in the original
SMAA	Shudokan Martial Arts Association
UNESCO	United Nations Educational, Scientific, and Cultural Organization
WKF	World Karate Federation
WWII	Second World War 1939–1945

EXPLANATIONS OF ASIAN TERMS

Explanations of Asian terms are provided in the text when used for the first time. In addition, and especially for our readers who are not as familiar with karate and martial arts, they are alphabetically listed here again for quick orientation.

Asian terms are complex and cover several facets. The explanations below are kept short and focused on a term's connotation as referred to in the text.

B

Bo	Staff, about six feet long, used as a weapon in *kobudo*.
Bubishi	Name of an ancient Chinese work on martial arts and traditional medicine.
Budo	Japanese term for modern Japanese sports martial arts derivatives from *bujutsu*.
Bujutsu or jujutsu	"Warrior skills"; term for traditional martial arts on ancient mainland Japan.
Bunkai	Application of kata moves and concepts in combat.
Bushido	Moral code for a samurai's attitudes, behavior, and lifestyle.

C

Ch'üan fa	Ancient term for traditional Chinese empty hand martial art.
Chi, Qi or Ki	Asian terms for the natural energy of the universe flowing through everything.
Chudan	Solar plexus level; often called "middle" in a karate move.
Chudan-uke	"Middle block"; in karate, a defending arm move using a forearm's radius bone.

D

Dachi	Stance/position in karate.
Daimyo	Feudal vassals of a Shogun in ancient Japan.
Dan	Ten black-belt ranks in martial arts; used to designate levels of proficiency.
Deshi	Student of an art.
Dentou or dento	Genuine, original.
Do	Never ending "way" or "path" of continuous improvement.
Dojo	Training hall.
Doriyoky	Hard work with total commitment.
Doshinkan	"Hall to study the way of the heart"; a Japanese karate style created by Ichikawa Isao in the 1960s based on the teachings of Tomaya Kanken's *Shudokan* (around 1930).

E, F

Eku	Often used term for an oar, about six feet long, used as a weapon in *kobudo*.
Fukyu (kata)	"Something to be spread and shared"; in karate a "*Fukyu* kata" is a basic kata of a style.

G

Gaijin or gaigene	Non-Japanese foreigner; has somewhat negative connotations.
Gedan	Lower-body level; often called "low" in a karate move.
Gedan-barai (uke)	"Low block"; an arm technique in karate to block the lower part of one's body.
Gi	Martial arts uniform worn during training and performance, traditionally white in karate.
Goju Ryu	Officially recognized umbrella karate style in Okinawa; created by Miyagi Chojun around 1930 based on the teachings of Higaonna Kanryo around 1870; literally "hard-soft-style."
Gojushiho	Name of a kata practiced in Okinawan karate.

H

Hachiji-dachi	"Natural stance"; an upright position in karate with feet shoulder-width apart and angled naturally.
Haito	"Knife-hand"; cutting move in karate with the edge of the hand at its thumb side.
Hanshi	Honorary title meaning "master, "most senior teacher," and "teacher of teachers"; used in many martial arts for the top few instructors of that style, sometimes translated as "Grand Master"; in many karate styles awarded to tenth Dan; in some styles to 9th Dan as well.
Heian	Name of a kata series in Japanese *Shotokan* karate created by Funakoshi Gichin as a modification of the Okinawan *Pinan* kata series.
Heiko-dachi	Comparable to *jigo-dachi,* "horse stance"; a karate position like riding a horse with feet set wide apart, knees bent, but feet parallel, not angled, and pointing forward.
Heisoku-dachi	An upright position in karate with feet placed parallel together; in some styles this is the "bow position."
Hiki	Ryukyu Islands' royal government organization under King Sho Shin in the 16th century.
Honbu dojo	Martial arts style's administrative headquarters and central training hall.
Honto	"Real," "true"; here, essence of kata concepts.

I, J

Ichidan	See *Shodan.*
Ichigeki hissatsu	The martial arts ideal of killing with a single blow.
Isshin Ryu	Karate substyle of *Shorin Ryu* in Okinawa (with considerable *Goju Ryu* elements); created by Tatsuo Shimabuku in the 1950s.
Jigo-/Jigotai-dachi	"Horse stance"; a karate position like riding a horse with feet set wide apart, knees bent, and feet pointing outward, angled in line with thighs.

Jo	Mid-sized staff up to 5 feet long, used as a weapon in *kobudo*.
Judan	Head-level; often called "high" in a karate move.
Jutsu	"Science of an art"; general Japanese term for combat martial arts.
Jujutsu	"Warrior skills"; traditional martial arts on ancient mainland Japan focused on grappling, pinning, joint locks, and throws, using attackers' energy against them.

K

Kama	Sickle used as a weapon in *kobudo*.
Kamaite	"Get ready" or "in position"; a command used in karate.
Karate	Japanese martial art, created and developed in Okinawa as the renaming of *Te* and *Tode*, the genuine fighting arts of the Ryukyus; initially meaning "China-hand," to be altered later to "open-hand."
Karatedo	Path of continuously practicing karate to combine physical, mental, and spiritual development.
Karateka	Karate practitioner (singular and plural).
Kata or gata	Standardized series of defending and attacking moves; literally meaning "form."
Kenpo	"Fist method"; traditional Okinawan martial art related to Chinese boxing.
Ki	See *Chi*.
Kiba-dachi	"Straddled leg stance" in Japanese karate, comparable to *heiko-dachi*.
Kihon (kata)	"Basic"; in karate a "*Kihon* kata" is a combination of fundamental moves.
Kyoku	Name of a kata series in *Doshinkan* Karatedo.
Kobayashi Ryu	Other word for the karate style of *Shorin Ryu*; created by Chibana Chosin in Okinawa around 1930 based on the teachings of Matsumura Sokon (around 1840) and Itosu Anko (around 1900).
Kobudo	Using everyday tools and trade equipment as extensions of the body in karate.

Kohai	"More junior student"; in this context, seniority refers to membership in the same organization, not to age.
Kokusaidori	Main street in central Naha, Okinawa, Japan.
Koryu	"Old school"; a Japanese term for any kind of traditional arts.
Kumite	Partner exercises; used in karate as formal drills or as sparring or free-fighting combat.
Kung-fu or gonfu	Modern term for Chinese empty-hand martial art.
Kyoshi	Honorary title meaning "polished senior teacher"; in some karate styles awarded to 7th and 8th Dan; in others awarded to sixth Dan and above.
Kyu	Ten colored (initially all white) belt ranks below the ten black-belt Dan ranks in karate and other martial arts to designate various levels or degrees of proficiency or experience.

M

Machi dojo	Privately owned dojo in Okinawa where traditional martial arts are taught and preserved.
Mae-geri	Forward kick; foot/leg technique used in karate.
Makiwara	Strong but flexible tapered wooden board, anchored to the ground and hit by karateka for hand, arm, foot, and leg conditioning.
Matsubayashi Ryu	Karate substyle of *Shorin Ryu* in Okinawa created by Nagamine Shoshin after WWII; the term is derived from kanji of *Shuri-Te* and *Tomari-Te* masters Matsumura/Matsumora.
Morote	Using one hand/arm to support the other one in a karate technique.
Musubi-dachi	An upright position in karate with heels together and feet open at a 45-degree angle; in many styles this is the "bow position."

N

Naihanchi	Name of a traditional Okinawan kata series that today has three forms.

Naihanchi-dachi	"Straddled leg stance" in Okinawan karate.
Naore	"Return to the starting position"; in some karate styles used as a command at the end of a kata performance.
Nekoachi-dachi	"Cat stance"; a position in karate with most of the weight on the back leg and bent knees.
Nukite	"Spear-hand"; a thrust move in karate with extended fingers tightly compressed together.
Nunchaku	String- or chain-connected short wooden pieces used as a weapon in *kobudo*.
Nunte Bo	Harpoon/boathook used as a weapon in *kobudo*.

O, P, Q

Obi	Belt worn by martial arts practitioners.
Okuden	A certain level of advanced training in Japanese arts.
Omote	"Outside" or "surface" of something. Here, the obvious application of a kata concept.
Pangainun Ryu	Initial name of an Okinawan karate style later renamed *Uechi Ryu*. Created by Uechi Kanbun in the early 1920s based on Okinawan *Te* and Chinese martial arts.
Pinan	"Peaceful (mind) and (stay) safe"; name of a karate kata series of five forms created by Itosu Anko around 1900 for educational purposes in the public school system.
Qi	See *Chi*.

R

Rei	"Bow and show respect"; used as a command in martial arts ceremonies.
Renshi	Honorary title meaning "polished Instructor." Skilled or expert teacher. Awarded in karate to fourth Dan and above.
Ryu	"School" or "system"; term used when naming martial arts styles.

S

Samurai	Military nobility and officer caste of medieval and early modern Japan from the twelfth century until their abolition in the 1870s.
Sanchin (kata)	Basic kata in some karate styles representing the most important fundamentals to synchronize breathing, focus, conditioning, moves, and body-weight transfer.
Satsuma	Southern Japanese former province led by the Shimazu clan that increased its feudal domain by invading and occupying the Ryukyus.
Seibukan	Karate substyle of *Shorin Ryu* in Okinawa created by Shimabukuro Zenryo in the 1960s.
Senpai	"Senior student"; in this context, seniority refers to membership in the same organization, not to age.
Sensei	General term for "teacher," "mentor"; not reserved for teachers of a particular Japanese art; doctors, lawyers, and certain other professionals may receive this designation too.
Shihan	Honorary title meaning "chief instructor." In some Japanese karate styles used as 9th Dan rank below Hanshi, in others it is not related to rank.
Shitei/seitei (kata)	Form/kata created in the early 1980s by JKF, based on traditional Okinawan forms as a prerequisite for karateka to qualify for JKF-facilitated tournaments. Used until 2013.
Shito Ryu	Officially recognized karate style on mainland Japan created by Mabuni Kenwa around 1935.
Shobayashi Ryu	Karate substyle of *Shorin Ryu* in Okinawa created and named by Shimabukuro Eizo around WWII.
Shogun	Historical term for Japan's military commander.
Shodan	First level; used to name a kata or rank level in karate.
Shomen	'Font'; in karate the dojo wall where symbols, flags, and sensei portraits are displayed.
Shorin Ryu	Officially recognized umbrella karate style in Okinawa based on the teachings of Matsumura

	Sokon around 1840, Shuri-Te, and Itosu Anko around 1900; literally "small forest style."
Shotokan	Officially recognized karate style on mainland Japan created by Funakoshi Gichin in the mid 1920s; named by Funakoshi's students sometime later.
Shudokan	"Hall to study the way"; a Japanese karate style created by Toyama Kanken in the 1930s.
Shuhari	Japanese martial arts concept that describes the stages of learning to mastery. In this context, used to explain individual training variances within an acceptable range of possible interpretations.
Shuto	"Knife-hand"; cutting move in karate with the edge of the hand below the pinky finger.
Soto-deshi	Student of an art who lives outside of a dojo.
Soto-uke	"Outside block"; in karate, a "middle" defending arm move using the forearm's ulna bone.
Suikendo	"Fists flowing like water"; a karate fighting style created by Yamashita Tadashi.

T

Tai Chi	A so-called "internal" Chinese martial art, having spiritual, mental, and qi-related aspects, practiced for defense training, health benefits, and meditation. An "external" martial art focuses more on physical aspects.
Tanbo	Short staff, about four feet long, used in *kobudo*.
Taikyoku	Name of a kata series used in several karate styles.
Te or Ti	Traditional Okinawan weaponless fighting art; literally meaning "hand."
Tekki	Name of a kata series in Japanese *Shotokan* karate created by Funakoshi Gichin as a modification of Okinawan *Naihanchi kata*.
Tekko	Net-hauling tool or modified horseshoes used as weapons in kobudo.
Tode	Renaming of "*Te*"; literally meaning "China hand."

Tonfa	Wooden handle used as weapon in kobudo.
Tsuki	Fist strike, punch; attack move in karate.

U, V, W

Uchi deshi	Full-time live-in student of an art at a dojo; literally "inside student."
Uchinaguchi	Native language on the Ryukyu islands.
Uechi Ryu	Officially recognized umbrella karate style in Okinawa created by Uechi Kanbun around 1900 based on Okinawan ^and Chinese martial arts.
Uechi-Hachiji-Dachi	"Inward natural stance"; an upright position in karate with feet less than shoulder-width apart, toes pointing inward and knees bent inward.
Uke	"Block"; a defending move with the arm in karate using the forearm bones.
Ura	"Back" or "behind." A side that is hidden from view; here, the hidden aspect of kata concepts.
Wado Ryu	Officially recognized karate style on mainland Japan created by Otsuka Hironori around 1935.

Y

Yakusoku	In the karate context used here it means "arrangement," "engagement," and, more specifically, "partner exercises" or "partner drills."
Yin / yang	Asian concept of dualism, describing how opposite or contrary forces may be complementary and interconnected in the natural world, defining each other by contrast and thus creating an overarching entity of mutual interdependence.
Yudansha	Martial artists holding Dan (black belt) ranks in karate or in other martial arts. (Singular and plural.)
Yumaru	Spirit of caring and helping one another in Okinawa.

LIST OF PHOTOS (P), TABLES (T) AND GRAPHS (G)

Title	P	T	G	Page
Shorin Ryu Shorinkan Honbu Dojo 1967 and 2019	X			8
Correct (and Incorrect) Fist Position for Bo Forward Strike Compared to Empty Hand Forward Punch	X			12
Correct (and Incorrect) Fist Position for Bo Outside Block Compared to Empty Hand Outside Block	X			13
Example of a Possible "Intent Time Line" Developing During a Real-Life Attack			X	19
Officially Recognized Karate Styles in Mainland Japan and in Okinawa		X		24
Officially Recognized Karate Styles in Okinawa and Mainland Japan			X	27
Nakazato Shugoro Sensei Correcting Sensei Noel Smith, 1967	X			39
Noel Smith Sensei, 8th Dan Shorin Ryu, Shorinkan	X			43
Shisa Figures at Shuri Castle Gate	X			49
Shisa Figures at the Shureido Karate Gear Store Entrance	X			49
Days of Karate in Naha/Okinawa 2019: Okinawan Masters after Demonstrating Kata at the Karate Kaikan, Oct 24	X			51
Okinawan Karate Intangible Cultural Asset Holders 1997–2020		X		53
Karate Kaikan and Budokan in Naha, Okinawa	X			55
Okinawan Masters Sent to the USA in 2017 by the Okinawa Prefecture Government to Promote Dentou Okinawan Karate Internationally	X			56
Okinawa Masters Seminar Attendants in Washington, DC—November 2017	X			57
Initial and Altered "Chambered" Fist Position Examples in Kobayashi Shorin Ryu	X			67
Kata Moves and Hidden Concepts (Iceberg Analogy)			X	73
"Schuhplattler" Dance—Example of an Intangible Bavarian Subcultural Heritage within Germany	X			79
"Eisa" Dance—Example of an Intangible Okinawan Sub-Cultural Heritage within Japan	X			80
Different Training Opening Etiquette in Japanese and Okinawan Karate		X		95
Different Training Closing Etiquette in Japanese and Okinawan Karate		X		96
Core Variances of Training Practices Between Kobayashi Ryu and Doshinkan		X		98
Nakazato Shugoro Sensei Directly Correcting Postures of Sensei Noel Smith and Sensei Frank Hargrove	X			101
Ichikawa Isao Sensei and Ichikawa Nabuo Sensei Demonstrating Defensive Moves	X			102
Karateka's Hands/Fists with and without Makiwara Conditioning	X			113
Sensei 10th Dan Shorin Ryu Doug Perry Instructing Makiwara Use	X			114
Sensei 10th Dan Shorin Ryu Doug Perry Instructing Knuckle Conditioning	X			115
Instructors at Okinawan Karate and Kobudo Winter Camp 2018	X			117
Yamashita Tadashi Sensei Teaching Suikendo 2019 at OBI Okinawan Budo Institute	X			118

173

Title	P	T	G	Page
Systematic Supervised Development of Kumite Skills in Kobayashi Ryu	X			122
Nakazato Shugoro Sensei Demonstrating Nekoachi-Dachi at 53 Years and Almost 80 Years of Age	X			126
Sayuri Iha Sensei and Shorin Ryu Shorinkan Yudansha at 2019 Day of Karate	X			128
Artificial Deep Stance/Position in Kata	X			129
Low Versus Deep Jigo-Dachi (Horse Stance)	X			130
A Karateka's Body in Equilibrium as a Lever to Deliver Maximal Strength into a Block/Counter			X	131
Explanation of Terms Used in the Law-of-the-Lever Analysis		X		132
Impact of Different Center of Gravity Positions on Block/Counter Strength		X		134
Today's Common High Cat Stances with Straight Back Leg	X			136
Yudansha in "Low" Cat Stance at OBI Okinawa Budo Institute	X			137
Naihanchi Ichidan Postures Displayed at a Training Camp 2020	X			138
Nakazato Minoru, Hanshi, Genka Noritsune, Hanshi, and Asato Sezaburo, Kyoshi at the Shorin Ryu Shorinkan Honbu Dojo in Okinawa	X			141
Traditional Naihanchi-Dachi in Okinawa and at OBI Okinawan Budo Institute	X			142
Traditional Naihanchi-Dachi Derived from Heisoku-Dachi via Hachiji-Dachi			X	143
"Modern Naihanchi-Dachi" as Kiba-Dachi Derived from Jigo-Dachi			X	144
Traditional and "Modern" Wide and Deep Positions/Stances in Naihanchi Kata	X			145
Step Sequence to Block with Traditional Naihanchi-dachi and Modern Kiba-dachi			X	147
Parameters to Evaluate "Distance per Time"		X		148
Alternative Calculations for Higher Step Velocity		X		151
Damaging Torque-Angles Between Knee-Bending Direction and Foot Placement in Modern Kiba-Dachi vs. Natural Bending Direction in Traditional Naihanchi-Dachi	X			153
Jigo-Dachi Version in Naihanchi Kata	X			155
Modern Naihanchi- (Kiba-) Dachi Variation with Feet Straight	X			156

REFERENCES

Abernethy, Iain (2010): *Naihanchi - Karate's Most Deadly Kata?* ; https://iainabernethy.co.uk/article/naihanchi-karates-most-deadly-kata, retrieved October 2, 2019

Abernethy, Iain (n.d.): *The Practical Application of Karate*; https://iainabernethy.co.uk/; retrieved 05/01/2020

Apsokardu, Matthew (2010): *Exploring the Value of Naihanchi Kata . . . and Putting It Into Action*; https://www.ikigaiway.com/2010/exploring-the-value-of-naihanchi-kata-and-putting-it-into-action/; retrieved 03/16/2020

Bayer, Hermann (2020): *Okinawan Kobayashi Shorin Ryu & Japanese Doshinkan Karatedo - A Research Paper on Experienced Differences of Purpose and Training between Genuine Okinawan Karate and Japanese Karate-Do*; © Dr. Hermann Bayer, https://hermannbayer.academia.edu/research

Bayer Hermann (2019a): *Is Altering the Traditional Stance/Position in Naihanchi Kata Impacting a Karateka's Vulnerability? A Research Paper on the Physics of a Kata Modification*; © Dr. Hermann Bayer https://hermannbayer.academia.edu/research

Bayer, Hermann (2019b): *The Lower You Are The Stronger You Are? A Research Paper On Karate Stances/ Positions in Kobayashi Shorin Ryu*; Research Paper © Dr. Hermann Bayer https://hermannbayer.academia.edu/research

Bayer, Hermann (2000): *Coaching-Kompetenz—Persönlickleit und Führungspsychologie*; München/ Basel: Ernst Reinhardt Verlag, 2nd German edition

Băiţel, Irina / Deliu Dan (2014*): Kinematic analysis of the cross punch applied in the full-contact system using inertial navigation technology and surface electromyography*; Procedia - Social and Behavioral Sciences; Volume 117, March 2014, pp. 335–340

Bellina, Christian (2018): *Tomaya Kanken—The Heritage of Shudokan*, Klagenfurt/Austria: © Christian Bellina, MSc, DAgrSc, Limited Edition, and www.tomaya-book.org

Bishop, Mark (1991): *Okinawan Karate—Teachers, Styles and Secret Techniques*, London: A & C Black Publishers Ltd., 2nd edition

Bowman, Paul (2010): *The Globalization of Martial Arts*; in: Green, Thomas A. and Svinth, Joseph R. (ed.) (2010*): Martial Arts in the Modern World*; Westport, CT: Praeger Publishers, Inc.; 2nd edition

CFA Classical Fighting Arts Magazine (diverse years, volumes and issues); cited as "CFA, Issue#, page#" in case no specific author is published

Chambers, David, Ikemiyagy, Taku, Dohrenwend, Robert (publ.) (2020): *Okinawa Karate—The Exquisite Art*; Naha/Okinawa: Dragon Associates. Inc. & Ikemiya Shokai Co., Ltd.; © Classical Fighting Arts; quoted as "Chambers et. al. 2020"

Chen, Yea-Wen & Lin, Hengjun (2016): *Cultural Identities*, printed from Oxford Research Encyclopedia, Communication (oxfordre.com/communication), © Oxford University Press USA, PDF retrieved 01/24/2020

Chibana, Chosin (2006): *Karate-Do No Kokoroe–The Teachings of Karate-Do*; Translation and Commentaries by Pat Nakata, Classical Fighting Arts Vol 1 Issue# 10, pp. 19–23

Clarke, Christopher M. (2012a): *Okinawan Karate–A History of Styles and Masters, Volume 1: Shuri-Te and Shorin Ryu*, Huntington, MD: Clarke's Canyon Press

Clarke, Christopher M. (2012b): *Okinawan Karate–A History of Styles and Masters, Volume 2: Fujian Antecedents, Naha-Te, Goju Ryu and other Styles*, Huntington, MD: Clarke's Canyon Press

Clarke, Michael (2012): *A Map: Knowing Where You Stand in the Dojo*; https://ymaa.com/articles/a-map-knowing-where-you-stand-in-the-dojo, retrieved 03/01/2020.

Clarke, Michael (2016): *Redemption–A Streetfighter's Path to Peace—A Martial Arts Memoir*; Wolfeboro, NH, YMAA Publication Center, Inc.

Clayton, Bruce D. (2010): *Shotokan's Secret—The Hidden Truth Behind Karate's Fighting Origins*; © Cruz Bay Publishing, Inc.; 3rd printing 2012

Clayton, Bruce D. (2012): *High Kicks: Why stretch to do something stupid?*; http://shotokanssecret.com/phpbb2/viewtopic.php?f=4&t=238&sid=7f8f3 26001478580ffeb9078d32849ff#p408; posted 09/23/2012; n.p.; retrieved 08/02/2020

Connor, Lucy (2019): *The Martial Arts Business Statistics You Need to Know*; https://www.glofox.com/blog/martial-arts-business-statistics/; retrieved 03/31/2020

Cummins, William / Scaglione, Robert (2002): *Shorin Ryu–Okinawan Karate Question and Answer Book*, New York, NY: Person-to-Person Publishing, Inc., 3rd edition

Dai Nippon Butoku Kai (n.d.): *History and Philosophy*; https://www.dnbk .org/history.php; retrieved 01/30/2020

Davey, H.E. (no date): *Your Guide to Budo & Koryu Bujutsu v 3-16-16*, Shudokan Martial Arts Association

Davey, H.E. (2018): *An Excerpt from "The Japanese Way of the Artist,"* SMAA Journal Vol. 23, Issue# 2, p. 9–13

Dollar, Allen (2017): *Secrets of Uechi Ryu Karate—and the Mysteries of Okinawa*; © Cherokee Publishing, 2nd revised edition

Donelly, Todd (n.d.): *A Survey of Historical Information on Naihanchi Kata*, Research Paper https://www.scribd.com/doc/153150604/A-Survey-of-Historical-Information-on-Naihanchi-Kata, retrieved 05/06/2019

Doria, Christian / Veicsteinas, Arsenio / Limonta, Eloisa / Maggioni, Martina A. / Aschieri, Pierluigi / Fabrizio, Eusebi / Fano, Giorgio / Pietrangelo, Tiziana (2009): *Energetics of karate (kata and kumite techniques) in top-level athletes*; European Journal of Applied Physiology, Issue#107, pp. 603–610; https://www.academia.edu/20118160/Energetics_of_karate _kata_and_kumite_techniques_in_top-level_athletes; retrieved 04/17/2020; quoted as "Doria et.al. 2009"

Dreikurs, Rudolf (1981): *Grundbegriffe der Individualpsychologie*; Stuttgart/Germany: Klett-Cotta, 4th German edition

Enkamp, Jesse (n.d. - a): *The WKF Shitei Kata Are Finally Removed (+ Historical Bonus Material!)*; https://www.karatebyjesse.com/wkf-shitei-kata-removed -nagamine-jkf-bonus/; retrieved 02/08/2020

Enkamp, Jesse (n.d.- b): https://www.youtube.com/user/KARATEbyJesse; div. videos retrieved 09/20/2020

Fuente, de la, Eduardo Gonzales / Niehaus, Andreas (2020): *From Olympic sport to UNESCO intangible cultural heritage : Okinawa karate between local, national, and international identities in contemporary Japan*; In G. H. Keum & Ch. H. Park (Eds.), *Traditional martial arts as intangible heritage;* University of Gent: ICHCAP / ICM; pp. 40–51; http://hdl.handle.net/1854/LU -8681889

Funakoshi, Gichin (1973): *Karate-do Kyohan—The Master Text*; Tokyo-New York-London: Kodansha International Ltd.

Funakoshi, Gichin (1983): *Karatedo–Mein Weg*, Tokyo & Weidenthal: Kodansha Int. & Werner Kristkeitz Verlag, 1st German edition

Giesen, Bernhard / Seyfert, Robert (2013): *Kollektive Identität*; Aus Politik und Zeitgeschichte Vo. 63, Issue# 13–14, pp. 39–43

Goodin, Charles C. (2006): *The Why of Bunkai–A Guide for Beginners*, Hawaii Karate Seinenkai https://www.scribd.com/document/271684275 /The-Why-of-Bunkai, © Charles Goodin, retrieved 05/20/2019

Grossman, David A. (2007): *On Combat—The Psychology and Physiology of Deadly Conflict in War and Peace*; PPCT Research Publications; © David A Grossman; 2nd edition (with Loren W. Christensen)

Haines, Bruce A. (1970): *Karate's History and Traditions*, Ruthland, VM & Tokyo: Charles E. Tuttle Company, Inc., 3rd edition

Hayes, William ("Bill") R. (2018): *My Journey with the Grandmaster— Reflections of an American Martial Artist on Okinawa*; ©1997 by William R. Hayes; Kearney, NE: Morris Publishing; 8th printing

Hayes, William ("Bill") R. (div. years): *Okinawan Shorin Ryu Karatedo Kenkyu Kai Shinbum Newsletters*; © Okinawan Shorin Ryu Karatedo Kenkyu Kai Shinbum, Stafford, VA & Fredericksburg, VA (since published seasonally as "Spring," "Summer," "Fall" and "Winter" issues in "Volumes," quoted as *"Hayes n.d., Vol. #, Issue #* [if available], *season*, p. #")

Hargrove, Frank (n.d., n. p): *Why should there be Nakazato-Ha Shorin Ryu?*; https://sites.google.com/site/nakazatokaratecom/why-nakazato-ha; retrieved 07/31/2020

Hashimoto, Akiko (2015): *The Long Defeat: Cultural Trauma, Memory, and Identity in Japan*; Oxford, NY: Oxford University Press

Henning, Stanley E. (2007): *Buddhism and East Asian Martial Arts*; Classical Fighting Arts Magazine, Vol 2 Issue# 12, pp. 37–40

Hein, Laura & Selden, Mark (ed.) (2003): *Islands of Discontent–Okinawan Responses to Japanese and American Power*; Lanham, MD: Rowman & Littlefield Publishers, Inc.

Higaonna, Hiroshi (2018): *The Way of Japanese Karate-do*, Translated and Explained by Henning Wittwer, Classical Fighting Arts Magazine, Vol. 3 Issue# 5, pp. 25–29

Hokama, Tetsuhiro (2000): *History and Traditions of Okinawan Karate*, Hamilton, Ontario, Canada: Master Publ.

Ionete, Gabriela L. / Mereuta, Elena / Mereuta, Claudiu / Tudoran, Marian S. / Ganea, Daniel (2011): *Experimental Study on Kinematics of Gyaku-Tzuki Punch*; Annals of the University Dunarea de Jos of Galati; Fascicle XV: Physical Education & Sport Management, Issue 1, p. 103–108 (quoted as "Ionete et. al.")

Johnson, Noah C.G. (2012): *The Japanization of Karate? Placing an Intangible Cultural Practice*; Journal of Contemporary Anthropology, Vol 3, Issue# 1, pp. 60–78

JKA (n.d.): *Japan Karate Association*; https://www.jka.or.jp/en/; retrieved 06/09/2019

Karate Kaikan Okinawa (n.d.): http://karatekaikan.jp/en/; retrieved January 12, 2020

Kadekaru, Tooru (2015): A study of the kata Sanchin in Goju Ryu, Uechi-ryu, Baihe-quan (White-Crane-Boxing), and Wuzu-quan (5-Ancestors-Boxing); in: Ryūkyū Karate no Rūtsu o saguru Jigyō—Chōsa Kenkyū Hōkokusho (Research and Study Report—Project to Explore the Roots of Ryūkyū Karate). Urasoe City Board of Education, March 2015, pp. 69–80. Translated by *Andreas Quast* and posted on http://ryukyu-bugei.com/?p=8464 on 02/20/2020; retrieved 05/30/2020

Kiyuna, Choko (2018): *A Conversation with Choko Kiyuna Sensei–Director-General, Okinawa Karate Do Shinkokai*, Classical Fighting Arts Magazine, Vol. 3, Issue# 5, pp. 11–13

Kinjo Tsuneo / Gima, Tesu (2020): *Karate No Hanashi - Talking about Karate with Tsuneo Kinjo, 9th Dan and Tetsu Gima, 9th Dan*; Classical Fighting Arts Magazine, Vol. 3, Issue# 58, pp. 31–39

Kotek, Ruthie (2016): *What is so Japanese about Shotokan Karate-Do? : Protection of Cultural Identity and Economic Rights in the Global Sphere*; Thesis submitted in Partial Fulfillment for the Master's Degree to the University if Haifa, Department of Asian Studies, May 2016

Kuramoto, Masaku (2020): *An Interview with Sensei Masaku Kuramoto . . . from the Higaonna Dojo in Naha, Okinawa during the CFA Spring Seminars at the Tenchi Martial Arts Center*; Classical Fighting Arts Magazine, Vol. 3, Issue# 58, pp. 16–22

Lind, Werner (1991): *Die Tradition des Karate–Meister und Stile der traditionellen Kampfkunst in Okinawa, China und Japan*; Heidelberg-Leimen/ Germany: Werner Kristkeiz Verlag

Macarie, Iulius-Cezar / Roberts, Ron (2010): Martial Arts and Mental Health; Contemporary Psychotherapy Vol 2, # 1, http://www.contempo rarypsychotherapy.org/vol-2-no-1/martial-arts-and-mental-health/; retrieved 04/08/2020

Martin, Damien (2006): *The Psychosocial Benefits Of Traditional Martial Arts Training: What Most Instructors Know But Can't Articulate*; © Damien Martin 2006; https://www.academia.edu/35947156/The_Psychosocial _Benefits_Of_Traditional_Martial_Arts_Training_What_Most_Instructors _Know_But_Cant_Articulate; retrieved 04/10/2020

May, Samantha (2016): *Uchinaaguchi Language Reclamation in the Martial Arts Community in Okinawa and Abroad*; Thesis Submitted to The University of the Ryukyus for the degree of Doctor of Philosophy; March 2016

May, Samantha (n.d.): *Practicing Peace: The International Okinawan Martial Arts Community as a Community of Practice*; PowerPoint Presentation at Department of Comparative Regional Cultures, University of the Ryukyus, Okinawa; https://www.academia.edu/9469670/Practicing_Peace _The_International_Okinawan_Martial_Arts_Community_as_a_Com munity_of_Practice; retrieved 04/17/2020

McCarthy, Patrick (n.d.): International Ryukyu Karate-jutsu Research Society IRKRS; http://www.koryu-uchinadi.com/; div. posts

McCarthy, Patrick (2016): *Bubishi–The Classic Manual of Combat*, Ruthland, VM & Tokyo & Singapore: Tuttle Publishing, revised and expanded edition

McCarthy, Patrick (2005): *Sometimes you don't know how to fit in until you break out*; http://www.koryu-uchinadi.org/KU_HAPV.pdf; retrieved 09/19/2020

McCarthy, Patrick (1987): *Classical Kata of Okinawan Karate*, Burbank, CA: Ohara Publications, Inc.

Mertz, Scot (n.d.) researched div. sources for Naihanchi, which Sensei Bob Young listed on 01/24/2020 at https://www.karate4theheart.com/2020/01 /nerd-life-origins-of-naihanchi.html; retrieved 06/08/2020

Meyer, Stanislav (2007): *Citizenship, Culture and Identity in Prewar Okinawa*; A thesis submitted for the Degree of Doctor of Philosophy at The University of Hong Kong; January 2007

Messner, Nicolas (2020): *The Belt: Myth and Reality of an Essential Symbol*; https://www.ijf.org/news/show/the-belt-myth-and-reality-of-an-essential -symbol; retrieved 07/31/2020

Moenig, Udo / Minho, Kim (2016): *The Invention of Taekwondo Tradition, 1945–1972: When Mythology Becomes History*; Acta Koreana Vol. 19, Issue #2, pp. 131–164; © Academia Koreana, Keimyung University

Mudric, Radomir / Rankovic, Velizar (2016): *Analysis of Hand Techniques in Karate*; SPORT - Science & Practice, Vol. 6, No 1 & 2, 2016, pp. 47–74

Muromoto, Wayne (2018): *Traditions in a Traditional Art*, SMAA Journal Vol. 23, Issue 4, pp. 7–12

Nagamine, Shoshin (1976): *The Essence of Okinawan Karate-Do*, Ruthland, VM & Tokyo: Charles E. Tuttle Co., Inc.

Nakazato Shugoro (n.d.): *Nakazato On Sport Karate*; https://sites.google .com/site/nakazatokaratecom/nakazato-on-sport-karate; translated by Steve Neal; edited by Chris Estes; retrieved 07/31/20

Nielson, Wesley K. (2006): *Annexation, Militarism, and Reversion—A Look into Okinawa Identity*, Paper Anthropology 504 Dr. Eric Canin, California State University Fullerton; https://www.academia.edu/12056898/Annexation _Militarism_and_Reversion_A_Look_into_Okinawa_Identity, retrieved 02/02/2020

Nitobe, Inazo / Kirov, Blago (2014): *Bushido—The Soul of Japan*, CreateSpace Independent Publishing Platform; 1st illustrated edition

Noble, Graham (2019a): *Chosin Chibana's Shorin Ryu–His Legacy and Students*; Classical Fighting Arts Magazine Vol 3, Issue# 56, pp. 28–47

Noble, Graham (2019b): *Chosin Chibana's Shorin Ryu–His Legacy and Students Part II*; Classical Fighting Arts Magazine Vol 3, Issue# 57, pp. 22–33

Noble, Graham (2019c): *Gichin Funakoshi's Exquisite Art*, Classical Fighting Arts Magazine, Vol 3, Issue# 57, pp. 33–51

Noble, Graham (2020): *Gichin Funakoshi's Exquisite Art Part II*, Classical Fighting Arts Magazine, Vol 3, Issue# 58, pp. 43–51

Nunberg, Noah (2012a): *The Martial Artist's Potential Civil and Criminal Liability - Part I - Civil Liability*; http://lbcclaw.com/news/the-martial -artists-potential-civil-and-criminal-liability-part-i-civil-liability; retrieved 04/12/2020

Nunberg, Noah (2012b): *The Martial Artist's Potential Civil and Criminal Liability - Part II - Criminal Liability*; http://lbcclaw.com/news/the-martial -artists-potential-civil-and-criminal-liability-part-ii-criminal-liability; retrieved 04/12/2020

OBI Okinawan Budo Institute—Virginia Shorin Ryu Shorinkan Karate School (no date), http://www.obikarateschool.com/, retrieved 04/18/2019

ODKS Okinawa Dentou Karatedo Shinkokai (n.d.): http://www.odks.jp/en/; retrieved 08/18/2019

OKIC Okinawa Karate Information Center within the Okinawan Karate Kai-kan (no date): http://okic.okinawa/en/, retrieved 06/30/2019

OPG Okinawa Prefectural Government (2003): *History of Okinawan Karate*, https://web.archive.org/web/20081011051605/http://www.wonder -okinawa.jp/023/eng/001/001/index.html, retrieved 08/30/19

Oyama, Masutasu (1987): *Der Kyokushin Karate Weg*; Leimen/Germany: Werner Kristkeitz Verlag; 1st German edition

Perry, Jason (2018): *An Old Man's Way: Doug Perry's Unlikely Journey Through Karate, War, and Life*; Pennsylvania/USA: Apsos Publishing, Apsos LLC

Partikova, Veronika (2018): *Psychological Collectivism in Traditional Martial Arts*; Martial Arts Studies Vol. 7, pp. 49–59. doi.org/10.18573/mas.72; retrieved 05/29/2020

Pflüger, Albrecht (1975): *Karate-Do: Das Handbuch des modernen Karate*, Sicker/Germany: Falken Verlag

Quast, Andreas (n.d.): Ryukyu *Bugei. Research Workshop*; http://ryukyu-bugei .com/; div. posts

Quast, Andreas (2013): Karate 1.0—Parameter of an Ancient Martial Art; Düsseldorf, Germany: © 2013 by Andreas Quast, www.ryukyu-bugei .com

Quast, Andreas (2015a): *A Stroll Along* Ryukyu *Martial Arts History*; Düsseldorf, Germany: ©Andreas Quast, www.ryukyu-bugei.com; printed in the USA, Middletown, DE January 2020

Quast, Andreas (2015b): Wanshū, Wansu, and Wang Ji; http://ryukyu-bugei .com/?p=4675; posted 09/13/2015; retrieved 05/10/2020

Quast, Andreas (2016): *The 36 Clans of the Min-People*; http://ryukyu-bugei .com/?p=6869; posted 08/18/2016; retrieved 05/10/2020

Quast, Andreas (2017): *'nchi means ti* 手; posted March 5, 2017 on Ryukyu Bugei; http://ryukyu-bugei.com/?tag=naihanchi, retrieved 04/06/2020

Roy, J. Maria / Ashwin, Felix P. (2014): *Mathematics of Karate Techniques - Dynamics & kinematics of karate; International Journal of Computing Algorithm*, Vol. 3, February 2014, p. 586–589

Shorin Ryu Shorinkan (no date), https://www.karateshorinkan.com/links .php, retrieved April 15, 2019

Singh, Anupam A. (2017): Analysis of force, time, energy, psychological demand and safety of common kicks in martial arts–A thesis submitted for the degree of Master of Science in Industrial Engineering at Iowa State University, © Anupam A. Singh

Shimabukuro, Eizo (1985): *Eizo Shimabukuro Interview*, September 5, 1985, https://www.usadojo.com/eizo-shimabukuro-interview/, retrieved Mai 10, 2019

Starr, Phillip (2020): *Something old, something new, something borrowed*; https://www.facebook.com/pg/Phillip-Starr-Books-and-DVDs-1037930 53032146/posts/?ref=page_internal, 01/08/20; retrieved 01/13/20

Swanson, John David ('J.D.') (2017): *Karate Science: Dynamic Movement (Martial Science)*, Wolfeboro, NH: YMAA Publication Center, Inc.

Swift, Paul (n.d.): Kanei Uechi's Strategy for Peace through Cultural Exchange of Karate-do; Bryant College Zhuhai, Beijing, Institute of Technology Zhuhai #6; https://www.academia.edu/26199863/Kanei_Uechis_Strategy_for _Peace_through_Cultural_Exchange_of_Karate_do; retrieved 07/05/2020

Takamiyagi Shigeru (2008): *OKKJ, Part 1: Karate. Chapter 1—Definition and Categories of Karate. 2. The Classification of Karate. (1) Martial arts karate (budō karate)*; in Takamiyagi Shigeru / Shinzato Katsuhiko / Nagamoto Nazahieo (2008): *Okinawa karate kobudo" jiten*; Tokyo: Kashiba Shoko, pp. 77–79; http://ryukyu-bugei.com/; posted by Andreas Quast 01/25/20; retrieved 01/28/20

Thalken, Jason (2015): *Fight Like a Physicist: The Incredible Science Behind Martial Arts (Martial Science)*, Wolfeboro, NH: YMAA Publication Center, Inc.

Thomas, Jason E. / Hornsey, Philip E. (2010): *Tae Kwon Do Kom Do Kwan: An Introduction for New Students*; Austin, TX: Custom Press; © 2010, Jason E. Thomas; 2nd edition

Tomaya, Kanken (2007): *Karate Styles*—Translated by Mario McKenne, Classical Fighting Arts Magazine Vol 2, Issue# 12, pp. 56–59

Virginia Shorin Ryu Shorinkan Karate School—OBI Okinawan Budo Institute (no date), http://www.obikarateschool.com/, retrieved 04/18/2019

Walter, Jearl D. (1975): *Karate strikes*; in: American Journal of Physics, Volume 43; pp. 845–849

Weller, Jenny (2019): *14 Martial Arts Industry Trends You Need to Know*; https:// www.glofox.com/blog/martial-arts-industry-trends/; retrieved 03/31/2020

Weiser, Mark / Kutz, Ilan / Jacobsen-Kutz, Sue / Weiser, Daniel (1995): Psychotherapeutic Aspects of the Martial Arts; American Journal of Psychotherapy, Vol. 49, p. 118–127; quoted as 'Weiser et.al. 1995'

Wichmann, Wolf-Dieter (1998): Karate Kata—Heian 1–5, Tekki 1, Bassai Dai; Niedernhausen/Germany: Falken Verlag GmbH

Wilder, Kris (2010): Sanchin Kata - Ancient Wisdom; https://ymaa.com /articles/sanchin-kata-ancient-wisdom; retrieved 05/15/2020

Wilk, Stephen R. / McNair, Ronald E. / Feld, Michael S. (1979): *The physics of karate*; American Journal of Physics, Volume 51, pp. 783–790; quoted as 'Wilk et.al. 1979'

Yagi, Meitatsu (2018*): Interview with Meitatsu Yagi 10th Dan*, Classical Fighting Arts Magazine, Vol. 3 Issue# 5, pp. 15–24

Yonaha-Tursi, Teiko (2017): *The Seminar Attendees Train Dedicatedly, Okinawa Traditional Karate Masters in Virginia*; Okinawan Times p. 25, November 29 (English Version sent to the author by email 11.27.2017)

INDEX

A

aggression, 62–65, 84
Ahagon Naonobu, 54
ambiguity tolerance, 38, 40
Americanization, v, 1, 33–34
Ananku, 107
Asato Sezaburo, 140–141, 143, 174

B

basic principles, 99
Bavaria, 78–80
Bo, 10–14, 163, 168, 173
body-weight-power, 66, 88, 92, 99–100,
   108–110, 119, 121, 133–134,
   139–140
Bubishi, 5, 65–66, 112, 163, 179
Buddhism, 30–31, 178
budo, ix, 15–17, 20, 23, 29, 48, 60, 62, 81,
   84–86, 93, 104, 118–119, 121, 126, 137,
   142, 161, 163, 173–174, 176, 181–182
budokan, 52, 54–55, 173
bujutsu, 14, 21, 81, 84–85, 112, 163, 176
bunkai, v, 16, 41, 43, 68–70, 72, 74–75, 98,
   103, 106, 108, 111–113, 116, 121, 124,
   127, 139, 146, 149, 163, 177
bushido, ix, 10, 18, 21, 32, 48, 81, 85–86,
   163, 180

C

cat stance, 68, 92, 124, 131, 133, 135, 137,
   168, 174
Center of Gravity, 99, 130–135, 140, 150,
   152, 154–156, 174
ch'üan fa, 3, 5, 7, 14, 107, 163
character development, 15, 104, 108, 159
Chibana Chosin, ix, 4, 7, 20, 24, 35, 42, 47,
   66, 75, 86, 106, 116, 125, 139–140, 157,
   166

Chinese martial arts, 3–7, 25, 31, 168,
   171
Classical Fighting Arts, xi, 23, 25, 58, 161,
   176, 178–180, 182–183
cognitive, 40
combat, v, x, 4, 18–20, 22, 31, 61–62,
   65–66, 68–73, 75–77, 84–85, 87, 89, 98,
   104, 108, 111, 113, 116, 118–122, 124,
   139, 159–160, 163, 166–167, 177, 179
creating maximal damage in the most
   efficient way, 31
creating the most possible damage in the
   most effective way, 15
cross stance, 140, 146, 154, 156
cultural heritage, v, c, 21, 45, 50, 53, 58, 60,
   78, 81–83, 160, 173, 177
cultural identity, v, 45, 53, 80–81, 83, 160,
   179
cultural symbol, 78, 160
curriculum, v, 7, 98, 104–105, 109–110

D

Dai Nippon Butoku Kai, 15, 60, 176
Day of Karate, 50, 127–128, 141, 174
delayed block/counter, 156
dentou Okinawan karate, x, 7, 25, 28, 31, 43,
   54, 56, 60, 62–63, 77, 85, 88, 97, 160,
   173
deshi, x, 10, 16, 35–37, 40–41, 60, 68,
   91–92, 100, 106, 109, 122, 124, 141,
   155, 164, 170–171
dichotomy of culture and citizenship,
   46–47
distance is time, 75, 147
Do, x, xi, 1, 4, 9, 16, 18, 20, 23, 25, 28, 31,
   36–37, 40–41, 44, 47, 61–62, 70, 75–78,
   80, 82–85, 87–88, 94–95, 97–98, 103,
   105, 110, 120–121, 124–125, 128, 144,
   150, 152, 157, 159–160, 163–164, 175–182

Doshinkan, ix, 91–98, 100, 103–104, 106–108, 110, 121–122, 159, 164, 166, 173, 175

E

Eisa, 80–81, 173
Eku, 10, 164
encyclopedia of moves, 105
equality of man, 36
equilibrium, 131–134, 174
etiquette, 29, 41, 60, 93–96, 109, 173
existentialism, 30

F

FAJKO, 22–24, 161
Fang Quiniang, 65
fighting capabilities, 21, 97–98, 110
Funakoshi Gichin, 14–15, 18, 20, 24, 46, 105, 144, 165, 170

G

Genka Noritsune, 140–141, 143, 174
genuine Okinawan karate, viii, x, 21, 34, 48, 86, 104, 122–123, 159–160, 175
gi, 41, 48, 74, 164
Goju Ryu, xi, 6–7, 23–25, 53–54, 56, 63, 76, 88, 105, 107, 111, 164–165, 176, 178

H

hara, 99, 103, 125
Heian, 61, 74, 76, 106, 110, 165, 182
Hichiya Yoshio, 53
hidden concepts, 69–70, 73, 75, 173
Higaonna Kanryo, 7, 24, 164
Higaonna Morio, 53
honbu, 8, 10, 44, 66, 91, 100, 103, 110, 127–128, 130, 140–141, 143, 156, 165, 173–174
Honbu, 8, 10, 44, 66, 91, 100, 103, 110, 127–128, 130, 140–141, 143, 156, 165, 173–174
Honbu Dojo, 8, 10, 44, 66, 91, 100, 110, 127–128, 130, 140–141, 143, 156, 165, 173–174
horse stance, 130, 135, 144, 154, 165, 174

I

ichigeki hissatsu, 18, 86, 165
Ichikawa Isao, 91, 93, 97, 100, 102, 106–107, 110–111, 164, 173
Ichikawa Nobuo, 37, 92, 100, 102, 111
Intangible Cultural Asset, 10, 53, 76, 80, 112, 173
Ishikawa Seitoku, 53
Isshin Ryu, 7, 165
Itokasu Seiki, 53
Itosu ('Anko') Yasutsune, ix, 4, 16–17, 24, 28, 31, 76, 157, 166, 168, 170

J

Japanese Karatedo, v, ix, x, 9, 15, 20–21, 28, 85, 89, 92, 105, 122–123, 158–160
Japanization, v, 1, 15, 17, 71–72, 76, 178
Japanized, 15–16, 21, 26, 29, 62, 71, 81, 92
JKF, 24–26, 28, 52, 161, 169, 177
Jo, 10, 166
jujutsu, 14, 163, 166

K

Kama, 10, 166
karate inflation, 32
Karate Kaikan, 51, 53, 55, 58, 161, 173, 178, 181
karate styles, ix, 6, 10, 24, 26–27, 54, 61, 76, 85, 92, 107–108, 116, 122, 124–125, 139, 144, 152, 154, 165, 167, 169–170, 173, 182
karate tourism, 57–59
karate tourists, 10, 40, 47, 58
kata alterations, 68, 124, 159
kata modifications, 66, 68, 76, 124, 160
kenpo, 7, 20, 166
Kiba-dachi, vi, 128, 139, 144–147, 150–151, 153–154, 156, 166, 174
Kinjo Kempo, 141
Kinjo Satoshi, 141
knees over the big toes, 135–137, 152
Kobayashi, ix, 7, 9, 16, 25, 43, 53, 66–67, 76, 86, 88, 91–94, 97–100, 103–104, 106–109, 113, 118, 122, 125–127, 140–141, 143, 146, 159, 166, 173–175

kobudo, 10–11, 14, 25, 41, 50, 52–54, 56, 59, 87, 105, 107, 116–117, 135, 141, 163–164, 166, 168, 170–171, 173, 182
kohai, 36, 167
Kokusaidori, 47, 50, 167
koryu bujutsu, 21, 81, 84–85, 176
kumite, v, 27, 47, 87–88, 98, 103, 106, 111–113, 116–123, 167, 174, 177
Kyoku, 106, 110, 166
Kyokushinkai, 88

L

Law of Physics, 152
law-of-the-lever, 132, 134, 174

M

Mabuni Kenwa, 24, 157, 169
machi dojo, 7–8, 35, 40, 43, 56–59, 139, 167
makiwara, 112–114, 167, 173
Masanari Kikugawa, 53
Matsubayashi, 7, 25, 53, 76, 105, 144–145, 167
Matsumura Sokon, 24, 166, 169
mechanics, 69–70, 72, 92, 124, 130, 139, 159
meditative athletics, ix, 18, 32
minimum requirements, 109–110
Miyagi Chojun, 7, 24, 61, 111, 164
Miyahira Katsuya, 53
Morinobu Maeshiro, 53
morote chudan-uke, 74
Motobu Choki, 14–15, 20, 155
muscle memory, 73, 77, 86, 100, 103

N

Nagamine Shoshin, 10, 26, 53, 76, 112, 140, 145, 167
Naha-Te, 6–7, 24–26, 53, 58, 105, 107, 157, 176
Naihanchi, vi, 4, 92, 96, 107, 109, 111, 118, 138–147, 149–158, 167–168, 170, 174–175, 177, 180–181
Naihanchi-dachi, vi, 138–147, 149–156, 168, 174
Nakamoto Masahiro, 53
Nakazato Jyoen, 53, 76

Nakazato Minoru, 57, 66, 110, 117, 127, 140–141, 143, 174
Nakazato Shugoro, xi, 10, 39, 43, 53, 60, 63, 66–67, 70, 76, 87, 92–93, 101, 104, 111, 116–118, 120–121, 125–127, 130, 133, 137, 140, 157, 173–174, 180
natural stance, vi, 128, 133, 135, 137, 165, 171
Nunchaku, 10–11, 168
Nunte Bo, 10, 168

O

Octoberfest, 79
Okinawa Dento Karatedo Shinkokai, 50, 52
Okinawa is the Birthplace of Karate, v, 1, 26, 52, 54
Okinawa Karate Information Center, xi, 5, 50, 52, 58, 161, 181
Okinawan masters, 10, 22–23, 26, 50–51, 54, 56, 58–59, 62–63, 68–69, 72, 76, 124, 173
Okinawan Prefectural Government, 50–54, 56–59, 161
Olympic Games, 29, 104
Olympic sport, 2, 22–25, 29, 177
Original Seven, 43, 69–71, 92, 126–127
Otsuka Hironori, 24, 171
over-compensation, 65

P

Pangainun Ryu, 7, 168
Passai, 26, 109
Pinan, 4, 61, 68, 74–76, 109–110, 131, 139, 157, 165, 168
posture/balance, 99, 103, 134
pre-emptive strikes, 19
psychomotor, 40
punch velocity, 148–151

S

Sai, 10–11, 21
Sanchin, 107, 111, 169, 178, 183
Satsuma, 3, 5, 169
Sayuri Iha, 127–128, 174
secret techniques, 68, 175
Seibukan, 7, 88, 169
Seikichi Iha, 53

self-control, 62, 87, 97, 120, 122
self-discovery, 30, 37, 40
self-perfection, ix, 15, 31, 93, 122–123, 159–160
self-protection, vii, ix, x, 4, 15, 17–18, 20, 22, 31, 60, 85, 93, 108, 159
senior karate authorities, 41, 125
senpai, ix, 36, 94, 109, 169
Shido Kan, 53
Shimabukuro Eizo, 23–24, 70–72, 169
Shintoku Takara, 53
Shiroma Jiro, 92, 127
Shisa, 48–49, 173
shitei kata, 25–26, 177
Shito Ryu, 24, 26, 63, 157, 169
Shobayashi Ryu, 7, 70, 72, 105, 169
shomen, 74, 94–96, 169
Shorin Ryu, ix, xi, c, 4, 6–10, 16–18, 21, 24–25, 41, 43–44, 47, 53–54, 56, 60, 62, 66–71, 76, 86, 92–100, 103–111, 113, 116–122, 125–128, 130, 133, 138–141, 143–146, 154, 156, 159, 165–167, 169, 173–176, 178, 180–182
Shorinji Ryu, 76
Shorinkan, xi, c, 8–10, 18, 41, 43–44, 47, 62, 66–67, 69, 71, 86, 92–96, 104–105, 108, 110, 116, 119, 126–127, 130, 139–141, 143, 154, 156, 173–174, 181–182
Shotokan, 2, 14–16, 24, 26, 74, 76, 88, 105–106, 139, 144, 165, 170, 176, 179
Shudokan, ix, 22, 84, 91, 93, 106–107, 122, 162, 164, 170, 175–176
shuhari, 66, 68, 76, 103–104, 108, 125, 170
Shuri-Te, ix, 6–7, 16, 21, 24–26, 53, 58, 105, 140, 167, 170, 176
si vis pacem para bellum, 61
sparring, v, 29, 47, 87, 97–98, 103, 111–112, 119–123, 167
speedy, fencing sport moves, 15, 17
spiritual karatedo, 29, 32
sports karate, v, 27, 29, 43, 56, 58, 64, 77, 84, 86–89, 120, 160
stance/position, v, vi, 125, 127–128, 130, 132–135, 137–141, 143–146, 150–152, 154–156, 158–159, 164, 174–175

stances/positions, vi, 92, 99, 125, 127–129, 131, 135–136, 145, 150, 152, 159
step velocity, 148–151, 174
Suikendo, 118–119, 170, 173
symbolism, 93

T
Taekwondo, 2, 22, 35, 180
Tanbo, 10, 170
Te, v, ix, 2–7, 9, 16, 20–21, 24–26, 36, 53, 58, 66, 84–85, 87, 94, 105, 107, 111, 116, 140, 157–158, 166–168, 170, 176
Tekko, 10, 170
The 1st Okinawa Karate International Tournament 2018, 54, 82
the lower you are, the stronger you are, vi, 116, 133–135, 150, 175
there is no first attack in karate, 18, 74
Tomari-Te, 6–7, 20, 24, 58, 105, 167
Tomaya Kanken, ix, 14, 22, 93, 106–107, 164, 175
Tomoyose Ryuku, 53
Tonfa, 10, 171
traditional Japanese karatedo, v, 92
traditional Japanese martial arts, 15, 84
Tsutomu Nakahodo, 53

U
Uchinaguchi, 59, 171
Uechi Kanbun, 7, 24, 28, 168, 171
Uechi Ryu, 6–7, 24–25, 28, 53–54, 56–57, 105, 111, 168, 171, 177
Uehara Takenobu, 53

V
velocity, 92, 139, 147–151, 174
vulnerability, vi, 12, 92, 124, 139, 146, 150–151, 158–159, 175

W
Wado Ryu, 24, 26, 171
Wakugawa Kosei, 53
weaponless fighting art, 9, 170
White Crane, 65, 111
WWII, ix, 2, 6, 15, 22, 30, 40, 46, 60, 162, 167, 169

Y

Yagi Maitatsu, 107
Yagi Meitoku, 53, 76
Yakusoku, 116–118, 123, 171
Yamakawa Tetsuo, 56
Yamashita Tadashi, 62, 71, 92, 118, 127, 170, 173
yang, x, 36, 42, 123, 171

Yilichuan Kung Fu, 82
yin, x, 36, 42, 123, 171
yumaru, 48, 171

Z

Zen, 17, 26, 31–32
zone defense, 88, 119, 121

ABOUT THE AUTHOR

Hermann Bayer, PhD Biography

Hermann holds degrees in economics, sociology, psychology, and business administration. He worked in German and US universities for eighteen years as a scientist, professor, campus dean, and multi-site dean. For another twelve years Hermann served as the CEO and executive coach of a German coaching and consulting firm. In addition, he had ten successful years of self-employment, another nine years working in the manufacturing industry, and two years serving in the (West) German army's corps of engineers. He immigrated to the USA in 2005.

The author of several books and numerous articles on industrial relations, coaching, and consulting, Hermann now publishes on karate-jutsu's and karate-do's socio-cultural roles and their development.

Hermann started to train and to study the art of karate—including its historical and socio-cultural development—in 1981. His experience covers traditional (non-sports) Japanese *Shudokan-Doshinkan* karate-do as well as classic Okinawan *Shorin Ryu* karate-jutsu. In 2016 he completely changed his life priorities from academics to "full-time-karate." To broaden his karate development beyond its Japanese form and to better understand today's misconceptions about the art's original orientation toward protecting and preserving life, he restarted from scratch with classic Okinawan *Kobayashi Ryu* karate-jutsu and kobudo. In addition, Hermann studies *suikendo*—meaning "the art of fists flowing like water," today's most advanced karate fighting system. Over the years, he has spent considerable time with renowned Japanese, Western, and Okinawan karate teachers, all the while researching the core essence of the style they represent.

Today, in his seventies, Hermann is still training hard, practicing karate daily and attends at least three, but mostly four, two-hour empty-hand and kobudo training sessions every week. To make a point about combining (not to be confused with "integrating") traditional karate-jutsu and sports karate, he successfully competes in martial arts tournaments and secures first place in his age bracket.

BOOKS FROM YMAA

101 REFLECTIONS ON TAI CHI CHUAN
108 INSIGHTS INTO TAI CHI CHUAN
A SUDDEN DAWN: THE EPIC JOURNEY OF BODHIDHARMA
A WOMAN'S QIGONG GUIDE
ADVANCING IN TAE KWON DO
ANALYSIS OF SHAOLIN CHIN NA 2ND ED
ANCIENT CHINESE WEAPONS
ART AND SCIENCE OF STAFF FIGHTING
ART AND SCIENCE OF STICK FIGHTING
ART OF HOJO UNDO
ARTHRITIS RELIEF, 3D ED.
BACK PAIN RELIEF, 2ND ED.
BAGUAZHANG, 2ND ED.
BRAIN FITNESS
CARDIO KICKBOXING ELITE
CHIN NA IN GROUND FIGHTING
CHINESE FAST WRESTLING
CHINESE FITNESS
CHINESE TUI NA MASSAGE
CHOJUN
COMPLETE MARTIAL ARTIST
COMPREHENSIVE APPLICATIONS OF SHAOLIN CHIN NA
CONFLICT COMMUNICATION
CUTTING SEASON: A XENON PEARL MARTIAL ARTS THRILLER
DAO DE JING
DAO IN ACTION
DEFENSIVE TACTICS
DESHI: A CONNOR BURKE MARTIAL ARTS THRILLER
DIRTY GROUND
DR. WU'S HEAD MASSAGE
DUKKHA HUNGRY GHOSTS
DUKKHA REVERB
DUKKHA, THE SUFFERING: AN EYE FOR AN EYE
DUKKHA UNLOADED
ENZAN: THE FAR MOUNTAIN, A CONNOR BURKE MARTIAL ARTS
    THRILLER
ESSENCE OF SHAOLIN WHITE CRANE
EVEN IF IT KILLS ME
EXPLORING TAI CHI
FACING VIOLENCE
FIGHT BACK
FIGHT LIKE A PHYSICIST
THE FIGHTER'S BODY
FIGHTER'S FACT BOOK
FIGHTER'S FACT BOOK 2
FIGHTING ARTS
FIGHTING THE PAIN RESISTANT ATTACKER
FIRST DEFENSE
FORCE DECISIONS: A CITIZENS GUIDE
FOX BORROWS THE TIGER'S AWE
INSIDE TAI CHI
JUDO ADVANTAGE
JUJI GATAME ENCYCLOPEDIA
KAGE: THE SHADOW, A CONNOR BURKE MARTIAL ARTS THRILLER
KARATE SCIENCE
KATA AND THE TRANSMISSION OF KNOWLEDGE
KRAV MAGA COMBATIVES
KRAV MAGA FUNDAMENTAL STRATEGIES
KRAV MAGA PROFESSIONAL TACTICS
KRAV MAGA WEAPON DEFENSES
LITTLE BLACK BOOK OF VIOLENCE
LIUHEBAFA FIVE CHARACTER SECRETS
MARTIAL ARTS ATHLETE
MARTIAL ARTS OF VIETNAM
MARTIAL ARTS INSTRUCTION
MARTIAL WAY AND ITS VIRTUES
MASK OF THE KING
MEDITATIONS ON VIOLENCE
MERIDIAN QIGONG EXERCISES
MIND/BODY FITNESS
MINDFUL EXERCISE
MIND INSIDE TAI CHI
MIND INSIDE YANG STYLE TAI CHI CHUAN
NATURAL HEALING WITH QIGONG
NORTHERN SHAOLIN SWORD, 2ND ED.
OKINAWA'S COMPLETE KARATE SYSTEM: ISSHIN RYU
PAIN-FREE BACK
PAIN-FREE JOINTS

PRINCIPLES OF TRADITIONAL CHINESE MEDICINE
PROTECTOR ETHIC
QIGONG FOR HEALTH & MARTIAL ARTS 2ND ED.
QIGONG FOR LIVING
QIGONG FOR TREATING COMMON AILMENTS
QIGONG MASSAGE
QIGONG MEDITATION: EMBRYONIC BREATHING
QIGONG MEDITATION: GRAND CIRCULATION
QIGONG MEDITATION: SMALL CIRCULATION
QIGONG, THE SECRET OF YOUTH: DA MO'S CLASSICS
QUIET TEACHER: A XENON PEARL MARTIAL ARTS THRILLER
RAVEN'S WARRIOR
REDEMPTION
ROOT OF CHINESE QIGONG, 2ND ED.
SAMBO ENCYCLOPEDIA
SCALING FORCE
SELF-DEFENSE FOR WOMEN
SENSEI: A CONNOR BURKE MARTIAL ARTS THRILLER
SHIHAN TE: THE BUNKAI OF KATA
SHIN GI TAI: KARATE TRAINING FOR BODY, MIND, AND SPIRIT
SIMPLE CHINESE MEDICINE
SIMPLE QIGONG EXERCISES FOR HEALTH, 3RD ED.
SIMPLIFIED TAI CHI CHUAN, 2ND ED.
SOLO TRAINING
SOLO TRAINING 2
SPOTTING DANGER BEFORE IT SPOTS YOU
SPOTTING DANGER BEFORE IT SPOTS YOUR KIDS
SUMO FOR MIXED MARTIAL ARTS
SUNRISE TAI CHI
SURVIVING ARMED ASSAULTS
TAE KWON DO: THE KOREAN MARTIAL ART
TAEKWONDO BLACK BELT POOMSAE
TAEKWONDO: A PATH TO EXCELLENCE
TAEKWONDO: ANCIENT WISDOM FOR THE MODERN WARRIOR
TAEKWONDO: DEFENSE AGAINST WEAPONS
TAEKWONDO: SPIRIT AND PRACTICE
TAI CHI BALL QIGONG: FOR HEALTH AND MARTIAL ARTS
TAI CHI BALL WORKOUT FOR BEGINNERS
THE TAI CHI BOOK
TAI CHI CHIN NA: THE SEIZING ART OF TAI CHI CHUAN,
    2ND ED.
TAI CHI CHUAN CLASSICAL YANG STYLE, 2ND ED.
TAI CHI CHUAN MARTIAL POWER, 3RD ED.
TAI CHI CONCEPTS AND EXPERIMENTS
TAI CHI CONNECTIONS
TAI CHI DYNAMICS
TAI CHI FOR DEPRESSION
TAI CHI IN 10 WEEKS
TAI CHI PUSH HANDS
TAI CHI QIGONG, 3RD ED.
TAI CHI SECRETS OF THE ANCIENT MASTERS
TAI CHI SECRETS OF THE WU & LI STYLES
TAI CHI SECRETS OF THE WU STYLE
TAI CHI SECRETS OF THE YANG STYLE
TAI CHI SWORD: CLASSICAL YANG STYLE, 2ND ED.
TAI CHI SWORD FOR BEGINNERS
TAI CHI WALKING
TAIJIQUAN THEORY OF DR. YANG, JWING-MING
TAO OF BIOENERGETICS
TENGU: THE MOUNTAIN GOBLIN, A CONNOR BURKE MARTIAL
    ARTS THRILLER
TIMING IN THE FIGHTING ARTS
TRADITIONAL CHINESE HEALTH SECRETS
TRADITIONAL TAEKWONDO
TRAINING FOR SUDDEN VIOLENCE
TRUE WELLNESS
TRUE WELLNESS: THE MIND
TRUE WELLNESS FOR YOUR GUT
TRUE WELLNESS FOR YOUR HEART
WARRIOR'S MANIFESTO
WAY OF KATA
WAY OF SANCHIN KATA
WAY TO BLACK BELT
WESTERN HERBS FOR MARTIAL ARTISTS
WILD GOOSE QIGONG
WINNING FIGHTS
WISDOM'S WAY
XINGYIQUAN

VIDEOS FROM YMAA

ADVANCED PRACTICAL CHIN NA IN-DEPTH
ANALYSIS OF SHAOLIN CHIN NA
ATTACK THE ATTACK
BAGUA FOR BEGINNERS 1
BAGUA FOR BEGINNERS 2
BAGUAZHANG: EMEI BAGUAZHANG
BEGINNER QIGONG FOR WOMEN 1
BEGINNER QIGONG FOR WOMEN 2
BEGINNER TAI CHI FOR HEALTH
CHEN STYLE TAIJIQUAN
CHEN TAI CHI CANNON FIST
CHEN TAI CHI FIRST FORM
CHEN TAI CHI FOR BEGINNERS
CHIN NA IN-DEPTH COURSES 1—4
CHIN NA IN-DEPTH COURSES 5—8
CHIN NA IN-DEPTH COURSES 9—12
FACING VIOLENCE: 7 THINGS A MARTIAL ARTIST MUST KNOW
FIVE ANIMAL SPORTS
FIVE ELEMENTS ENERGY BALANCE
INFIGHTING
INTRODUCTION TO QI GONG FOR BEGINNERS
JOINT LOCKS
KNIFE DEFENSE: TRADITIONAL TECHNIQUES AGAINST A DAGGER
KUNG FU BODY CONDITIONING 1
KUNG FU BODY CONDITIONING 2
KUNG FU FOR KIDS
KUNG FU FOR TEENS
LOGIC OF VIOLENCE
MERIDIAN QIGONG
NEIGONG FOR MARTIAL ARTS
NORTHERN SHAOLIN SWORD : SAN CAI JIAN, KUN WU JIAN,
    QI MEN JIAN
QI GONG 30-DAY CHALLENGE
QI GONG FOR ANXIETY
QI GONG FOR ARMS, WRISTS, AND HANDS
QIGONG FOR BEGINNERS: FRAGRANCE
QI GONG FOR BETTER BALANCE
QI GONG FOR BETTER BREATHING
QI GONG FOR CANCER
QI GONG FOR DEPRESSION
QI GONG FOR ENERGY AND VITALITY
QI GONG FOR HEADACHES
QI GONG FOR HEALING
QI GONG FOR THE HEALTHY HEART
QI GONG FOR HEALTHY JOINTS
QI GONG FOR HIGH BLOOD PRESSURE
QIGONG FOR LONGEVITY
QI GONG FOR STRONG BONES
QI GONG FOR THE UPPER BACK AND NECK
QIGONG FOR WOMEN
QIGONG FOR WOMEN WITH DAISY LEE
QIGONG FLOW FOR STRESS & ANXIETY RELIEF
QIGONG MASSAGE
QIGONG MINDFULNESS IN MOTION
QI GONG—THE SEATED WORKOUT
QIGONG: 15 MINUTES TO HEALTH
SABER FUNDAMENTAL TRAINING
SAI TRAINING AND SEQUENCES
SANCHIN KATA: TRADITIONAL TRAINING FOR KARATE POWER
SCALING FORCE
SHAOLIN KUNG FU FUNDAMENTAL TRAINING: COURSES 1 & 2
SHAOLIN LONG FIST KUNG FU: ADVANCED SEQUENCES 1
SHAOLIN LONG FIST KUNG FU: ADVANCED SEQUENCES 2
SHAOLIN LONG FIST KUNG FU: BASIC SEQUENCES
SHAOLIN LONG FIST KUNG FU: INTERMEDIATE SEQUENCES
SHAOLIN SABER: BASIC SEQUENCES
SHAOLIN STAFF: BASIC SEQUENCES
SHAOLIN WHITE CRANE GONG FU BASIC TRAINING: COURSES 1 & 2
SHAOLIN WHITE CRANE GONG FU BASIC TRAINING: COURSES 3 & 4
SHUAI JIAO: KUNG FU WRESTLING
SIMPLE QIGONG EXERCISES FOR HEALTH
SIMPLE QIGONG EXERCISES FOR ARTHRITIS RELIEF
SIMPLE QIGONG EXERCISES FOR BACK PAIN RELIEF

SIMPLIFIED TAI CHI CHUAN: 24 & 48 POSTURES
SIMPLIFIED TAI CHI FOR BEGINNERS 48
SIX HEALING SOUNDS
SUN TAI CHI
SUNRISE TAI CHI
SUNSET TAI CHI
SWORD: FUNDAMENTAL TRAINING
TAEKWONDO KORYO POOMSAE
TAI CHI BALL QIGONG: COURSES 1 & 2
TAI CHI BALL QIGONG: COURSES 3 & 4
TAI CHI BALL WORKOUT FOR BEGINNERS
TAI CHI CHUAN CLASSICAL YANG STYLE
TAI CHI CONNECTIONS
TAI CHI ENERGY PATTERNS
TAI CHI FIGHTING SET
TAI CHI FIT: 24 FORM
TAI CHI FIT: FLOW
TAI CHI FIT: FUSION BAMBOO
TAI CHI FIT: FUSION FIRE
TAI CHI FIT: FUSION IRON
TAI CHI FIT: HEART HEALTH WORKOUT
TAI CHI FIT IN PARADISE
TAI CHI FIT: OVER 50
TAI CHI FIT OVER 50: BALANCE EXERCISES
TAI CHI FIT OVER 50: SEATED WORKOUT
TAI CHI FIT OVER 60: GENTLE EXERCISES
TAI CHI FIT OVER 60: HEALTHY JOINTS
TAI CHI FIT OVER 60: LIVE LONGER
TAI CHI FIT: STRENGTH
TAI CHI FIT: TO GO
TAI CHI FOR WOMEN
TAI CHI FUSION: FIRE
TAI CHI QIGONG
TAI CHI PUSHING HANDS: COURSES 1 & 2
TAI CHI PUSHING HANDS: COURSES 3 & 4
TAI CHI SWORD: CLASSICAL YANG STYLE
TAI CHI SWORD FOR BEGINNERS
TAI CHI SYMBOL: YIN YANG STICKING HANDS
TAIJI & SHAOLIN STAFF: FUNDAMENTAL TRAINING
TAIJI CHIN NA IN-DEPTH
TAIJI 37 POSTURES MARTIAL APPLICATIONS
TAIJI SABER CLASSICAL YANG STYLE
TAIJI WRESTLING
TRAINING FOR SUDDEN VIOLENCE
UNDERSTANDING QIGONG 1: WHAT IS QI? • HUMAN QI
    CIRCULATORY SYSTEM
UNDERSTANDING QIGONG 2: KEY POINTS • QIGONG BREATHING
UNDERSTANDING QIGONG 3: EMBRYONIC BREATHING
UNDERSTANDING QIGONG 4: FOUR SEASONS QIGONG
UNDERSTANDING QIGONG 5: SMALL CIRCULATION
UNDERSTANDING QIGONG 6: MARTIAL QIGONG BREATHING
WATER STYLE FOR BEGINNERS
WHITE CRANE HARD & SOFT QIGONG
YANG TAI CHI FOR BEGINNERS
YOQI QIGONG FOR A HAPPY HEART
YOQI QIGONG FOR HAPPY SPLEEN & STOMACH
YOQI QIGONG FOR HAPPY KIDNEYS
YOQI QIGONG FLOW FOR HAPPY LUNGS
YOQI QIGONG FLOW FOR STRESS RELIEF
YOQI SIX HEALING SOUNDS
WU TAI CHI FOR BEGINNERS
WUDANG KUNG FU: FUNDAMENTAL TRAINING
WUDANG SWORD
WUDANG TAIJIQUAN
XINGYIQUAN
YANG TAI CHI FOR BEGINNERS

more products available from . . .

YMAA Publication Center, Inc. 楊氏東方文化出版中心

1-800-669-8892 • info@ymaa.com • www.ymaa.com

Lightning Source UK Ltd.
Milton Keynes UK
UKHW021413021221
394981UK00020B/370

9 781594 398438